"Responses to opera performances can be ecstatic and overpowering. Using insights from a variety of human sciences, Joseph Cone applies a 'stereo' perspective to explore how and why opera as a living performance affects our emotions so deeply. A book like no other, *Seeing Opera Anew* is well-researched, informative, and a pleasure to read."

Ellen Dissanayake, *author of* What Is Art For? *and* Homo Aestheticus: Where Art Comes From and Why

"Joseph Cone's *Seeing Opera Anew* strikes out many new connections between the arts, especially music-drama, and human nature. He lucidly scans about a score of masterpieces, discerning patterns outlined by evolutionary psychology and citing recent findings in anthropology and the psychology of emotions. In effect, he sketches out an enormous sphere of influences on our experiences in this, the most ambitious of the arts. Readers new to opera and established fans alike will find much to learn and enjoy in this truly multifaceted volume."

Brett Cooke, *Professor of Russian, Texas A&M University*

"This innovative and illuminating collection of short essays critically explores the history of opera through new realms of connection and serendipity. Cone has assembled a diverse representation of operatic style, period, and practice; inviting the reader to devolve further. Rich in imagery, color, and anecdote, each essay situates an enduring operatic example within contemporary modalities, providing the art form with enhanced relevance, sustainability, and impact in an increasingly complex and challenging global market. Cone's innate knowledge, passion, and humor shine through, ensuring the storytelling remains inclusive and accessible to all readers. I highly recommend this publication as a key work that affords historic operatic practice a new 'home' within contemporary locales – with surprising and compelling results."

Nicole Panizza, *Assistant Professor, Music,*
Coventry University, UK

SEEING OPERA ANEW

What people ultimately want from opera, audience research suggests, is to be absorbed in a story that engages their feelings, even moves them deeply, and that may lead them to insights about life and, perhaps, themselves.

How and why can this combination of music and drama do that? What causes people to be moved by opera? How is it that people may become more informed about living and their own lives? *Seeing Opera Anew* addresses these fundamental questions.

Most approaches to opera present information solely from the humanities, providing musical, literary, and historical interpretations, but this book offers a "stereo" perspective, adding insights from the sciences closely related to human life, including evolutionary biology, psychology, anthropology, and neuroscience. It can be hoped that academic specialists less familiar with the science will find points of interest in this book's novel approach, and that open-minded students and inquisitive opera-goers will be stimulated by its "cultural and biological perspective."

Joseph Cone graduated from Yale University (literature, music, science) and the University of Oregon (communications), and for four decades at Oregon State University his faculty position involved research in, and the practice of, science communication with the public. His love and knowledge of opera began at home and school and grew through years of enjoyment, study, and attending performances. This book is his sixth.

SEEING OPERA ANEW

A Cultural and Biological Perspective

Joseph Cone

LONDON AND NEW YORK

Cover image: iStock

First published 2024
by Routledge
4 Park Square, Milton Park, Abingdon, Oxon OX14 4RN

and by Routledge
605 Third Avenue, New York, NY 10158

Routledge is an imprint of the Taylor & Francis Group, an informa business

© 2024 Joseph Cone

The right of Joseph Cone to be identified as author of this work has been asserted in accordance with sections 77 and 78 of the Copyright, Designs and Patents Act 1988.

All rights reserved. No part of this book may be reprinted or reproduced or utilised in any form or by any electronic, mechanical, or other means, now known or hereafter invented, including photocopying and recording, or in any information storage or retrieval system, without permission in writing from the publishers.

Trademark notice: Product or corporate names may be trademarks or registered trademarks, and are used only for identification and explanation without intent to infringe.

British Library Cataloguing-in-Publication Data
A catalogue record for this book is available from the British Library

Library of Congress Cataloging-in-Publication Data
Names: Cone, Joseph, author.
Title: Seeing opera anew: a cultural and biological perspective/Joseph Cone.
Description: [1.] | Abingdon, Oxon; New York: Routledge, 2023. | Includes bibliographical references and index. |
Identifiers: LCCN 2023030726 (print) | LCCN 2023030727 (ebook) |
ISBN 9781032184289 (hardback) | ISBN 9781032184272 (paperback) |
ISBN 9781003254478 (ebook)
Subjects: LCSH: Opera. | Opera—Psychological aspects. | Social evolution.
Classification: LCC ML1700 .C665 2023 (print) | LCC ML1700 (ebook) |
DDC 782.1092/2—dc23/eng/20230630
LC record available at https://lccn.loc.gov/2023030726
LC ebook record available at https://lccn.loc.gov/2023030727

ISBN: 978-1-032-18428-9 (hbk)
ISBN: 978-1-032-18427-2 (pbk)
ISBN: 978-1-003-25447-8 (ebk)

DOI: 10.4324/9781003254478

Typeset in Sabon
by Deanta Global Publishing Services, Chennai, India

CONTENTS

Preface   *ix*

PART 1
Music-Dramas, Evolutionary Biology, and Psychology   **1**

Part 1 Introduction: What Science has to Offer   3

1 *Orfeo*: Stories, Singing, and Sexuality   11

2 *Rodelinda*: Emotion, Music, and Drama   26

3 *L'Elisir d'Amore*: Mate Choice, Comedy, and Consonance   40

4 *Le Nozze di Figaro*: Marital Commitment and Challenges
   to It   54

5 *Don Giovanni, Wozzeck*: Assessing Adult Character   69

6 *Die Walküre, Simon Boccanegra*: Parenting, Power, and
   Posterity   84

7 *The Tempest, Lear, Falstaff*: Aging and Wisdom   99

viii Contents

PART 2
Cultural Considerations Regarding Opera   **113**

Part 2 Introduction: What is meant by "Culture"   115

8 Attracting Audiences: *War and Peace, Omar, Song from the Uproar*   123

9 Origins and Innovations: Before and After *La Bohème* (the movie)   138

10 Affording Extraordinary Experiences: *Les Troyens, Akhnaten*   153

Index   *169*

PREFACE

People have been expressing themselves through music for thousands of years, and probably far longer.[1]

And during more than 400 years, generations of people in Europe, the Americas, and elsewhere where European music is listened to have been attracted to a combination of music, words, and drama that emerged in Italy as "opera." Today, millions of people listen to and watch operatic performances.[2]

But why?

They—*we*, complex human beings—may certainly be drawn to, and enjoy, any of opera's components, including the singing, instrumental music, drama, stagecraft, dance and movement, as well as the unique features of a particular performance, for opera is a performing art. For many, going to the opera is a *special* occasion, differing in quality and expectation from the daily round.

But what people ultimately want from opera, audience research suggests,[3] is to be absorbed in a story that engages their feelings, even moves them deeply,[4] and that may lead them to insights about life and, perhaps, themselves.[5]

How and why can this combination of music and drama do that? What causes people to be moved by opera? How is it that people may become more informed about living and their own lives? This book addresses these fundamental questions.

Traditional discussions of opera present musical, literary, and other historical information, examining such elements as the composer's historical period, the development and influence of the composition, and performance

x Preface

practices and performers. In more recent years, music-dramas sometimes have been viewed for what they might reveal about cultural biases of their time and place. Such elements may be interesting to know and are clearly important to specialists; and fruits of research in musicology and other disciplines of the academic "humanities" are presented in this book. But why people may be affected by opera has deeper roots, in our psychology and, ultimately, in our biology.

We are, of course, mammals, with biological characteristics common to our species, *Homo sapiens*. A large brain, upright walking, and the ability to speak and sing may come to mind as among these characteristics. But we "Sapiens" —and since it's us we're talking about, we can be a little informal and call us just that without confusion—we are also social animals and have been so during the approximately 200,000 years of our species.[6] Living in social groups molded our psychology,[7] and learning from one another led to the development of distinctly human culture,[8] ultimately including the arts we know today.

Although most approaches to opera present information solely from the humanities, this book offers a "stereo" perspective, adding insights from the sciences closely related to human life, including evolutionary biology, psychology, anthropology, and neuroscience. (As biology is the science of life and living organisms, these may be summed as a "biological" perspective.) It can be hoped that academic specialists less familiar with the science drawn upon in *Seeing Opera Anew* will find points of interest in this book's novel approach. Adding to understanding, not taking away from it, is, naturally, the goal.

Inquisitive students and opera-goers who are open to understanding more about how and why opera affects them may be especially curious. The students may be as intrigued by human behavior as they are by music and other arts. Such a "multidisciplinary" interest might well be encouraged as a cornerstone in the development of well-rounded, critical thinkers[9] who can be capable in complex modern societies. For their part, opera audiences, who pay to witness a music-drama performance, likely hope to carry some value from it back into their daily lives. What value they may obtain will be a recurring interest. And those with little previous exposure to or interest in the uncommon blend of music and drama that is opera are especially invited to discover the qualities which lie ahead.

The book is in two parts, the first emphasizing the biological perspective, the second a cultural one, but both are combined in each chapter. *Evolution*—biological, cultural—is an organizing concept throughout, and it will be introduced and developed in the pages ahead. Each part of the book is led with its own introduction to the chapters that follow, and each of those chapters discuss one or more operas composed during the five centuries from the 1600s to today. Overall, *Seeing Opera Anew* intends to show

Preface **xi**

that relevant sciences can contribute to the understanding and appreciation of subjects that traditionally have been the province of other disciplines.

I came to write this book because of my long devotion to opera. I grew up in a family of amateur musicians, and from early childhood I heard operatic arias sung by my father. My parents collected and played opera recordings, and my sister and I sometimes joined our parents in listening to Metropolitan Opera radio broadcasts. Feeling the excitement of live performances in foreign languages, I was motivated as an adolescent to study librettos and puzzle out French and Italian. By the time I was in high school (an American "prep school"), I branched out and wrote my senior project on three music-dramas by Richard Wagner.

In college I studied literature, music theory, and pre-med sciences because I found them all fascinating, but music wasn't just a study, as I also sang in several Yale singing groups, sometimes as a soloist. I determined to keep music, literature, and science prominent in my adult life.

While I continued to delight in and study opera performances and also sang for many years as a chorister, after graduate school I became a writer and editor, and then an academic, specializing in communicating with the public about science, primarily biological research and earth systems science. For three decades as a faculty member, I led a science communication office at Oregon State University, presenting the results of others' research and conducting my own communication research. Over a 50-year career, I have written hundreds of popular articles as well as academic publications. As a storyteller, I have also written, shot, and edited more than a dozen documentary films about scientific and environmental concerns, and I have researched and written five other books, including a biographical screenplay about Giuseppe Verdi.

My hybrid career as research communicator and a creative and performing artist is relevant here. The investigative habits I've developed over the years and the fascination about music, literature, and science that I have long held join with my continuing love of opera in this book.

I owe Heidi Bishop, the senior music editor at Routledge, my special acknowledgment, as she supported the different approach of this book throughout its development and was always collegial, flexible, and acute.

In addition, I am glad to acknowledge those scholars who generously reviewed drafts of chapters relating to their expertise. A diverse group, I include their academic homes at the time: Joseph Carroll (Univ. Missouri—St. Louis), L. Brett Cooke (Texas A&M), Gregory Decker (Bowling Green), Ellen Dissanayake (Univ. Washington), John H. Falk (Oregon State Univ.), Iain Fenlon (Cambridge), Alf Gabrielsson (Uppsala Univ.), Tony Jackson (Univ. North Carolina), Christopher Morris (Maynooth Univ.), Dale Purves (Duke), Mary Ann Smart (U.C. Berkeley), Brian Soucek (U.C. Davis), and

xii Preface

Francesca Vella (Cambridge). Comments of three anonymous reviewers were also helpful.

A few readers commented extensively. The close reading of Sandy Ridlington, a professional editor, my colleague, and opera devotee, was a great benefit. The observations and encouragement of Brett Cooke and Ellen Dissanayake reflected both their scholarship and their kindness. My thinking about most of the operas highlighted in this book has benefited from conversations with all the members of the opera club that I led in Corvallis, Oregon, notably Jeff Weber, Guillermo Giannico, Leslie Lundborg, my wife; and particularly, again, Sandy Ridlington. Over many years, stimulating conversations with other good friends, John Falk, Paul Guida, Bill Huck, and Jon Schwartz helped shape my thinking about the cultural and biological content of this book. Three voice teachers whom I greatly admired, Dan Ferro, Don Brown, and David York, taught me how demanding and inspiring is the singer's art; and I gained much from those who also taught me music composition and choral singing when I was an undergraduate at Yale.

To all who helped me, I give my sincere thanks.

Notes

1 Some early written evidence is of love songs in Ancient Egypt, ca. 1300 BCE, 3,300 years ago: A. G. McDowell, *Village Life in Ancient Egypt: Laundry Lists and Love Songs* (Oxford: Clarendon Press, 1999). But song may date back tens of thousands of years: I. Morley, "A Multi-disciplinary Approach to the Origins of Music: Perspectives from Anthropology, Archaeology, Cognition and Behaviour," *Journal of Anthropological Sciences* 92 (2014): 147–177.
2 My estimate based on U.S.-only data from 2019 would total some 10 million adults. National Endowment for the Arts, "U.S. Patterns of Arts Participation: A Full Report from the 2017 Survey of Public Participation in the Arts," (Washington, DC, 2019), 57.
3 I am mainly referring to quantitative research: National Endowment for the Arts, "A Decade of Arts Engagement," (Washington, DC, 2015), and Marketing Research Professionals Inc., "Building Millennial Audiences: Barriers and Opportunities," (The Wallace Foundation, 2017). Also Sinéad O'Neill, Joshua Edelman, and John Sloboda, "Opera and Emotion: The Cultural Value of Attendance for the Highly Engaged," *Participations* 13, no. 1 (2016): 24–50.
4 Such as the "self-transcendence" detailed in Claudio E. Benzecry, *The Opera Fanatic: Ethnography of an Obsession* (Chicago: University of Chicago Press, 2011), 126ff.
5 Marketing Research Professionals Inc., "Millennial Audiences," 45.
6 The date of origin of our species continues an active area of research, but about 200,000 years ago is the current, prevailing understanding. For a succinct account of human evolution, see S. Condemi and F. Savatier, *A Pocket History of Human Evolution: How We Became Sapiens*, trans. Emma Ramadan (New York: The Experiment, LLC, 2019).
7 David M. Buss, "Evolutionary Psychology Is a Scientific Revolution," *Evolutionary Behavioral Sciences* 14, no. 4 (2020).

8 R. Boyd, P. J. Richerson, and J. Henrich, "The Cultural Niche: Why Social Learning Is Essential for Human Adaptation," *Proceedings of the National Academy of Sciences of the United States of America* 108 Suppl 2 (2011): 10919.

9 Massimo Pigliucci, *Nonsense on Stilts*, 2nd ed. (Chicago: University of Chicago Press, 2018), 139.

PART 1

Music-Dramas, Evolutionary Biology, and Psychology

Included in Part 1:

Introduction: What Science Has to Offer
1. *Orfeo*: Stories, Singing, and Sexuality
2. *Rodelinda*: Emotion, Music, and Drama
3. *L'Elisir d'Amore*: Mate Choice, Comedy, and Consonance
4. *Le Nozze di Figaro*: Marital Commitment and Challenges to It
5. *Don Giovanni, Wozzeck*: Assessing Adult Character
6. *Die Walküre, Simon Boccanegra*: Parenting, Power, and Posterity
7. *The Tempest, Lear, Falstaff*: Aging and Wisdom

DOI: 10.4324/9781003254478-1

PART 1 INTRODUCTION

What Science has to Offer

In this overview, many statements will, of necessity, not present the detail or the complexity of a later, closer view. But, to start with the basics, opera is commonly defined as a dramatic work in which all or most of the words are sung to music.[1] This definition can be refined to operas are dramas presented *through* music,[2] which, in most cases, is heard throughout the drama. Music adds expressive features to the words and behavior of the dramatic characters; and, as a whole, a music-drama serves as a lens through which human characteristics and behaviors are revealed.

Those characteristics and behaviors have been discussed by many with a scientific understanding as, at least in part, a product of evolution,[3] ever since the pioneering research and influential publications of Charles Darwin[4] in the nineteenth century. While sometimes called the "theory" of evolution, that term should not be interpreted as indicating untested ideas or a matter of conjecture. To the contrary, biological evolution is well established by evidence,[5] as this part of the book will develop. The strength of science is its systematic approach to understanding the natural, physical world through collecting data that test hypotheses about how that world works.[6]

Since Darwin, biological evolution has had a special sense as the unfolding of forms of life over long periods of time. Fossil evidence reveals that we *Homo sapiens*, for example, are descended with many modifications from ancestral species that lived in trees some seven million years ago.[7] No preordained plan directs the unfolding, nor is there a prescribed endpoint. Over time variations arise in a species, Darwin observed, and a "natural selection" occurs that preserves the variations which benefit the organism under its conditions of life.[8] For a species to persist in the world, enough of its

DOI: 10.4324/9781003254478-2

4 Music-Dramas, Evolutionary Biology, and Psychology

individuals must first survive long enough to produce a next generation. For individuals, survival and the rather clinically named "reproduction" become basic drives. This is true for humans as for other living things.

From an evolutionary perspective, many human behaviors and physical characteristics (such as our unusually large brains) arose because they provided some advantages for survival and reproduction. The rapid assessment of a threat of becoming something else's dinner, for example, is a behavior with survival value,[9] not only for ancestral humans confronting an environment with dangerous predatory beasts, but also for every other animal in the roughly 500 million years of animal evolution.[10] It is worth taking just a few seconds to dwell on that long period of time, since it is so much outside the realm of human experience that 500 *million* can understandably seem both extremely big and incomprehensible, without a reference point. An exceptional human life may last 100 years, but one million years is ten thousand times that duration, and the number of years of animal evolution *500 times longer* still. During all that time it should seem very plausible that crucial behaviors aiding survival would have become ingrained in living beings.

Human evolution will be seen not as a bystander but, instead, a participant in three main ways with respect to music-drama. As a creative art designed to communicate with others, opera will be examined as a product of evolved human minds and bodies, in many specific ways. Likewise, for the audiences of this performing art, our human capacities enable responses to the various stimuli that opera presents. Better understanding of those capacities, the inborn potential[11] of *us* "Sapiens," may enhance appreciation of this art.

Third, nearly all music-dramas, regardless of their date or place of composition, are grounded in pivotal concerns of stages of human life,[12] particularly adolescence, adulthood, and agedness, although the preceding birth, infancy, and childhood are not ignored. The sequence of stages, ending in death, is commonly called a life "cycle"[13] because additional births may flow out of it. But "human life-history" is becoming the more useful framework as it focuses on the distinctive and evolved life patterns of our species, such as our unusually long lifespan and the substantial contributions males make to the support of females and children.[14] "Life-history theory" examines the dynamic allocation of energy to support survival and reproduction,[15] an allocation always present but not always recognized by individuals. Operas most commonly center on adulthood[16] and the allocation of energy during that stage, often dramatized through typical challenges and conflicts involved in mating and fidelity; parenting and care for progeny; and surviving and succeeding in society.

The relationships between biology and culture on the substance of music-dramas are the continuing interest of this book. "Culture" can be defined in different ways. For many attuned to the arts, "culture" (or "high" culture) is likely to mean the products of human knowledge and creativity, such as an opera, a painting, or a cathedral. Human culture does include such representations and products of knowledge, but the word can also mean *all* the collective learning passed forward over time[17] that enables not only these products but also the myriad of other human activities. The common humanist perception that culture stands apart and is not connected to human evolution is being contested in recent decades with a new and scientific understanding. "We are a *cultural* species," evolutionary scholar Joseph Henrich has argued, and that "cultural" characteristic is "the key to understanding how humans evolved and why we are so different from other animals."[18]

Briefly, the argument of Henrich and colleagues is that the main reason that humans are the dominant species on our planet is that not only do we learn from others but also that information accumulates over time and is put to use. This cumulative "cultural learning" process began probably millions of years ago with practices like the making of stone tools for chopping and cutting. Over the generations, the knowledge available to individuals was considerably more than any one person, no matter how intelligent, could figure out during their own life.[19] Once useful skills and practices accumulated and improved over generations, those who possessed such cultural information would have been favored by natural selection: and so the products of this cultural evolution, such as better tools and fire for cooking food, would have become selective pressures shaping the genetics of human minds and bodies.[20] From this perspective, human biology and culture co-evolved.

One line of evidence that culture and biology both have evolved,[21] influencing each other often profoundly in a "coevolutionary"[22] process, is research in archaeology and anthropology. Ancestors of humans slowly evolved to have larger brains; and our ancestors also slowly evolved increasingly more effective and sophisticated stone tools. The quantity of skulls and sharpened stones that have been collected in various places and dated by scholarly methods support the interpretation that these two phenomena influenced each other.[23] The genes shaping brains and the cultural factors shaping tool use interacted. Such is a foundation of "gene-culture coevolution theory."[24]

These are exciting times in the fields of biological and cultural evolution and their interplay, as data and ideas are put out and tested. In the last two decades some pioneer thinkers have been viewing the dynamic links between biology and culture through such frames as biopoetics,[25] biocultural theory,[26] and the gene-culture coevolutionary theory; and, in general, a "biocultural" perspective recognizes that the human life cycle is organized and developed by evolving culture in its many manifestations, including the institutions of society, beliefs, technology, and the arts. Human psychology is itself seen to have an evolutionary grounding, as supported by dozens of research articles and books.[27] One of its leaders, David M. Buss, has argued

6 Music-Dramas, Evolutionary Biology, and Psychology

that evolutionary psychology provides the solid theoretical foundation that psychological studies have lacked[28] and "focuses primarily on psychological adaptations: mechanisms of the mind that have evolved to solve specific problems of survival or reproduction. But "in evolutionary psychology, culture also has a major effect on psychological adaptations."[29]

The chapters ahead will offer examples of the explanatory value of evolutionary psychology, gene-culture coevolution theory, and a biocultural perspective, while not ignoring criticism of these scholarly programs.[30] In presenting and examining an enriched, contemporary view of culture and biology, this book hopes to advance the insight of philosopher of science Massimo Pigliucci, that "understanding in the broadest sense, goes through a continuous—and respectful—dialogue between the various disciplines that contribute to human knowledge and experience."[31] Pigliucci, also an evolutionary biologist, considers the sciences that domain of knowledge and the humanities the domain of experience. Both domains are vital and valuable, and human understanding needs them both and their continuing improvement. For its part, science is never done, is always subject to revision, and, indeed, some revisions may challenge the science presented in this book. That is to be expected and is completely normal.

However, it would be naive to ignore the very sharp divide that separates scholars whose disciplinary training and commitments are in the natural sciences, the social sciences, and the humanities. Becoming a specialist in any scholarly discipline takes a long time, during which the aspirant usually becomes in close accord with what the field considers its appropriate knowledge, methods, and purview. When new ideas appear to present challenges to established views, those with careers invested in their practices are understandably wary. This response is particularly strong, sometimes hostile,[32] when a major change to its "paradigm"—the way of thinking in a field, its methods and standards—appears under threat.[33]

A survey of scholarly contributors to top journals in more than 20 disciplines provides insights about the divide among those who study human behavior.[34] Both the motivation for the survey and the findings of it deserve direct quoting. "Are the social sciences and humanities moving toward consensus about the biological underpinnings of human. behavior and cultural experience?" the developers of the survey wanted to know. Or "do whole blocs of disciplines face off over an unbridgeable epistemic gap?"[35]—that is, over what constitutes valid knowledge.

The researchers produced detailed statistical analyses of the responses of more than 600 diverse scholars regarding their beliefs about human nature, culture, and science. They found two main blocs of disciplines. Genetic influences (on human nature) were emphasized in the evolutionary social sciences, evolutionary humanities, psychology, and empirical study of the arts, philosophy, economics, and political science.[36] This bloc had confidence in scientific explanations of human behavior and culture. On the opposite side were disciplines that did not have that confidence and emphasized non-evolutionary "environmental" (primarily cultural) influences on human behavior and culture. These disciplines were "most of the humanities," including music, drama, anthropology, education, history and philosophy of science, religious studies, sociology, and women's or gender studies.[37]

In addition to the statistical analysis, the 2017 journal article quoted many opinions of participants, striking in their convictions and stark differences, although rarely showing much familiarity with the knowledge held by disciplines not their own. Such attitudes have been common in scholarship for generations. In the 1950s, for example, the novelist and physical chemist C. P. Snow commented on his experience of attending gatherings of people "thought highly educated and who have with considerable gusto been expressing their incredulity at the illiteracy of scientists":

> Once or twice I have been provoked and have asked the company how many of them could describe the Second Law of Thermodynamics. The response was cold: it was also negative. Yet I was asking something which is the scientific equivalent of: *Have you read a work of Shakespeare's?*[38]

Snow lamented the existence of the separate "two cultures" then, and the reader should be aware of this persistent disciplinary divide because it will permeate other discussions of music-drama by specialists in the various fields. But fair-minded exploration is the spirit of this book. Opera's joy and depth and possibilities deserve a friendly curiosity.

Seeing Opera Anew is organized thematically and somewhat chronologically. The chapters discuss seventeen important operas composed between 1607 and 2022, presented in mostly historical order. Six of the composers[39] represent half of the dozen whose operas are most performed in very recent years, and some of their operas discussed are very frequently performed, to the tune of hundreds of performances annually (*La Bohème*, *Le Nozze di Figaro*, and *Don Giovanni*).

In this first part of the book, the thematic emphasis will be understanding operas as they represent human stories based on stages of human life and how the audience of those stories may respond to them because of their evolved human capacities. One basic way to think of artistic communication is the communication model[40] of sender-message-receiver-effect-feedback. What "messages" or information does a music-drama "send" and what do audiences receive and how do they respond?

The first chapter examines the origins of opera, of singing itself, and the purposes of dramatic stories in the context of Monteverdi's seminal *Orfeo*. In chapter 2, Handel's *Rodelinda* provides the first opportunity to

8 Music-Dramas, Evolutionary Biology, and Psychology

look closely at the relationship between music, drama, and human feelings, the latter from the most recent scientific understandings. Considered next, in Donizetti's sparkling *L'Elisir d'Amore*, are the what, how, and why of human courtship, which is a central event in many lives and the foundation of romantic comedies. Chapter 4 is devoted to Mozart's *Marriage of Figaro*. Its sophisticated examination of adult amorous relationships will be considered through the lens of evolutionary psychology.

The next chapters focus on other challenges of adult life. In chapter 5, how observers assess the very troubling protagonists, Don Giovanni and Wozzeck, brings to the fore that essential human task, strongly influenced by evolved human capacities. Parenting occupies much energy and attention, and always has for humans, as producing progeny is an evolutionary drive. Chapter 6 examines the behavior of very different fathers and children portrayed by Wagner and Verdi in the course of two of their major music-dramas. Human life-history permits substantial aging, and the three operas in chapter 7 are considered for how they present, musically and dramatically, a core psychological challenge of the last phase of life, which is acquiring and demonstrating wisdom.

Together, the chapters intend to develop understanding of how and why music-drama may affect us and how from operas we may obtain vivid insight into ourselves, other persons, and human lives.

A final note: No recordings or performances are recommended in this book because preferences differ, new recordings arise, and discovery should be a keen personal pleasure. However, three general suggestions can be offered. As a performing art, opera is made to be seen, so it is preferable to view a whole opera, "live," if possible. Again, if a recording, watching the whole opera, even divided over days, rather than excerpts only, is best. Many audio-only recordings of operas, arias, and other excerpts are also available and can be valuable and stimulating supplements to an audio-visual presentation of the whole work.

Notes

1 *Oxford Learner's Dictionary*, s.v. "opera," accessed Oct. 21, 2022. http://www.oxfordlearnersdictionaries.com/us/definition/english/opera.
2 Joseph Kerman, *Opera as Drama*, new and rev. ed. (Berkeley: University of California Press, 1988), 5.
3 For summaries, see L. Workman and W. Reader, *Evolutionary Psychology: An Introduction* (Cambridge, UK: Cambridge University Press, 2021); J. Cartwright, *Evolution and Human Behaviour: Darwinian Perspectives on the Human Condition* (Basingstoke, UK: Palgrave Macmillan, 2016).
4 Of greatest relevance here: Charles Darwin, *The Descent of Man, and Selection in Relation to Sex* (Princeton, NJ: Princeton University Press, 1981; repr., Reprint of 1871 first edition).

Part 1 Introduction **9**

5 R. Dawkins, *The Greatest Show on Earth: The Evidence for Evolution* (New York: Bantam, 2009). One account of many that might be cited.

6 Massimo Pigliucci, *Nonsense on Stilts*, 2d ed. (Chicago: University of Chicago Press, 2018), 40.

7 An accessible recent summary: S. Condemi and F. Savatier, *A Pocket History of Human Evolution: How We Became Sapiens*, trans. Emma Ramadan (New York: The Experiment, LLC, 2019), 6.

8 Charles Darwin, *On the Origin of Species by Means of Natural Selection, or the Preservation of Favoured Races in the Struggle for Life; 3d Edition, with Additions and Corrections* (London: John Murray, 1861), http://darwin-online .org.uk/converted/pdf/1861_Origin NY_F382.pdf.

9 See R. L. Rosier and T. Langkilde, "Behavior under Risk: How Animals Avoid Becoming Dinner," *Nature Education Knowledge* 2.11 @011): 8; and Joseph LeDoux, *Anxious* (New York: Viking, 2015), 41.

10 Sören Jensen, Mary L. Droser, and James G. Gehling, "Trace Fossil Preservation and the Early Evolution of Animals," *Palaeogeography, Palaeoclimatology, Palaeoecology* 220, no. 1 (2005).

11 APA Dictionary of Psychology, s.v. "capacity." Accessed Dec. 26, 2022. http:// dictionary.apa.org/capacity.

12 Barry Bogin and B. Holly Smith, "Evolution of the Human Life Cycle," *American Journal of Human Biology* 8, no. 6 (1996).

13 A thorough, expansive discussion: B. Bogin et al., "Human Life Course Biology: A Centennial Perspective of Scholarship on the Human Pattern of Physical Growth and Its Place in Human Biocultural Evolution," *American Journal of Physical Anthropology* 165, no. 4 (2018): 834–854.

14 Peter J Richerson and Robert Boyd, "The Human Life History Is Adapted to Exploit the Adaptive Advantages of Culture," *Philosophical Transactions of the Royal Society B* 375, no. 1803 (2020).

15 Hillard S. Kaplan and Steven W. Gangestad, "Life History Theory and Evolutionary Psychology," *The Handbook of Evolutionary Psychology* (Wiley Online Books, 2015), http://doi.org/10.1002/9780470939376.ch2.

16 Brett Cooke, "Cliches Worth Singing: Narrative Commonplaces in Opera," *The Evolutionary Review*, vol. 1, no. 1 (2010). This offered an early but preliminary statistical review of opera subjects.

17 Gary Tomlinson, "Introduction," *Culture and the Course of Human Evolution* (Chicago: University of Chicago Press, 2018), 1.

18 Joseph Henrich, *The Secret of Our Success* (Princeton, NJ: Princeton University Press, 2016), 3.

19 R. Boyd, P. J. Richerson, and J. Henrich, "The Cultural Niche: Why Social Learning Is Essential for Human Adaptation," *Proceedings of the National Academy of Sciences of the United States of America* 108 Suppl 2 (2011)

20 Ibid., 116.

21 A review of cultural evolution: Catherine Driscoll, "The Evolutionary Culture Concepts," *Philosophy of Science* 84, no. 1 (2016).

22 Peter J Richerson and Robert Boyd, *Not by Genes Alone: How Culture Transformed Human Evolution* (Chicago: University of Chicago Press, 2008).

23 See Driscoll, "The Evolutionary Culture Concepts."

24 P. J. Richerson, R. Boyd, and J. Henrich, "Colloquium Paper: Gene-Culture Coevolution in the Age of Genomics," *Proceedings of the National Academy of Sciences of the United States of America* 107 Suppl 2 (2010).

25 Brett Cooke, "Literary Biopoetics: An Introduction," *Interdisciplinary Literary Studies* 2, no. 2 (2001).

26 Joseph Carroll et al., "Biocultural Theory: The Current State of Knowledge," *Evolutionary Behavioral Sciences* 11, no. 1 (2017).

10 Music-Dramas, Evolutionary Biology, and Psychology

27 A few examples: T. K. Shackelford, *The Sage Handbook of Evolutionary Psychology: Integration of Evolutionary Psychology with Other Disciplines* (Thousand Oaks, CA: SAGE, 2020). Workman and Reader, *Evolutionary Psychology: An Introduction*. David M. Buss, *The Handbook of Evolutionary Psychology*, volume 1: *Foundation* (Hoboken, NJ: John Wiley & Sons, 2015).

28 David M. Buss, "Evolutionary Psychology Is a Scientific Revolution," *Evolutionary Behavioral Sciences* 14, no. 4 (2020).

29 David M Buss, "4.2 Evolutionary Theories in Psychology," *Introduction to Psychology* (2019): 5.

30 Skepticism and sharp debate are basic to science. Evolutionary psychology, for example, has sometimes received challenges over its validity: e.g., Subrena E. Smith, "Is Evolutionary Psychology Possible?" *Biological Theory* 15, no. 1 (2020). Other works cited in this Introduction would refute the criticism; also see John Alcock, "Evolutionary Psychology and Biology," in *The SAGE Handbook of Evolutionary Psychology: Integration of Evolutionary Psychology with Other Disciplines*, ed. T. K. Shackelford (Thousand Oaks, CA: SAGE, 2020).

31 Pigliucci, *Nonsense on Stilts*, 261.

32 An example is the mid-twentieth-century dispute in the geological sciences over plate tectonics, discussed in Joseph Cone, *Fire under the Sea* (New York: William Morrow, 1991).

33 Thomas S. Kuhn, *The Structure of Scientific Revolutions*, vol. 111 (Chicago: University of Chicago Press, 1970).

34 Joseph Carroll et al., "A Cross-Disciplinary Survey of Beliefs about Human Nature, Culture, and Science," *Evolutionary Studies in Imaginative Culture* 1 (2017): 1.

35 Carroll, "Cross-disciplinary survey," 1.

36 Ibid.

37 Ibid., 19.

38 C. P. Snow, *The Two Cultures and the Scientific Revolution* (Cambridge, UK: Cambridge University Press, 1959), 16.

39 Verdi, Mozart, Puccini, Donizetti, Wagner, and Handel in that order. The international opera seasons of 2015/2016 and 2019/2020 provided the baseline. "Statistics," Operabase, http://www.operabase.com/statistics/en

40 Uma Narula, *Communication Models* (New Delhi: Atlantic Publishers & Distributors (P) Limited, 2006), 24.

1

ORFEO

Stories, Singing, and Sexuality

Invited to a special occasion in Mantua in 1607, privileged guests would have appreciated much about this handsome city in north-central Italy. The city held a favored place along the Mincio River on what was, in effect, an island connected only by bridges to the shore. This gave the rulers of Mantua a strategic position; and, well defended there for over three centuries, the Gonzaga dynasty had accumulated, then lavished, its wealth to make the city a monument to high art and architecture.

Inside the giant and sumptuous palace of the duke, guests would have been directed to a hall for music[1] and handed a little printed book, a "libretto," *L'Orfeo: Favola in Musica* (*Orpheus: A Tale in Music*) and seated. It is not known if on this occasion, the duke himself, Vincenzo Gonzaga, welcomed his guests. But since it was the Carnival season prior to the constraints of Lent, and the 45-year-old duke was known for his flamboyance and his love of singing, he may have stood at the front of the hall. Speaking while being admired for a ruff of the most exquisite white and of perfect folds, and his rakish goatee,[2] he may have told the gentlemen seated before him that he hoped that the novelty of the performance—this premiere that they were about to witness—would meet with their approval.

Duke Vincenzo would have acknowledged his aristocratic secretary, the author of the libretto, Alessandro Striggio, and then turned attention to *Orfeo*'s composer, Claudio Monteverdi, the accomplished, 40-year-old maestro of music for the Gonzaga court.

The audience looked to Monteverdi, seated with a small group of instrumentalists assembled in front of a stage, perhaps noticing the composer's piercing eyes or his ears that seemed rather too large for his head. He certainly heard things differently. Monteverdi's five earlier books of

DOI: 10.4324/9781003254478-3

12 Music-Dramas, Evolutionary Biology, and Psychology

part-songs for men and women, his madrigals, had expanded the world of melody and harmony to portray intense verses about love.

With a gesture from their maestro, the instrumentalists began to play. A brisk opening presented versions of the same melody, contrasting the smoothness of the stringed instruments with the more assertive wind instruments, which introduced the first singer on stage, dressed in costume and holding a lyre, who declared:

> I am Music, who in sweet accents
> Can make peaceful every troubled heart,
> And so with noble anger, and so with love,
> Can I inflame the coldest minds.[3]

The singer illustrated the words, the audience would have noticed, singing "sweet accents" with notes of particular tenderness, and "inflame" with agitation. Music can affect the feelings, the listeners heard and even more so perhaps experienced right then. So primed by Music, and music, they would have begun being led into the sound-world of the drama.

The legendary tale of Orpheus, a semi-god and spell-binding singer, would probably have been known by the audience, at least in outline,[4] and the most sophisticated among them would have recognized, in general, the forms of the music that they now heard. But very few would have been prepared for exactly what Monteverdi and Striggio made of the story.

A pastoral scene unfolded on stage, as shepherds sang of the circumstances that had brought Orpheus to this happy day when his love, Eurydice, had consented to marriage. A chorus of shepherds and "nymphs" celebrated the god of marriage, singing "bring these lovers peaceful days, and forever banish the horrors and shadows of torments and grief."

Those sentiments would have deepened as the tenor portraying Orpheus came forward to sing to the "rose of heaven," the Sun: "Tell me, have you ever seen/ A happier and more fortunate lover than I?"

The audience heard Eurydice sing of her own contentment, watched the shepherds and shepherdesses dance energetically to a lively tune; and then Orpheus's lovely young wife went off innocently with friends to pick flowers. Orpheus and shepherds stayed behind, singing happily of the pleasures of the woodlands and meadows and his good fortune.

Abruptly a friend of Eurydice appeared, downcast, declaring "Ah! bitter fate, *ah!* wicked and cruel destiny!" All the texture went out of the instrumental accompaniment as this messenger haltingly delivered to Orpheus the news, "Your wife is dead; she was bitten by a snake."

At that exact moment at the premiere on February 24, 1607, how did men in the audience react?[5] Did their eyes widen? Did they feel a sudden chill? Feel frightened, somehow? Unfortunately, no first-hand accounts from the

Orfeo **13**

invited guests have come down. But those who were paying attention would likely have been affected by two fundamental causes.

The first was long before identified clearly by Aristotle, who in his *Poetics,* written down some 1900 years before *Orfeo,*[6] had argued[7] that "imitation" was an "instinct, implanted in man from childhood."[8] Moreover, "through imitation he learns his earliest lessons." Imitation is a path to learning.[9] "No less universal is the pleasure felt in things imitated," the philosopher added, even though what is imitated "may be painful to see." The foundation of drama's effects, he continued, is an imitation of what does, or could, happen in life.[10] A spouse's death could and did and does happen in life.

But perhaps the brilliant Aristotle, writing in the 300s BCE about imitation ("mimesis" in Greek), was describing an exclusively cultural phenomenon to aid learning which might have arisen only with the clever Greeks? Or perhaps arose with a preceding civilization, such as the Egyptians of the Pharaohs?

As the Introduction previewed, evidence from fossils and stone tools points to a different and far earlier origin for imitation among our distant ancestors. *Homo sapiens* are hominins,[11] a subgroup of all great apes. Although *Homo sapiens* arose as a species some 200,000 years ago, we were preceded by several other *Homo* species dating back about 2.8 million years.

Over the roughly two million years from one relative, *Homo habilis,* to *Homo sapien*s the skull's cranial capacity increased about two and one-half times.[12] Our species has greater abilities to think and affect the world more than our predecessors. But even with brains smaller than ours, our distant relatives' needs to survive in their environments led them to develop stone tools, likely used as long as 3.3 million years ago[13] by the related "hominid" species[14] that preceded our *Homo* group. Over millions of years through the hominins, stone tools became used for pounding, splitting bones, and cutting flesh and other matter.

Toolmaking behaviors, involving repeated purposeful gestures that would have proved vital to survival, would have been passed down over a great many generations. Gradually, over all those years, they became more sophisticated in design and apparent purpose.[15] The interplay between increasing brain size and tool sophistication suggests the gene-culture coevolution[16] highlighted in the Introduction. But without language as we know it until our own species, all this "passing down" of stone tool fabrication would have been accomplished by imitation.

Imitation was very likely not limited to the making and use of such tools. However, scientists can be sure about this at least because stone can be preserved, while, for example, the close watching of the master by the young apprentice, to learn how to turn a stone into a tool, is not preserved, although it must have happened. Such "cultural learning" depends upon the fundamental human capacity to share attention.

14 Music-Dramas, Evolutionary Biology, and Psychology

Infants show the ability at about nine months of age to attend to the same objects as a parent does, such as a nearby child's toy. "With joint attention we may say that the infant and partner understand themselves to be attending to the same thing together, from different perspectives but at the same time they understand that they are doing so," according to developmental psychologist Michael Tomasello.[17] The psychological "package" of joint attention but different perspectives is a skill unique to our species,[18] and would seem to be essential to so much of human communication, including that of the men watching the first performance of *Orfeo* in 1607.

Imitation, born of attention, appears then fundamental to human life. By saying that drama was an "imitation" of what could happen in life, Aristotle did not mean, however, a direct copying of a process, as might happen with fashioning stones. A drama was to him, as to the Mantuans and to people today, a fiction: something made, created to represent life and from which a person might learn. A representation of actions would be necessary to engage a person's interests, even though each individual might respond to it differently.

Indeed, the second fundamental cause of an audience response is that *Orfeo* is a particular representation of human actions—a story, and of a certain kind. Why and how people attend to stories will be our recurring interest, so it is best to begin with what they are and why stories are told at all. However, adopting a perspective from contemporary consumer cultures with the constant bombardment of "stories" presented through many media (books, television, films, YouTube, etc.) can obscure underlying fundamentals. Adults might say they watch sit-coms just to be entertained or murder mysteries to be distracted from the realities of their daily life. But there is likely more to it for them than just entertainment and distraction.

The sit-coms and detective dramas, in fact, hold the essence of story[19] in two ways. First, stories are a social phenomenon; they begin with a teller and presume a listener who can be interested in the tale. Second, a story usually involves a situation in which a leading character wants, or needs to do, something. From an initial condition, that character encounters complications and challenges, and ultimately comes to some sort of resolution of that starting point, accompanied by some increase in understanding by him or her, or by others in the story.

Those who attend to a story may, in turn, be affected by it in how they feel and think. Such effects could be a distinct advantage; as the American essayist Joan Didion observed, "We tell ourselves stories in order to live."[20] That common human experience of the purpose and effects of story makes a case to those with an evolutionary-perspective that telling and receiving stories may be an ancient human adaptation. An "adaptation"[21] is a behavior, trait, or feature shaped by natural selection that promotes, or once promoted, survival and, ultimately, reproductive success. "Art and storytelling are adaptations," Brian Boyd, a professor of literature, was one of the first to argue.[22]

> Art is a form of cognitive play with pattern . . . engaged in spontaneously by all normal individuals. Literature and other arts have helped extend our command of information patterns, and that singular command makes us who we are.

Early stories would not have been murder mysteries or police procedurals, not exactly. But they very well could have told or shown what situations to avoid in the environment and what to do to survive if caught up in them, through extending human "command of information patterns." As Boyd observed, "Because the world swarms with patterns, animal minds evolved as pattern extractors, able to detect the information meaningful to their kind of organism in their kind of environment and therefore to predict and act accordingly."

Whether making and receiving stories are indeed adaptations and therefore, in effect, "hard-wired" in us, or not, deserves fuller attention, later. But it is fair to say that *Orfeo* is a common and even, arguably, a primary type of story, a family tragedy, and more so, an intimate, relationship tragedy. Before the dreadful moment when his wife's death is reported, Orpheus had sung: "So happy was the day, My love, when first I saw you / And happier the hour when I sighed for you." And happiest, "most fortunate" when she had accepted him.

To this point, the drama is one of courtship and marriage, which daresay most of the men in the 1607 audience and many people before and since have had an interest in. Perhaps in their own lives those listening to Orpheus would also have crowed in triumph or briefly wept in gratitude at similar good fortunes, and perhaps even felt like singing. But the significance of courtship, marriage, and the spouse's immediate death is more than personal. It's about sex, of course. Living things make copies of themselves. Birds do it, bees do it, trees do it, and humans do it. For men and women, sexual reproduction passes some of the genes inherited from parents on to the next generation. People generally like that idea of personal continuity, and it's a good thing for a species, because the recombining and shuffling of genes that is involved helps make evolution of populations possible.

But what does Orpheus do as his wife is now dead? How will the story proceed? For tragic drama, Aristotle had argued in the *Poetics* that plot was the most important element.[23] Essential to a good plot was a unified action with a coherent sequence of events. It would be "complete" unto itself, a slice of time with a beginning and end, even though before and after could be pointed to. Within a drama, time and the sequence of events would often

16 Music-Dramas, Evolutionary Biology, and Psychology

include sharp punctuations.[24] One punctuation would involve reversals of fortune for the leading characters; another would be moments of recognition or discovery, in which something or someone previously not understood or recognized becomes so.

These punctuations, usually sudden, sometimes violent, sometimes occurring together, could prompt "pity and fear" in the audience. But a successful tragedy would "purge" those negative emotions that it had prompted. Aristotle called this "catharsis," a term and concept that later passed into more common use. *Orfeo* generally reflects Aristotle's understanding and overall formula for tragedy. That first tragic "reversal of fortune" is what has happened to Eurydice. What could be a greater shock to a new spouse, or more pitiable; and how might a composer best present the moment?

Monteverdi did not immediately overwhelm the audience with sound. Instead, he initially understated the music, presenting the exchange between Orpheus and the messenger within a restricted vocal range and dynamic, scarcely accompanied by instruments. This restriction reflects that the characters are stunned in the moment (as may be members of the audience).

Finally, Orpheus begins to express himself, slowly, and within the limited musical bounds of a recitation style of vocalism, close to speech:

Tu sei morta, mia vita; ed io respiro?
Tu sei da me partita,
Per mai più non tornare, ed io rimango?
You are dead, my life, and I (still) breathe?
You are departed from me,
Never to return, and I remain?[25]

Gradually, Orpheus's expression expands into a melody that, still closely inflecting the poetic verses, suggests his resolve to venture into the underworld and bring Eurydice back. His voice and the accompaniment first ascend up the scale—"Farewell, Earth. Farewell, Sky"—and then descend decisively with "Sun, farewell!"

The wedding guests close the scene in an impassioned chorus that, similar to a traditional Greek chorus, expressively reflects on the unexpected events, emphasizing their own pity and fear: "Ah, bitter blow! Ah, wicked cruel Fate! Ah, baleful stars! Ah, avaricious heaven!"

From this point, if drama is imitation and imitation is bound up with learning, what can be said about what more the audience may learn about human life from what Orpheus does in the remainder of the opera? Orpheus is no ordinary man; he is a semi-god, and that imaginary split in nature brings forward what is godlike and what is not in the character's behavior. So, he goes to Hell to retrieve Eurydice, which only a god might manage, but librettist Striggio and Monteverdi take pains to emphasize the human quality of the behavior of Orpheus. He does not tell Charon, "I am a god and you should comply with my request," to ferry me across the River Styx, but instead Orpheus sings, "I am not alive, for after the death of my wife my heart is no longer with me, and without a heart how could I live?"

For the rest of the opera, in which Orpheus goes to Hell and comes back, *Orfeo* passes beyond dramatic imitation of a natural world to the world of myth, to an underworld repeatedly imagined over centuries in Greek and Roman stories. In Hades, Pluto's wife Proserpine persuades him to release Eurydice, but Orpheus is told that he may not look at her until emerged from the underworld. Yet Orpheus turns to see her, impetuously saying that what Pluto forbids the more powerful Cupid commands. But Orpheus has been warned, and Eurydice must return down to Hell forever.

This second, terrible reversal of fortune provides a dramatic exclamation point, emphasizing the learning that the audience might take from it. Striggio's Eurydice makes the Aristotelian "recognition" explicit: "Ah! A view too sweet and too bitter. Have you lost me through too much love?" Too much self-indulgence, too little self-control, it would rather seem, by the all-too-human Orpheus. Such a tale, of a man who fails to bring back alive his wife (or sister) is reported as common in many world cultures.[26] Here, one would like to have heard Eurydice's fuller thoughts on what happened to her, but *Orfeo* does not offer them.[27] She is more the occasion for male experience than a woman herself, which is consistent with the prevailing role of women as subordinates at the time.[28]

Afterwards Orpheus sings of his grief, praises the absent Eurydice, and vows to renounce women. The original version is not entirely sympathetic to him; it concludes with the morose Orpheus being berated by a chorus of Bacchantes,[29] the female followers of Bacchus (in Greek known as Dionysus, whom Orpheus was a follower of). In a revised version of *Orfeo*, the Bacchantes are replaced by Orpheus's father, the god Apollo, who suddenly "descends from heaven on a cloud," a deus ex machina. Apollo consoles his son and brings him up to heaven, where he tells Orpheus he will see Eurydice in the stars. This happier ending to the opera from 1609 is the one performed today and probably preferred as soon as it was produced. A spectacular ending where a god ascends into heaven might be popular anytime but would have been a familiar trope, or theme, in Catholic Mantua in the early 1600s. The ascension does provide a catharsis, a purging of pity and fear.

Although grounded in human biology, any artwork is also a product of its time and the circumstances of its creators and their social world. As employees of the duke, Monteverdi and Striggio, for example, would have had no illusions about what stories to tell. The idea that a drama could be presented that would reflect, for example, the despotic, back-stabbing political reality of the Gonzaga dynasty would never have crossed their minds or, at least,

18 Music-Dramas, Evolutionary Biology, and Psychology

their lips. As court entertainment, opera began as subtle flattery. *Orfeo* was, in part, a compliment to the Gonzagas, as Striggio's drama was based on an earlier one, written for a previous duke's banquet.

Orfeo, this "tale in music," was something quite new, with music the signal novelty of the work. Probably some of the attendees told Duke Vincenzo that this music-drama affected them. In any case, the duke considered the premiere a success, as indicated by his demanding a second performance a week later.[30] He may have known that he was giving new life to the ancient past. Perhaps he or Striggio or Monteverdi had read Aristotle's *Poetics* by that time and been struck by the description of the features of tragedy and its relevance to *Orfeo*.[31] The *Poetics* had been in Italian translation since the 1540s and in Latin translation for more than a century (and educated men read Latin). The *Poetics* was a frequent topic of discussion and debate among Italian intellectuals concerned about the future of literature and their own culture.[32]

In defining tragic drama as "an imitation of an action that is serious, complete, and of a certain magnitude," Aristotle emphasized that spectacle, staging, costumes, movement, and the playing of some musical instruments were important elements of a performance. But most critical, he wrote, was "language embellished with each kind of artistic ornament … I mean language into which rhythm, 'harmony' and song enter." In fact, what is known of the performance of classical Greek tragedy is that it had characteristics of the musical work that Mantua had witnessed.

The discovery that Greek tragedy was in some way sung had been discussed in Italy since the mid-1500s, a half-century earlier, and intellectuals in Florence[33] came to propose the creation of new dramatic works that would enhance drama through music. Drama—fictions performed—was their goal, for they clearly recognized the power of performance. Costumes, dancing, and staging would be employed, but the words themselves were to be emphasized and sung accompanied in a style called *recitativo*, in which the rhythms and inflections of speech prompted the musical accompaniment. The Florentine Jacopo Peri composed and presented the first opera, *Euridice*, in 1600. Monteverdi exploited this declamatory style very flexibly and richly to create continuity throughout the drama of *Orfeo*, augmenting that style periodically with more distinct and extended melodic singing.

But why singing, for the Athenians who listened to the dramas of Aeschylus, Sophocles, and others? And why singing, for the Renaissance Italians? Why, after all, do people sing? It seems odd. People have other ways to communicate information if that were the main goal. But as any pre-verbal infant would tell you (if they could) the ability to make sounds with voices can communicate feelings, *shares* feelings. Nevertheless, people have other ways, more immediate ways of sharing feelings—through touch, for example—than singing. Perhaps something additional may be going on.

For a vivid clue, here is composer Hector Berlioz apparently describing a performance in the 1830s by Gilbert-Louis Duprez, the tenor who became famous as the first able to sing a high C[34] using "chest" voice—a full, masculine sound, very different from the high notes of earlier tenors.[35] Berlioz describes when the tenor "gives out some high chest notes with a resonance, an expression of heart-rending grief, and a beauty of tone that so far no one had been led to expect":

> Silence reigns in the stupefied [opera] house, people hold their breath, amazement and admiration are blended in an almost similar sentiment, fear; in fact there is some reason for fear until that extraordinary phrase comes to an end; but when it has done so, triumphantly, the wild enthusiasm may be guessed ... Then from two thousand panting chests break forth cheers.

With Duprez and with the dramatic tenors who followed him (and the dramatic sopranos as well), audiences appear to be responding to something more primal than well-crafted music or even the sentiments in the lyrics. Clarion, ecstatic high notes represented a physical feat in-the-moment way beyond the ability of normal people, an athletic exertion that harnessed strength and self-discipline in a peak moment that would, as Berlioz said, stupefy, amaze, and generate "wild enthusiasm." In nineteenth-century Italy and France, opera singers like Duprez commonly received the enthusiasm "usually reserved today for rock stars," as one scholar has noted.[36]

Berlioz and his audience were perhaps too genteel to emphasize the word in public, but underneath their aesthetic response is something to do with sex. That is unlikely a surprise, but it does merit some explanation.

Charles Darwin is better known for *On the Origin of Species*[37] in which he focused on "natural selection," which usually results in animals that are well adapted to the environment of their time. Later, in *The Descent of Man, and Selection in Relation to Sex*, Darwin described a second, related process. "Sexual selection" results in traits that affect an organism's ability to obtain a mate and successfully produce progeny. Living organisms, in this instance, rather than impersonal "nature," drive the selection. Darwin suggested singing as such a trait:

> When we treat of sexual selection we shall see that primeval man, or rather some early progenitor of man, probably first used his voice in producing true musical cadences, that is in singing, ... this power would have been especially exerted during the courtship of the sexes, serving to express various emotions, as love, jealousy, triumph, and serving as a challenge to their rivals.[38]

20 Music-Dramas, Evolutionary Biology, and Psychology

Darwin suggested two ways in which a singer might have an advantage for being selected. Singing "challenges rivals" in competition for a mate, analogous to when the biggest, strongest buck in the herd, possessing the largest rack of antlers, intimidates other males. Singing also "expresses various emotions," a behavior to which the (female) prospect would positively respond.[39]

In the decades following Darwin, evolutionary biology itself evolved as research prompted new insights, although there have been no fundamental changes to the Darwinian paradigm[40] (and, in general, the breadth of those insights is beyond the scope of this book). But, as an example, since Darwin the understanding of sexual selection has advanced through the notion of the "costly signal,"[41] some feature of the prospective mate that puts a "cost" or burden on him (or her) and which signals quality. Consider the peacock. Surely that male did not really need such an outrageously showy display of colorful iridescent feathers. Not only are they flashy and large, the feathers also make him vulnerable to predators that snatch at them. So why did the peacock evolve to have such a dangerous, beautiful attribute? The peacock's risky plumage can be understood as a costly signal, and choosy peahens choose showy and risky male attributes because they considered them "honest advertisements" of greater reproductive potential.

A different model of sexual selection makes more of beauty itself. As evolutionary biologist Richard Prum has argued, limiting explanation of mate preference to the idea of costly signaling is similar to a theory of "efficient" economic markets in which all actors are honest and rational and thus information leads to correct valuations. By contrast, his aesthetic model of sexual selection is "a lot like irrationally exuberant markets" in which choices are driven by subjective preferences and trend-following. "The peacock's tail as it evolves is transforming the female's brain and her capacity to understand what beauty is," Prum has said, "and her preferences are also transforming the tail; they evolve along an entrained path together."[42]

Arguably, vocal display can be at least a costly signal. Note Berlioz's description of tenor Duprez and the "panting" response of the audience: "from two thousand panting chests break forth cheers." A singer, like Duprez, who suddenly has to rise up to full, concert hall–filling volume on a high note is as exposed and vulnerable as a tightrope walker doing a backflip, with the singer's additional challenge that the note is not merely a physical feat—a high-pitched yell, as it were—but the culmination of some musical and dramatic statement. Mating with a person who could put on such a display might seem a pretty good bet: he has endurance, strength, intelligence, sensitivity, all there to witness in the moment when performance counts.

Consider another and familiar operatic example. Virtually every tenor who can sing the aria "Nessun dorma!" from Puccini's *Turandot* does so, in a concert or in the opera itself, singing he "will triumph" (vincerò) and win the unattainable princess. How? At the musical climax, as the orchestra swells, the tenor rises to the loud high B and then the A below it, and usually holds them triumphantly, *loudly*—even though Puccini did not score the final notes that way. "Nessun dorma!" in its musical form as well as its verbal content sounds a prime exhibit for sexual courtship as a biological function of singing.[43]

"Music," evolutionary psychologist Geoffrey Miller noted, "is used conspicuously in courtship [and] reaches its peak in young adulthood during the period of most intense courtship,"[44] as any young singer-songwriter or member of a garage band would likely confirm.

Yes, but if evolution linked music and sex, wouldn't one expect to see them also somehow linked in the brain? Peak pleasure in listening to music, it is known, is often accompanied by chills, also known as "goosebumps," and often chills arise at the climax of emotion and physiological arousal.[45] Those peaks are marked in the brain by strong flows of dopamine, a neurotransmitter, a chemical released by nerve cells to send signals to other ones. Research over the past two decades has found that dopamine transmission is a cause of pleasurable reactions to music.[46] Dopamine also increases during sex and during psychoactive drug use, and when dopamine flows it has the effect of stimulating the brain to repeat what it just did, to get more of this pleasurable reward.[47]

The "rewarding" flow of dopamine follows a buildup of anticipation, and Western music is adroit at constructing anticipation and release in time. "Nessun dorma!" does that, as does one of the most familiar and rousing examples of operatic music, the overture to *William Tell* by Rossini. The overture concludes with a famous "gallop,"[48] which appears to be racing toward a climax but then, repeatedly, the music does not end, the key changes, and the anticipation ratchets up further. This pattern of increasing the anticipation and delaying the climax became a staple of the conclusion of music compositions since at least the time of Bach, and it is also very common in popular music, such as rock 'n' roll.[49]

That singing may have been a factor in human sexual selection over perhaps tens of thousands of years is very difficult to "prove," as evidence from long ago is not directly available. No one is claiming that singing would be the only behavior that would attract mates, nor that all prospective mates would be attracted to singers. Formal empirical research into the genetic, physiological, and behavioral links that may exist between music and sexual selection has been limited.[50] Even so, those outside the laboratory may not need too much convincing about singers.

Intense female orientation devoted toward many male singers is quite apparent, as are males to female singers, and all happy permutations in between. Apart from their singing abilities, with the distinctive qualities that Darwin noted were intended to "charm,"[51] many performers

22 Music-Dramas, Evolutionary Biology, and Psychology

also present a certain physical attractiveness, and, today, with the help of modern marketing, appearance and ability can amplify each other, readily spawning, it is not difficult to imagine, mating fantasies. Beauty has power.

Singing is about more than sex, of course; and it would be remiss to skip over the fact that both in Athens in the fourth century BCE and in Mantua in the early sixteenth century CE, most and perhaps all the singers in dramas were male. Still, those specific cultural practices do not invalidate a broad-based biological argument for the appeal of singers. Anyway, female voices were quickly added to opera.

Orfeo retains the prestige of being the earliest opera still performed regularly today. In the years after its premiere, the people of seventeenth-century Italy came to consider opera the highest form of music and also the most appealing.[52] Opera rapidly became popular entertainment throughout Italy, in Venice, Rome, Naples, and other major cities. Many new operas were created to meet the demand: more than 400 operas premiered in Venetian theaters alone from 1637 until the end of the century.[53]

Monteverdi passed away in 1643, having composed at least another half-dozen operas.[54] But new composers and new audiences of the 1600s gradually moved opera away from its comparatively austere, courtly beginnings. Why certain artistic forms succeed, grow, and persist, while others do not, must be due, at least in part, to the benefits people perceive. With music, drama, acting, singing, dancing, stage spectacle all combined and in a social occasion, opera would have offered many stimuli and occasioned personal experiences distinctive in their collection at the time in a work for the theater. Key among the experiences were feelings and emotions.

Notes

1 Knowing which room was used might further illuminate performance practices. See Paola Besutti, "The 'Sala Degli Specchi' Uncovered: Monteverdi, the Gonzagas and the Palazzo Ducale, Mantua," *Early Music* 27, no. 3 (1999); those being seated included members of the local intellectual "academy," the Accademia degli Invaghiti, which had sponsored the work.
2 See the portrait: http://sv.wikipedia.org/wiki/Vincenzo_I_Gonzaga#/media/ Fil:Frans_Pourbus_the_younger_-_Portrait_of_Vincenzo_Gonzaga,_Duke_of _Mantua,_wearing_armour_and_the_Order_of_the_Golden_Fleece.jpg
3 Translation used in this chapter, except where noted: Claudio Monteverdi, *Orfeo: Favola in Musica (Orfeo* [sic]: *A Tale in Music)*, Italian libretto by Alessandro Striggio. English translation by Gilbert Blin (http://monteverdi.co.uk/downloads /Monteverdis_Orfeo_-_Libretto_and_translation.pdf; 2012).
4 Perhaps from the Latin version by Ovid or by an Italian drama from 1480 written for the Gonzaga court and that had been republished subsequently.

5 As far as is known, women were not invited to the first performance.

6 Which appear to be the notes of lectures given to his students about 330 BCE.

7 Aristotle, *The Poetics of Aristotle*, trans. S. H. Butcher (London: Macmillan and Co., 1902).

8 Aristotle's word "mimesis" scholars examine in great detail and sometimes interpret as slightly different from "imitation." Paul Woodruff, "Aristotle on Mimesis," in *Essays on Aristotle's Poetics*, ed. Amelie Rorty (Princeton, NJ: Princeton University Press, 2012).

9 Modern learning is more complex than what the *Poetics* describes. Engineering National Academies of Sciences and Medicine, *How People Learn II: Learners, Contexts, and Cultures* (Washington, DC: National Academies Press, 2018).

10 For Aristotle's statement of this (in English translation), see Woodruff, "Mimēsis," 81.

11 See Laura van Holstein and Robert A. Foley, "Hominin Evolution," *Encyclopedia of Evolutionary Psychological Science* (2017), http://doi.org/10.1007/978-3-319 -16999-6_3416-1. A more "popular" account is S. Condemi and F. Savatier, *A Pocket History of Human Evolution: How We Became Sapiens*, trans. Emma Ramadan (New York: The Experiment, LLC, 2019).

12 From about 611 to 1457 cubic centimetres, i.e., about 2.4 times. Table 2 in van Holstein, "Hominin Evolution," 8.

13 Jessica C. Thompson et al., "Taphonomy of Fossils from the Hominin-Bearing Deposits at Dikika, Ethiopia," *Journal of Human Evolution* 86 (2015).

14 *Australopithecus.*

15 Petar Gabrić, Marko Banda, and Ivor Karavanić, "Palaeolithic Toolmaking and the Evolution of Cognition and Language" (paper presented at the Proceedings of the 21st International Multiconference INFORMATION SOCIETY – IS Ljubljana, Slovenia, 2018).

16 Ibid.

17 M. Tomasello, "How Children Come to Understand False Beliefs: A Shared Intentionality Account," *Proceedings of the National Academy of Sciences of the United States of America* 115, no. 34 (2018): 8494.

18 Ibid.

19 See Dan P. McAdams, "First We Invented Stories, Then They Changed Us: The Evolution of Narrative Identity," *Evolutionary Studies in Imaginative Culture* 3 (2019): 2.

20 Joan Didion, *The White Album* (New York: Simon & Schuster, 1979), 11.

21 Discussed by many, including J. Cartwright, *Evolution and Human Behaviour: Darwinian Perspectives on the Human Condition* (Basingstoke, UK: Palgrave Macmillan, 2016), 14.

22 All Boyd quotes from Brian Boyd, "The Art of Literature and the Science of Literature," *American Scholar* 77, no. 2 (2008).

23 Aristotle, I. Bywater, and G. Murray, *On the Art of Poetry* (Oxford: Clarendon Press, 1920), 702.

24 Aristotle called reversals "peripitea" and discoveries "anagnorisis."

25 My translation.

26 Paul Harvey, ed., *The Oxford Companion to Classical Literature* [Reprinted with corrections]. (Oxford: Clarendon Press, 1959), 299.

27 But as one example, the recent opera, *Eurydice*, by Matthew AuCoin, does.

28 Some women in Renaissance Italy were exceptions to this norm, as reviewed in Holly S. Hurlburt, "A Renaissance for Renaissance Women?," *Journal of Women's History* 19, no. 2 (2007).

29 See John Whenham, "'Orfeo,' Act 5: Alessandro Striggio's Original Ending" in Whenham and Wistreich, *The Cambridge Companion to Monteverdi*.

24 Music-Dramas, Evolutionary Biology, and Psychology

30 This and many other details in Iain Fenlon, "The Mantuan *Orfeo*" in John Whenham and Richard Wistreich, eds., *The Cambridge Companion to Monteverdi* (Cambridge, UK: Cambridge University Press, 2007).

31 Lodovico Castelvetro's 1570 translation and commentary in Italian had given the best interpretation of Aristotle available, largely consistent with the Greek original: W. Rhys Roberts, *Greek Rhetoric and Literary Criticism* (New York: Cooper Square Publishers, 1963), 113.

32 Stephen Halliwell, "Epilogue: The *Poetics* and Its Interpreters" in Amélie Rorty, *Essays on Aristotle's Poetics* (Princeton, NJ: Princeton University Press, 1992), 413.

33 Claude V. Palisca, *The Florentine Camerata: Documentary Studies and Translations* (New Haven, CT: Yale University Press, 1989).

34 This tone, an octave above middle C, is normally the highest for a tenor voice, though a very few can sing higher.

35 Henry Pleasants, *The Great Singers: From the Dawn of Opera to Our Own Time* (New York: Simon and Schuster, 1966), 165. Berlioz does not mention Duprez by name but he would be the model.

36 Bernard Zelechow, "The Opera: The Meeting of Popular and Elite Culture in the Nineteenth Century," *History of European Ideas* 16, nos. 1–3 (1993): 92.

37 Charles Darwin, *On the Origin of Species*, 1859 (1st ed.). (London: Routledge, 2003), http://doi.org/10.4324/9780203509104

38 Charles Darwin, *The Descent of Man, and Selection in Relation to Sex.* (Princeton, NJ: Princeton University Press, 1981; repr., Reprint of 1871 first edition), 56.

39 These two ways are now referred to as "intrasexual" and "intersexual" selection, respectively.

40 Christina L Richards and Massimo Pigliucci, "Epigenetic Inheritance: A Decade into the Extended Evolutionary Synthesis," *Paradigmi* 38 (2020): 467.

41 Robust discussion: Geoffrey Miller, "Evolution of Human Music through Sexual Selection," in *The Origins of Music*, ed. B. Merker, N. L. Wallin, and S. Brown (Cambridge, MA: MIT Press, 2000).

42 Richard Prum, "Duck Sex, Aesthetic Evolution, and the Origin of Beauty," *Edge* (2014), http://www.edge.org/conversation/richard_prum-duck-sex-aesthetic-evolution-and-the-origin-of-beauty.

43 Miller, "Sexual Selection," 330.

44 Ibid.

45 Oliver Grewe, Reinhard Kopiez, and Eckart Altenmüller, "The Chill Parameter: Goose Bumps and Shivers as Promising Measures in Emotion Research," *Music Perception* 27, no. 1 (2009): 73. The effect was quite individual, however.

46 L. Ferreri et al., "Dopamine Modulates the Reward Experiences Elicited by Music," *Proceedings of the National Academy of Sciences of the USA* 116, no. 9 (2019): 3796.

47 The "sex, drugs, and rock 'n' roll" that the old expression put together would appear linked by dopamine in peak experiences.

48 As used in the 1950s American television show, *The Lone Ranger*.

49 Two diverse examples: the emphatic final moments of Beethoven's Ninth Symphony and "Southbound" by the Southern rock band, the Allman Brothers (http://youtu.be/oUyjeiWz_6c).

50 A review: A. Ravignani, "Darwin, Sexual Selection, and the Origins of Music," *Trends in Ecology & Evolution* 33, no. 10 (2018): 716–719.

51 "The progenitors of man, either the males or females, or both sexes ... endeavoured to charm each other with musical notes and rhythm." Darwin, *Descent*, 337.

52 Claude V. Palisca, *Music and Ideas in the Sixteenth and Seventeenth Centuries*, Music and Ideas (Urbana: University of Illinois Press, 2006), 129.
53 Evan Baker, *From the Score to the Stage: An Illustrated History of Continental Opera Production and Staging* (Chicago: University of Chicago, 2013), 13,15.
54 An accessible summary: Wikipedia contributors, "Lost operas by Claudio Monteverdi," Wikipedia, The Free Encyclopedia, http://en.wikipedia.org/w/index.php?title=Lost_operas_by_Claudio_Monteverdi&oldid=1021427496 (accessed September 2, 2021).

2

RODELINDA

Emotion, Music, and Drama

Anticipation thrummed the air that Saturday evening for some in London, for a new opera by the excellent Mr. Handel was to be presented at the King's Theatre, and the extraordinary Senesino would be heard in a leading role. *The Daily Courant* had cried out[1] the opera's name in all capitals, "RODELINDA," and also the ticket price of half a gold coin, a guinea.[2]

At that price, primarily gentlemen and their betters could afford attendance for the "Six a-Clock" start,[3] and as they entered the wooden theater on Market Lane and perhaps purchased a cup of tea or an orange on the way to their seats, they looked around to spy members of the court or King George himself. Whatever else they anticipated, the gentry could be confident of three things about this new opera: it would be in Italian, present a situation congenial to their interests, and feature singing whose qualities would quite likely charm, impress, and even thrill them.

By the premiere of *Rodelinda* in February 1725, opera had spread from Italy to France, Germany, England, and elsewhere in Europe. The 1700s saw even more construction of opera houses throughout Europe: more than 35 were built, renovated, or enlarged in the first half of the century.[4] While some of these were court theaters, most were open to the public, like the King's Theatre in London, although that "public" was mainly the well-to-do. Their appetite for operas in Italian by the German-born George Frideric Handel and by his Italian contemporaries prompted the annual creation of several new operas for the city and the return in repertory of as many more. Opera may have been sophisticated, but it was also keenly pleasurable.

The appeal of Italian operas in England, sung in a language that few understood, mystified those of a satirical outlook, such as the essayist Joseph Addison, who wrote in 1711[5] how "curious" it was that English opera-goers

DOI: 10.4324/9781003254478-4

"sit together like an audience of foreigners in their own country" to hear them.[6] Other observers recognized, however, that the appeal lay in the extraordinary singing of the *castrati*, such as Senesino and Farinelli, performers so popular they were known by their stage names. Such singers were men who had been castrated before puberty, a practice that had begun in Italy more than a century before to supply singers for church music. The *castrati* came to adulthood brilliantly trained and possessing a man's vocal power with a woman's agility and range.[7] An appreciation from 1709 captured the reaction to their singing:

> No Man or Woman in the World can boast of a Voice like Theirs, they are clear, they are moving, and affect the Soul itself ... a Voice the most clear, and at the same time equally soft, pierces the Symphony, and tops all the instruments with an agreeableness which they that hear it may conceive, but they will never be able to describe.[8]

"A voice they will never be able to describe," suggests there may be something inexpressible about singing. Until the advent of sound recordings in the early twentieth century, to experience opera always meant to witness a "live" performance, and the Italian *castrati* serve poignantly to remind that the human voice, singing live in performance, can be an unsurpassed musical instrument. As the novelist Stendhal enthused about some great singers and their art, "the *mystic powers of the human voice* ... could ultimately lead to *transports of delirium and rapture*"[9] (italics in original). Such musical transports are not limited to opera, Italians, or previous centuries, of course, but listeners of Handel's time simply could not get enough of these male singers (or of their equally well-trained female counterparts). The appeal of the voices of the *castrati*—"they are moving and affect the Soul itself"—highlights the vital place of emotion and feelings in opera.

Everyone, or nearly everyone, experiences what are routinely called emotions, and they affect much of human life, including what is considered important[10] and what is remembered. Decisions are affected, often swayed, by emotions. Circumstances associated with strong emotions, such as extraordinary performance of music, often create lasting memories.[11] And yet understanding the nature of emotion has proven a challenge.[12] The English word "emotion" derives from the Latin, meaning to "move out from," but that only raises more questions of what and why. What are emotions? Why do people have them? What functions do they serve? And to our immediate purposes, what is the relationship between them, music, and music-drama? Scientific inquiry provides valuable insights to all these, starting with some definitions and distinctions between phenomena that often seem to blur together, like feelings and emotions. Even "experts" have not agreed.

28 Music-Dramas, Evolutionary Biology, and Psychology

"What are emotions? This is a vexed and tricky question still unresolved by over 100 years of scientific research," the author of a textbook on human behavior, John Cartwright, wrote in 2016.[13] The "concepts of emotion" that researchers are using are "vastly different ... [and] we need a common vocabulary," a leading researcher, Ralph Adolphs, summarized in 2019.[14]

So apparently important to life as they are, emotions have been examined and described by philosophers since at least the time of the ancient Greeks, by psychologists for more than a century, and by neuroscientists in the last few decades. Because emotions are phenomena of our nervous systems and brains, neuroscience may offer the closest scientific view through the "labyrinth of emotion theories."[15] In 2022, a major report by a taskforce of 173 scientists from 26 countries provided the latest, interdisciplinary, collective understanding of emotion and related "affects"—feelings and moods.[16]

To discriminate terms, consider what might happen when a person sees that the vehicle they are driving is in the direct line of another vehicle suddenly approaching head-on. This possible collision arouses attention; is recognized as potentially very bad and harmful; and motivates a quick response. In the moment, "affect" changes, as given by those changes in "arousal," in the assessment of the condition as negative (its "valence"), and in the "motivation" to act. The driver may suddenly feel tense and acts to reduce the risk of a collision and death. And then afterwards perhaps expresses emotions of fear or anger. Such tracking, anticipating, and responding to the external environment are the core functions of "affective states," which include feelings, emotions, and also moods. All are subjective and conscious experiences that an individual may have, though not necessarily as prominently nor in as extreme an experience as the collision example.

As staying alive is always a priority, humans have two complementary internal processes to cope with the dynamic circumstances of life.[17] One, "allostasis," from the Greek meaning other-stability, orchestrates the organism's function based on anticipated needs coming from the environment.[18] All affective states serve allostasis by indicating the current state of the organism and its trajectory relative to a so-called comfort zone. The other internal process, "homeostasis," works to stabilize bodily functions around a set point, such as temperature control around 98.6 F.; and as the experience of a high fever indicates, physiological feelings again may be involved. Homeostasis is not only vital but also appears foundational to life (to be discussed further in chapter 8).

Recent neuroscience recognizes both emotions and moods as subsets of feelings, the latter broadly defined as anything a person experiences, including thoughts and physical sensations.[19] Emotions are rooted in evolution.[20] They differ from physiological feelings[21] in involving, typically, a conscious evaluation of a particular phenomenon or event in relation to the individual's allostatic comfort zone. So, afterwards, the driver may express anger at the other "stupid, reckless guy" who could have caused a collision, while the passenger in the front seat may now realize how fearful she was, and the teenager in the back seat says "Wow, great driving, mom!"

"Mood" differs from emotion by not being directed at a particular event or trigger but rather is a more extended episode of feeling, and it is marked by valence, positive or negative, or good or bad ("After hearing that great performance, I was in a good mood the rest of the evening"). While emotions often suggest goals for action ("I'm so angry, I could have punched that guy"), moods do not.[22] These summaries of feelings, emotion, and mood from a neuroscientific perspective suggest some caution about readily assigning the words "emotion" or "emotional" to every affective state, which often occurs in discussion of the arts.

But to return to Handel, the music historian Charles Burney introduced two key questions concerning music and emotion.[23] Handel's operas, Burney wrote in 1789, had quitted an earlier "tranquil and unimpassioned state" of music and "could now paint the passions in all their various attitudes [and make them] intelligible to the heart." By "passions" Burney may have meant both distinct and intense emotions, such as anger or joy, and also physical feelings, in "their various attitudes."[24] Burney also asserted that Handel made these emotions or feelings "intelligible to the heart," that is, able to be recognized and felt. But can music do these things? Dozens of psychologists have studied whether music by itself can *express* emotions, or if music can *evoke* or induce or make emotions "intelligible."[25]

Rodelinda provides a case in point. No doubt Handel himself could be quite "emotional." "You *dog*!" the composer angrily wrote to one of the *castrati* who objected to his vocal part because it did not showcase him well enough: "You think you know better than I do what is best for you to sing?"[26]

Strong sentiments also seem central to the appeal of Handel's operas, like *Rodelinda*, which is critically regarded today as one of his best. On the whole, it conformed to the conventions of *opera seria*, "serious opera," which gave preference to exposition of characters and to depiction of their feelings rather than preference to unique stories. These stories repeatedly featured convoluted conflicts of love, duty, and honor among the aristocracy.

Rodelinda was the eighth libretto provided to Handel by Nicola Francesco Haym (and the one in which the obscure, ungainly Italian names of the main characters are all of four syllables). To simplify the opera's main plot, the drama begins as King Bertarido has been deposed and is believed to be dead, and the usurper covets the deposed king's wife to become his queen. She, Rodelinda, will have none of it, only agreeing when the usurper, Grimoaldo, threatens to murder her young son if she does not. Rodelinda makes one condition: Grimoaldo must kill her son in front of her before she consents

30 Music-Dramas, Evolutionary Biology, and Psychology

to marry. This the usurper refuses—raising the possibility that he may not be totally bad.

Later Rodelinda discovers that her husband, Bertarido, is, in fact, alive; they are reunited but discovered together by Grimoaldo, who, furious, imprisons his rival and plans to have him executed. Through the intervention of a loyal friend, Bertarido is secretly freed, but the friend is injured in the process and blood is spilled. Under these extreme circumstances Grimoaldo reflects on what he has become.

A brief, turbulent orchestral prelude introduces and then similarly underscores an initial recitative by Grimoaldo, who declares—almost spits out— "I've three furies armed with many whips/in my heart: jealousy, disdain and love."[27] The agitated orchestral accompaniment continues as he furiously adds that others are "calling me faithless,/ perjurer, usurper, villain and tyrant." Apparently overcome by his violent feelings, he temporarily stops, perhaps to get a grip on them. Whether the singing actor feels the emotions himself or just portrays them is an interesting and separate matter, but to our main concern: is *music by itself* evoking an emotional response in the listener or expressing specific emotions?

No question that music and emotion are deeply connected for many people, usually since infancy. Research has demonstrated that infants and mothers communicate through babbling and soothing baby-song from the very first weeks of a child's life.[28] Children are born prepared to interact with others and imitate their facial expressions, such as blinking eyes and open mouths, very early, also demonstrating how fundamental imitation is to human behavior.[29] At the same time, combined with the facial expressions, a parent's sing-song voice and comforting touches provide a range of caring interactions, from calming and reassuring to lightly stimulating[30] ("peek-a-boo"). Such a parent-child interaction is mutual, "an impromptu multimedia duet," as music anthropologist Ellen Dissanayake recognized.[31] Such attunement can regulate moods and actions and restore a kind of balance of life functions, with music activating homeostasis-related neural systems, according to recent research.[32]

Beyond childhood, musical occasions clearly can continue to provoke feelings. Nearly all people have participated in music associated with special occasions, such as "Happy birthday, dear [Your Name here], happy birthday to you!" Such singing intends to induce some positive affect; the recipient may well feel happy about the others' caring and comfort. The "Happy Birthday" song shows that music can stimulate social bonds, and the scholarly case has been made that social cohesion was likely an evolutionary function of music,[33] a theme to which we will return.

Music is involved in many effects that people experience. But the question is still whether Handel's instrumental music itself, such as that underscoring Grimoaldo's verbal outburst, evokes emotion. "Although most musicians and listeners would seem to take the emotional powers of music for granted, it has been the matter of some controversy whether music really can evoke emotions,"[34] one leading music psychologist, Patrik Juslin, noted in 2015. Studies have "obtained evidence in terms of various emotion components," wrote Juslin, including feelings reported by research participants, their physiological reactions, and "activation of brain areas associated with emotions."

As to which "emotions" psychologists have associated with music, Juslin's review found a "very wide range" of terms, such as "interest," "arousal," and "pleasure."[35] The range suggests that among these psychological studies, some at least are describing "emotions" very differently from the understanding of neuroscience, which would characterize interest, arousal, and pleasure as associated with any feelings, not necessarily "emotions."

Music psychologists generally appear to have concluded that music does induce emotions, *per se*, because of how they understand emotions.[36] And while the argument that psychologists have associated "basic" emotions with music might give the impression that, well, if music can do that, the connection must be pretty basic and evident, that interpretation would be strongly challenged. In science, theories guide research, and "basic emotion theories" are only one type of emotion theory.[37]

This "basic" type claims that there are specific sets of emotion types that are natural and innate, with each emotion having its own physical essence that distinguishes it from others. A small group of emotions are said to be basic and will reliably arise from certain stimuli. What those emotions are, however, has differed among researchers, for example Anger, Fear, Surprise, Sadness, Disgust, Contempt, and Happiness[38] by one, or Seeking, Rage, Fear, Lust, Care, Panic, and Play by another,[39] or maybe also Love or "Tenderness."[40] The absence of a consensus about which emotions are in fact "basic" does raise questions about the research and its theoretical underpinnings.

A rather opposite set of theories[41] of emotion are known as "construction theories."[42] Neuroscience indicates that the brain *predicts* everything that humans do, using memory upon incoming data collected by our senses. Prediction, rather than reaction, would have been favored during the evolution of the brain, because it is faster, aiding survival. "We don't passively recognize emotions but actively perceive them," constructivist researcher Lisa Feldman Barrett has argued.[43] Consider happiness. The same individual might say they were happy when anticipating a romantic date for the opera, staying home alone, helping another person, or drinking a delicious milkshake. Moreover, the diverse phenomena those who speak English refer to as "happiness" are likely subtly different from what those who speak Italian mean by "felicità," or those who use apparently identical words[44] in any of the world's thousands of languages.[45] There is no underlying causal mechanism for and no "basic" essence to happiness, a constructivist would say.

32 Music-Dramas, Evolutionary Biology, and Psychology

The claim that a musical passage itself can reliably *evoke* specific emotions is not at all settled.

Whether music *expresses* basic emotions, which many music psychologists have claimed that it does, one comprehensive review and analysis of such research in 2018 found the claim generally wanting on theoretical and empirical grounds.[46] While the details are beyond our scope here, the critique of basic emotion *theory* is that its advocates have not explained why music would be able to express specified basic emotions. However, of the research they examined in detail, the reviewers did find a number of coincidences between acoustic patterns in music and in speech "prosody," the patterns and variations of rhythm and sound as people speak. For example, both human speakers and music sometimes are pitched lower, move downwards, or go slower; and the participants in music psychology research often judge such patterns to indicate "sadness." Higher pitched, upward moving, and faster sounds are sometimes judged to indicate "happiness" (but also "anger" or "fear").[47]

The scientific debate and inquiry continues, as the following year a group of psychologists, asking the question about music and emotion somewhat differently, found that "subjective experiences associated with music" are organized on "at least 13 dimensions,"[48] including "beautiful," "triumphant," and "scary." Doubtless scientific research will continue to try to understand the varied and often intense subjective experiences people report in response to music. But music is rarely heard by itself and arguably has its effects from its performance contexts. Instrumental "program music," for example, often flags in its title a potential story which the listener may then imagine and develop while listening: Beethoven's "Pastoral" symphony, Vivaldi's *Four Seasons*, Elgar's "Pomp and Circumstance" marches are clear examples. For our immediate purposes in attending to a music-drama, again it is not music alone that may evoke a subjective response, a feeling, an emotion. As with childhood lullabies or later "happy birthdays!" it is the marriage of words and music and circumstances that may prompt them in music-drama.[49] Returning to Handel's Grimoaldo can demonstrate this.

Handel created a soliloquy for the character that captures in its musical form the best and most expressive means that the composer had at his disposal. Instrumental music had become formally more sophisticated in the century since Monteverdi; at about the same time Handel was writing *Rodelinda*, Bach, for example, was writing his keyboard Partitas, and Vivaldi was publishing *The Four Seasons*. Following Grimoaldo's initial violent outburst, as he pauses to reflect, the music begins again in a new mode, a gentler *arioso*, partly recitative, partly melody. The tenor haltingly sings of "gentle breezes" that would lull him toward rest and a "peaceful heart."

A third musical form now emerges, an aria, "Pastorello d'un povero armento" (A little shepherd of a poor flock) in which Grimoaldo enters more deeply into that change of heart, singing throughout. The aria is of the conventional type referred to as *da capo* (Italian for repeating "from the beginning"). Its first section, an "A ," repeats after a contrasting "B" section. In this instance, Grimoaldo first imagines a shepherd tending to his flock and sleeping contentedly in the A verse. But the contrasting B section finds him again noting that in his life as king he finds no peace. When the A verse returns a sensitive singer can communicate quite subtly that his desires are changing through emphases on particular repeated words about the shepherd, such as "dorme contento" (sleeps contentedly). Crucially, the orchestral accompaniment throughout the A sections is marked by a leaping interval played by the strings, as if reflecting the usurper's unresolved question about how else he might live. But at the end of the repeat, the orchestra and singer resolve themselves into a short, graceful melody as Grimoaldo, indeed, falls asleep.

Without any words, what "emotion" would a leaping interval express or evoke? "None" is the default answer; and the burden of proof must be on those who would argue otherwise. But taken as a whole dramatic moment of words, musical accompaniment, and action, Grimoaldo's soliloquy can be affecting. Handel shows the character in authentic, common experiences shared by a great many adults: the torment over competing desires and ambitions, and the wish at times to escape them to a more wholesome, less-conflicted sense of self in another setting. An audience member may or may not be affected by the scene, as much depends on both the actual performance that is observed and the individuals themselves.

It is quite likely that members of the audience attending the King's Theatre that February evening in 1725 were there because they were drawn to seek out and enjoy experiences that prompt affect and emotion.[50] Some significant number of opera enthusiasts have a strong need for affect, as available audience research indicates.[51] Operas, as performance of stories which "imitate" life, have certain advantages in drawing observers into their imagined worlds for those effects. Media scholars call the phenomenon of being absorbed in stories through dramas, films, operas, dances, and reading novels, "transportation."

Transportation into a narrative world is a real phenomenon measurable with questions such as "While I was reading the narrative, I could easily picture the events in it taking place."[52] How great is a person's need for affect has been found to influence whether and to what extent transportation into the story-world occurs.[53] Transportation, say its researchers, is understood as a desired personal condition that resembles the phenomenon of "flow," an intensely focused, deeply satisfying mental state in which individuals often lose track of time. The originator of the flow concept, the Hungarian, Mihaly Csikszentmihalyi, identified reading as the most frequent flow activity partaken in by individuals worldwide.[54] It is not a leap to see that other

34 Music-Dramas, Evolutionary Biology, and Psychology

narrative and theatrical arts, like opera, can transport the observer and, presumably, generate flow.

Music is flow in itself. It also increases transportation, according to research that involved two experiments with films.[55] In the first, observers were shown a film with and without its original soundtrack. In the second, music was added to a film produced without it. In both experiments, participants found that music increased the feeling of being transported into an imagined world. Although this research was conducted using films, not opera, the use of music in film is closely related to its use in opera.

For all the distinctions and elaborations about music's effects, it remains that most people do listen to music for the effect it has on them, which does raise the question of how this human proclivity arose. Some evolutionary musicologists point to what must have been an incremental development of the mental and physical capacities leading, before music, first to "musicality" in the evolution of our species.

A sensitivity to pitch and the ability to distinguish different levels between pitches is one of the core components of musicality. Another biological capacity exploits timbre, the particular color or character of a sound: a scream versus a coo, for example. A third is the capacity to produce a rhythm and to repeat it in a sustained pulse or meter: two people linking arms and walking together toward another place, say. The development of such capacities over time and their combination would eventually lead to "music" as is usually thought of.

But musicality appears to have slowly arisen over hundreds of thousands of years, not with an intended goal to create music but rather, according to recent theorizing, within the social circumstances of our primitive forebears. Archaeologist Steven Mithen argued that "musical" variations in the pitch, rhythm, and timbre of human vocal calls may have arisen more than a million years ago as early hominins began inhabiting open savannah environments in Africa.[56] In those vulnerable spaces they would have banded together in groups for protection from other animals, and would have "had to be highly emotional beings to have survived."[57] Lacking language, "they would have become expert at expressing their emotions and reading those of others" by way of their vocal calls, Mithen inferred.[58] Moreover, the archaeologist suggested, "our [Sapiens] emotional sensitivity to music arose from this context."

Mithen's concept of a music-emotion link sees music not as an independent agent but as part of a larger context with consequences for survival.

Survival becomes prominent again in *Rodelinda* with Grimoaldo asleep. His ambitious henchman, Garibaldo, emerges and is about to murder him. But then Bertarido also emerges from hiding and stops Garibaldo. Only a little before, Grimoaldo was Bertarido's sworn enemy, but the latter has

Rodelinda **35**

presumably heard and was moved by the usurper's recent ruminations. In the finale, Grimoaldo, consistent with a change of heart, returns his kingship to Bertarido, who rejoices with the faithful Rodelinda.

In a drama that had veered close to tragedy, the reversals of fortune are completed as Grimoaldo takes up with Bertarido's sister, who once had been betrothed to Grimoaldo and had continued hoping for him. The evolutionary undercurrents in this opera appear to be a driving force. Mating and progeny are on everyone's minds. Grimoaldo had wanted to steal Rodelinda away from her husband, but that primary aim has been unsuccessful against the desire of husband and wife to be reunited, to sustain their original pairing, and to protect their son. Sheer survival has been at least as equal a concern, as all the main individuals face mortal danger because of the scheming of others. All the men are involved in who will dominate and exert power over others, one of the basic and evolved modes of human social behavior.[59] "Handel's audience expected to be able to learn from serious art and liked to tease out lessons by comparing and contrasting behaviour," the Handel specialist Ruth Smith observed, writing about *Rodelinda*.[60] The opera very likely obliged them.

For the composer, how best to conclude his opera and "tease out lessons by comparing and contrasting behaviour"? What would evolution suggest? Given the characters' recent animosity, it might seem dramatically improbable, but Handel and librettist Haym end with a chorus. The two couples (plus loyal friend) sing, "After the dark night/brighter, clearer/lovelier, dearer/appears the sun here below."[61] Such a happy chorus signals the return of social norms and may well echo the primitive evolutionary function of singing together. "In human prehistory and history," Ellen Dissanayake proposed, "it was *participation* in music that produced its group-bonding and group-maintaining effects, which were its adaptive contribution to life and reproduction."[62] Social bonding would have aided cooperation[63] and thus survival and even reproduction, making bonding an evolutionary advantage for Sapiens.[64]

In the finale, just before the chorus and before the two couples depart to a life of contentment (presumably), Rodelinda sings a final da capo aria declaring that "all the anguish has left her heart." For three and a half minutes. That da capo aria, graceful, bright, and up tempo, wants to express relief and joy but nevertheless is more than the tenth time that such an aria has brought *Rodelinda* to a sudden halt, as the singer repeats exactly the words she or he has sung a minute or two earlier. Handel was decidedly not naive, so he had a decent reason for repeating things, other than that he did have a gift for appropriate melody. That reason was spectacular singers, like the *castrati*, and their ability to ornament and otherwise inflect a repeat.

But the musical repeat usually compromised the ongoing drama; and, after Handel's time, the insistent use of such arias would pass out of favor.

36 Music-Dramas, Evolutionary Biology, and Psychology

Christoph Willibald Gluck and his librettist Ranieri de' Calzabigi get the main credit. They declared their new principles for operatic drama in a preface to the published score of *Alceste*, signed by Gluck in 1769:

> When I undertook to write the music for *Alceste*, I decided to strip it completely of all those abuses, introduced either by the ignorant vanity of singers or by composers over-eager to oblige, abuses which have for so long disfigured Italian opera ... I thought to restrict music to its true function of helping poetry to be expressive and to represent the situations of the plot, without interrupting the action or cooling its impetus with useless and unwanted ornaments.[65]

Mozart in the 1780s followed Gluck's lead to make his own operas less interrupted and thereby more engaging, to great effect. By 1832, a century after *Rodelinda*, Gaetano Donizetti's *L'Elisir d'Amore* possessed only the similarities of style of a distant cousin to Handel's.

But again, the perennial concerns with love and its trials are the focus.

Notes

1 Handel database, Stanford University, http://web.stanford.edu/~ichriss/HRD/1725.htm#_ftnref18
2 Named for the African country-source of the gold.
3 For Handel's audience: David Hunter, "Patronizing Handel, Inventing Audiences: The Intersections of Class, Money, Music and History," *Early Music* 28, no. 1 (2000): 32–49.
4 Evan Baker, *From the Score to the Stage: An Illustrated History of Continental Opera Production and Staging* (Chicago: University of Chicago, 2013), 43, 81.
5 *The Spectator*, March 21, 1711. See Joseph Addison and Richard Steele, *The Spectator*, Volumes 1, 2, and 3: A New Edition (1891) (Project Gutenberg), http://www.gutenberg.org/files/12030/12030-h/12030-h/12030-h.htm
6 However, "many audience members were apparently interested in the lyrics and the plot of the operas they were seeing, and you could buy copies of the libretto translated into English at many performances." Gregory Decker, PhD, email to author, July 21, 2020.
7 Kaylyn Kinder, "Eighteenth-Century Reception of Italian Opera in London" (University of Louisville, 2013), 21. Cites Raguenet; see next endnote.
8 François Raguenet, *A Comparison between the French and Italian Musick and Operas*. Translated from the French; With Some Remarks. (etc.) London: Printed for William Lewis, 1709. Repr. ed. Introduction by Charles Cudworth (Westmead, UK: Gregg Int. Pub. Ltd, 1968), 37–38.
9 Henry Pleasants, *The Great Singers: From the Dawn of Opera to Our Own Time* (New York: Simon and Schuster, 1966), 134.
10 See John H. Falk, *The Value of Museums: Enhancing Societal Well-Being* (Lanham, MD: Rowman & Littlefield, 2022), 23.
11 James L. McGaugh, "Making Lasting Memories: Remembering the Significant," *Proceedings of the National Academy of Sciences of the United States of America* 110, no. supplement 2 (2013): 10402–10407.

12 "no one can define 'emotion.' I don't even mean a fancy formal definition. Just a pragmatic one." Alan J. Fridlund, "Review: Weisfeld, Glenn. 2019. Evolved Emotions: An Interdisciplinary and Functional Analysis," *Evolutionary Studies in Imaginative Culture* 4.1 (Spring 2020).

13 J. Cartwright, *Evolution and Human Behaviour: Darwinian Perspectives on the Human Condition* (Basingstoke, UK: Palgrave Macmillan, 2016), 190.

14 R. Adolphs, L. Mlodinow, and L. F. Barrett, "What Is an Emotion?" *Current Biology* 29, no. 20 (2019): R1064.

15 Daniela Schiller et al., "The Human Affectome," (2022): 18.

16 Much of the content in the following four paragraphs derives from Schiller, "Human Affectome."

17 The "two complementary processes are presumed to maintain a balanced organismic state": Ibid., 10.

18 Ibid., 10.

19 Ibid., 11.

20 Another recent review: Kristen A Lindquist et al., "The Cultural Evolution of Emotion," *Nature Reviews Psychology* 1, no. 11 (2022): 669–581.

21 Schiller, "Affectome," 21. Summary.

22 Ibid., 19.

23 Charles Burney, *A General History of Music* (1935; New York: Harcourt, Brace and Company, Original publication 1789), http://archive.org/details/generalhist oryof00burn2. 747.

24 L. F. Barrett, "The Theory of Constructed Emotion: An Active Inference Account of Interoception and Categorization," *Social Cognitive and Affective Neuroscience* 12, no. 1 (2017): 6.

25 See Patrik N. Juslin, "Emotional Reactions to Music," ed. Susan Hallam, et al., *The Oxford Handbook of Music Psychology* (Oxford: Oxford University Press, 2018). http://www.oxfordhandbooks.com.

26 Cited by Alan Riding, "In Opera, a Different Kind of Less Is More: 'Handel and the Castrati,'" *New York Times*, April 19, 2006. Giovanni Carestini was the offending *castrato*.

27 George Frideric Handel, *Rodelinda*, Italian libretto by Nicola Haym. English translation by Peter Jones. Outhere Music, 2020, 60. http://booklets.idagio.com /691062065825.pdf.

28 Ellen Dissanayake, "The Earliest Narratives Were Musical," *Research Studies in Music Education* 34, no. 1 (2012): 3–14.

29 For neonate discussion: A. N. Meltzoff and W. Prinz, *The Imitative Mind: Development, Evolution and Brain Bases* (Cambridge, UK: Cambridge University Press, 2002), 48.

30 S. E. Trehub, N. Ghazban, and M. Corbeil, "Musical Affect Regulation in Infancy," *Annals of the New York Academy of Sciences* 1337 (2015): 186–189.

31 Ellen Dissanayake, "The Art of Ritual and the Ritual of Art," in *The Nature of Craft and the Penland Experience* (North Carolina: 2004). See also Ellen Dissanayake, "Antecedents of musical meaning in the mother-infant dyad," *Biopoetics: Evolutionary Explorations in the Arts*, Brett Cooke and Frederick Turner, eds. (Lexington, KY: ICUS Books, 1999), 367–397.

32 Assal Habibi and Antonio Damasio, "Music, Feelings, and the Human Brain," *Psychomusicology: Music, Mind, and Brain* 24, no. 1 (2014): 99.

33 Patrick E. Savage et al., "Music as a Coevolved System for Social Bonding," *Behavioral and Brain Sciences* 44 (2021). A. R. Harvey, "Music and the Meeting of Human Minds," *Frontiers in Psychology* 9 (2018): 762.

34 Juslin, "Emotional Reactions," 3.

38 Music-Dramas, Evolutionary Biology, and Psychology

35 Ibid., 4. "[M]usic may arouse both basic (e.g., *sadness, happiness, interest*) and complex (e.g., *pride, nostalgia*) emotions ... [And] the most frequent emotional states across studies include the following categories: *calm-relaxation, happiness–joy, nostalgia–longing*. . . as well as different synonymous terms."

36 Note that Juslin's review article is titled "Emotional Reactions to Music."

37 Schiller, "Human Affectome," 15.

38 P. Ekman and D. Cordaro, "What Is Meant by Calling Emotions Basic," *Emotion Review* 3.4 (2011): 364–370. doi: 10.1177/1754073911410740

39 J. Panksepp, "Neurologizing the Psychology of Affects: How Appraisal-Based Constructivism and Basic Emotion Theory Can Coexist," *Perspectives on PsychologicalScience*2.3(2007):281–296.doi:10.1111/j.1745-6916.2007.00045.x

40 P. N. Juslin, "What Does Music Express? Basic Emotions and Beyond," *Frontiers in Psychology* 4 (2013): 596. doi: 10.3389/fpsyg.2013.00596

41 A third set are usually described as "Appraisal theories," but will not be detailed here as they do not clarify the discussion. For a summary of them, see Schiller, "Human Affectome," 15.

42 Or "constructivist": Ibid.

43 L. F. Barrett, "What Faces Can't Tell Us," *New York Times*, March 28, 2014.

44 A. P. Fiske, "The Lexical Fallacy in Emotion Research: Mistaking Vernacular Words for Psychological Entities," *Psychological Review* 127, no. 1 (2020): 95–113.

45 See http://www.linguisticsociety.org/content/how-many-languages-are-there-world

46 J. Cespedes-Guevara and T. Eerola, "Music Communicates Affects, Not Basic Emotions - A Constructionist Account of Attribution of Emotional Meanings to Music," *Frontiers in Psychology* 9 (2018): 5.
These two critics argue that much of basic emotion music psychology has been compromised by limitations of methods, for example that participants were asked to listen to stereotypical Western music and report their "emotions" from a plausible but limited list of familiar options.

47 Ibid., 9–10. See chart for details.

48 A. S. Cowen et al., "What Music Makes Us Feel: At Least 13 Dimensions Organize Subjective Experiences Associated with Music across Different Cultures," *Proceedings of the National Academy of Sciences of the United States of America* 117, no. 4 (2020): 1924–1934.

49 People "draw heavily (if unwittingly) on a wide variety of contextual clues — a body position, a hand gesture, a vocalization, the social setting and so on," as neuroscientist Lisa Barrett noted about emotion construction. L. F. Barrett, "What Faces Can't Tell Us," *New York Times*, March 28, 2014.

50 Gregory R. Maio and Victoria M Esses, "The Need for Affect: Individual Differences in the Motivation to Approach or Avoid Emotions," *Journal of Personality* 69, no. 4 (2001): 583–614.

51 Sinéad O'Neil, Joshua Edelman, and John Sloboda, "Opera Audiences and Cultural Value: A Study of Audience Experience," CreativeWorks London Working Paper No. 2 (University of London, 2014); Claudio E. Benzecry, *The Opera Fanatic: Ethnography of an Obsession* (Chicago: University of Chicago Press, 2011).

52 Melanie C. Green and Timothy C. Brock, "The Role of Transportation in the Persuasiveness of Public Narratives," *Journal of Personality and Social Psychology* 79, no. 5 (2000): 704–721.

53 Markus Appel and Tobias Richter, "Transportation and Need for Affect in Narrative Persuasion: A Mediated Moderation Model," *Media Psychology* 13, no. 2 (2010): 101.

54 M. Csikszentmihalyi, *Flow. The Psychology of Optimal Experience* (New York: Harper Perennial, 1990). Chapter 5 identifies reading in this way.

55 Kristi A. Costabile and Amanda W. Terman, "Effects of Film Music on Psychological Transportation and Narrative Persuasion," *Basic & Applied Social Psychology* 35, no. 3 (2013): 316–324.

56 S. Mithen, "The Music Instinct: The Evolutionary Basis of Musicality," *Annals of the New York Academy of Sciences* 1169 (2009): 3–12.

57 Ibid., 5.

58 Ibid., 6–7.

59 Joseph Henrich, *The Secret of Our Success* (Princeton, NJ: Princeton University Press, 2016), 122–128. Also: Joseph Carroll, "Evolutionary Social Theory: The Current State of Knowledge," *Style* 49, no. 4 (2015): 512–541.

60 Handel, *Rodelinda*, tr. Jones, "Constructing the Drama," 19.

61 Handel, *Rodelinda*, tr. Jones, 65.

62 Ellen Dissanayake, "If Music Is the Food of Love, What about Survival and Reproductive Success?" *Musicae scientiae* 12, no. 1_suppl (2008): 182.

63 A selection of relevant scholarship: (1) Ellen Dissanayake, "Ritual and Ritualization: Musical Means of Conveying and Shaping Emotion in Humans and Other Animals," in *Music and Manipulation: On the Social Uses and Social Control of Music*, ed. Steven Brown and Ulrich Voglsten (Oxford and New York: Berghahn Books, 2006); (2) Robin Dunbar, "On the Evolutionary Function of Song and Dance," in *Music, Language, and Human Evolution*, ed. Nicholas Bannan (Oxford: Oxford University Press, 2012); (3) M. Tomasello and A. Vaish, "Origins of Human Cooperation and Morality," *Annual Review of Psychology* 64 (2013): 231–255.

64 See Dissanayake, "If Music."

65 Gluck to Archduke Leopold of Tuscany, Vienna, 1769, in *Alceste* (Vienna, 1769), pp. xi–xii; Translation by P. Howard in Patricia Howard, *Gluck: An Eighteenth-Century Portrait in Letters and Documents* (Oxford: Clarendon Press, 1995), 84.

3

L'ELISIR D'AMORE

Mate Choice, Comedy, and Consonance

"Doctor Bittersweet" is pouring drinks into shot glasses, and the twenty-something is feeling pretty good about his bartending prowess and himself.

"Hey, you folks!" he calls out. "Listen up."

"This marvelous drink will cure your toothache," he starts singing. "It will also kill mice and lice." Amused, Belcore and Giannetta stop flirting out on the balcony, not that Dulcamara ("Bittersweet") especially notices. In the kitchen, putting a dozen tiny glasses of liquor onto a tray, he continues to riff on all the amazing things these drinks can do. "An ailing seventy year old became a father to ten ... Thanks to this elixir, many widows stop weeping in a week."

As Dulcamara glides into the living room with the glasses, Nemorino perks up when hearing that the drinks can help "lover boys" with their romances (and "young ladies" with their skin). What the heck? Nemorino, Belcore, Giannetta, and Adina, just returned to her living room, wearing a slinky red dress, all start grabbing glasses and gulping them down.

The drinking whirls to a conclusion with Dulcamara ending his rap triumphantly standing on a sofa as the others laugh. Well, except Nemorino. This rich craziness is out of his class. He's wearing a simple t-shirt and high-top black sneakers; but though he may feel out of place, Nemorino has picked up the main idea of use to him. Taking Dulcamara aside, he asks if he can make him a special drink so that Adina, the rich, unattainable girl he loves, will love him in return? Oh, sure! says Dulcamara—for a price, so Nemorino takes off a sneaker and plucks his last dollar out of it.

Taking the money and turning to the others, Dulcamara laughs at how naive this other guy is.

Whether performed by lithe and talented young singers in this updated Dutch staging in 2021[1] or by less lithe, older singers in a traditional staging

DOI: 10.4324/9781003254478-5

that hearkens back to nineteenth-century Italy, Gaetano Donizetti's *L'Elisir d'Amore* (*The Elixir of Love*) is pretty much sure-fire with audiences.

The reasons are intriguing but not all evident.

People generally like to laugh. That laughter is "good medicine" is proverbial,[2] and it turns out some science backs that up. Laughter, not surprisingly, is reported to reduce stress,[3] including the hormone cortisol, which messes with the immune system and is implicated in disease (or "dis-ease," as the emphatic write). And laughter, as a pre-linguistic utterance, may have evolved to smooth out and lighten relations between long-ago hominins.[4] Maybe that's where slipping on a banana peel started.[5]

Surprise and laughter go together, like Nemorino's sneaker, a banana-peel slip, or "I'm a busy man, and I can't be bothered to punch you at the moment, but here is my fist. Kindly run towards it as fast as you can."[6]

Laughter is a funny thing. Maybe not everyone will laugh at that. But as this bit of script suggests, a laugh often also depends on the tone of voice and physical manner that reflect the speaker's attitude. Here it's the satiric, sharp-tongued Blackadder, of the BBC sitcom, again ridiculing his dim-witted servant, Baldrick, who has devised a "cunning plan" to save the doomed King Charles I from being beheaded by placing a pumpkin on the king's head and chopping off the pumpkin instead. But now hearing Black Adder, Baldrick runs at his fist.

Comedy is of two kinds, probably more.[7] But at least one involves something like this Black Adder–Baldrick gambit, attacking the cluelessness or foibles of others. Another one of the kinds is the same, except the illusions of other people are not attacked from some position of superiority. Instead, the story reveals that we are all clueless at times, and our illusions get in the way of understanding what is real. That is the bigger comedy of life. Arguably, the greatest comedies ascend into such good-hearted laughter.

The Elixir of Love is one of them. But as the laughter *at* Nemorino suggests, this comedy occasionally has an edge. Audience members who are adolescents or older and have ever been in love and thought a bit about it will know about the edge. And they are often very interested in romantic comedies because courting comes with the territory of being human, so it is easy to see oneself in the situation. Indeed, no other single decision in life may stand more important than the choice of a mate.[8] A good choice can bring many benefits to the partners (and their children); a bad choice, quite the opposite.

At the start of *L'Elisir*, Nemorino, the naive young fellow, sees Adina, an attractive, rich young woman, and right away sighs, "How beautiful she is; how dear. The more I see her, the more she pleases me."[9] But "I don't have the ability to inspire her slightest affection." These statements reveal that, on the one hand, Nemorino has typical qualities of a romantic lover, in idealizing his beloved and desiring her to love him.[10] But he is not blind to his limitations.

42 Music-Dramas, Evolutionary Biology, and Psychology

In a traditional production, he's an illiterate farmer, and she's a rather worldly local farm-operator.[11] Adina, who has been reading alone, turns to read the story aloud to the assembled villagers, including Nemorino. The legend of Tristan and Isolde could not be plainer: Isolde was hard-hearted and aloof; the handsome knight Tristan "had not the slightest hope of winning her" but went to a magician who gave Tristan a love potion and, voilà, Isolde no longer keeps away from him.

Adina comments, "I wish I knew the recipe of so perfect an elixir" (ne sapessi la ricetta ...). With this setup the plot of *L'Elisir* would seem to come into full view, and the audience would just have to watch relationship magic play out. But what, ask librettist Felice Romani[12] and composer Donizetti, would be the truth or the dramatic novelty of that? So, as dramatists they play with simple expectations about how easily a courtship between Nemorino and Adina might go.

Some magic is a common element in "romantic comedies" and reflects that such comedies often integrate the literary form of "romance,"[13] which historically takes place in a world that saunters a bit above reality, featuring chivalrous knights devoted to desirable ladies and animated by unnoticed powers outside conventional experience. The 1987 American movie *Moonstruck* gives a modern instance. A superstitious widow is about to marry her dull fiancé, but under the mysterious influence of the moon she gets swept off her feet by his somewhat dangerous, passionate brother. As the movie's theme song has it, "When the Moon hits your eye like a big pizza pie, that's amore."[14]

Although no one would wish to downplay the distant magic of the moon, Donizetti's opera about "amore" opts for a more usable elixir. While the drink that the quack Doctor Dulcamara sells to Nemorino is nothing other than cheap wine, it does provide what "magic" does in probably all romances. It lowers inhibitions. The elixir of love gives Nemorino hope, even confidence, that Adina will love him. Marry him, maybe even.

Naturally, humans look for sexual partners. Not all want to have children at any given time, and some not at all. Heterosexual coupling is most common in all cultures, and it is how our *species* persists, not that many, if any (not even evolutionary biologists) enter into relationships for that reason. But in most circumstances in most cultures, and certainly in Donizetti's Italy, courtship would normally precede sex. And there's very little, if any, overt suggestion in *L'Elisir* that the characters' goals are simply for sex and its possible pleasures rather than for durable, long-term love.

Courtship tests the suitability of the prospective partners, as most participants come to understand, if they do not understand to begin with. But women and men are, typically, testing for somewhat different qualities, although that is not always clear to the other. *L'Elisir* provides a lesson.

Nemorino, as the suitor, goes through a number of trials, starting when he asks to talk with Adina. Their encounter in Act 1, scene 3 conveys the initial challenges of courting, in which the individuals try to express who they are and what they want. Adina begins by reassuring Nemorino that he is "good and modest"—and she would like him to forget about her. She's a flirt, she tells him, and like a breeze touches down naturally on one flower and then another. Her melody and its slowly unrolling contours suggest both a natural metaphor of breeze and her attempt at candor. The melody also exemplifies the trademark "bel canto" style of "beautiful singing" that the opera features. Melody is more prominent than any other component of Donizetti's art, here helping to express character but doing so in a way likely ingratiating to the singer and to the listener.

Nemorino takes up Adina's melody with its contours but more seriously describes himself as a river that is drawn persistently to the sea. "It is drawn by a power it cannot explain," but, like the river, he wishes to follow it and lead to her. She appears to be taken by his sincerity but resumes in another verse, cautioning him to do as she does and take a new lover every day, as "one nail drives out another." While this may seem a surprising metaphor for a female character to express in 1832, it does convey Adina's stated determination to have her freedom to choose. To which Nemorino replies, again in melodic imitation, that her advice is impossible because he cannot drive out his "first love" for her.

Nemorino does not have money, but something may be happening to Adina's estimation of him, as Donizetti shows through his musical imitation that Nemorino is listening, attuned to her, and sincere. He just might make a reliable, committed spouse. Without the music, the words alone could not make this attunement as clear. This raises a very interesting question about virtually all romantic vocal duets in opera: Why do the two voices imitate, harmonize, or otherwise blend with each other? Is this just an operatic or musical convention, created by Monteverdi or some other musician?

Researchers who study conversational vocal patterns have found that, in general, even individuals unacquainted with each other actively match the vocal register and the pacing of their speech. But heterosexual singles *converge* in their vocal register and range over time.[15] In addition, in its parallel verses, Romani's and Donizetti's music-drama also reflects the ritualized nature of successful courtship, which is a complex process[16] of communication and trust-building, and follows a certain order.

Ritual involves performing an act or acts in a set manner for a purpose. Humans developed rituals, psychological research suggests, to regulate emotions, social connections, and their performance of activities.[17] Following prescribed steps exerts some control over the uncertain circumstances of life[18] and can generate confidence. In courting, attraction may be followed by increasing emotional intimacy and, then, with increasing physical

44 Music-Dramas, Evolutionary Biology, and Psychology

intimacy. Other sequences tend not to last because of uncertainties in the missing parts. A suitor who asks: "Will you marry me?" on the first date is unregulated and unlikely to be successful.

Regarding attraction and increasing emotional intimacy, the on-stage "chemistry" between the performers portraying Adina and Nemorino, their glances and body language, can underline what may be happening unspoken. Through this first scene of courting and self-disclosure, Donizetti does not lose a light touch. But more tests lie ahead for Nemorino.

Adina has tried to put off Nemorino by saying that she's a flirt and unreliable as a prospective partner, and never saying anything about loving him. But these do not disqualify her, apparently; and when explaining does not have its effect, she actively flirts with the itinerant Sergeant Belcore, who appears in town with his soldiers. She stokes Nemorino's jealousy and despair by even agreeing to marry Belcore, who certainly appears to be an unworthy lothario, although as a military man, he has higher status than Nemorino.

Donizetti mines Nemorino's crushed hopes and Belcore's hostility without flooding the mineshaft with the dark waters of tragedy. In a tableau that develops over about seven minutes and concludes Act 1, the composer first establishes a halting, plaintive, then impassioned melody for Nemorino, which is met with Belcore's haughty dismissal and attempt to end the discussion. But then the assertions of the rivals, the reflections of Adina, and the observations of the townsfolk spill over into a complex multi-voice finale. All the individual melodies may seem in keeping with individual characters' sentiments, but ultimately Donizetti organizes the whole into a concerted scene that could sound nearly as fine performed only on instruments. At the end, the whirling, *vivace* dance-form of the conclusion leaves Nemorino apparently rejected, pathetic, and mocked.

The first of two acts of the drama ends with Nemorino in despair; and it would seem that, superficially, Adina is just being the capricious rich girl who happens to be playing with the feelings of the poor country dreamer because she can. Her socioeconomic status, a sociologist might say, gives her that prerogative.

However, more is going on under the surface of her behavior, and Nemorino's, than either of them declare. As courtship commonly leads to childbearing and childrearing, prospective partners are often choosy, in their own ways.[19] A cross-cultural study of mate choices in 33 countries distributed throughout the globe, questioning more than 10,000 participants, found men and women typically have clearly differing concerns.[20] Evolutionary psychologist David Buss found that in 97% of the cultures women valued ambition and earning potential ("resource acquisition") in mates more than men did. And in 92% of the cultures, men valued physical attractiveness and "reproductive potential" in mates more than women did.

Refinement of such research and analyses have continued, but *L'Elisir* would broadly confirm these modern norms also in Nemorino, who said from the start that he found Adina beautiful and was attracted to her "the more he saw her," and in Adina, who appears to have little motivation to ally herself with a simple *contadino*.

Act 2 steadily increases the courtship challenges besetting Nemorino and Adina, which Donizetti and Romani portray vividly. The community gathers for a feast to celebrate her wedding to Belcore, but at the last minute Adina delays, saying that Nemorino has not shown up and she wants him there to get back at him ("vendetta") for .... something. She's frustrated, disappointed, knows not what, but she puts off the wedding until the evening.

In turn, Nemorino becomes desperate to obtain more "elixir" from Dulcamara so that he can get Adina to love him right away, he thinks. Dulcamara gives him 15 minutes to get the money, so he can quickly depart before his fake potions are recognized for what they are. To get the needed money Nemorino finds Belcore and enlists in the army. The wily sergeant figures this will get rid of his silly rival, while the rival figures that being able to buy the elixir will win Adina and get rid of the sergeant. Their cross-purposes and illusions are captured in a hilarious summary duet of self-confident up-tempo patter-song, from which one could imagine Charles Darwin (who enjoyed opera)[21] getting his idea about singing presenting "a challenge to rivals" in male-male sexual competition.

As he gets tipsy drinking more wine, Nemorino seems very unlikely to secure Adina's love, so his elation seems foolish. He's on a knife's edge and does not even see it. But then another reversal of fortune—literally—happens. Nemorino's rich uncle has died, leaving him his fortune. Learning this, the eligible townswomen repeat over and over, "he's a millionaire," and "don't tell anyone." Right.

When Nemorino appears on the scene, the women all show a newfound interest in him, which he credits to the drink and its amazing abilities to attract women. He does not know about the money he now has. But their elixir, clearly, is money and the magic it proffers. Dulcamara and Adina, separately, observe the scene, and she attempts to draw Nemorino aside because she has learned that he has joined the army, but "you're making a big mistake" (Tu fai gran fallo). Nemorino believes the elixir has also caused Adina to love him, but he drifts off with the other women, saying he'll come back to hear what Adina wants to tell him.

Alone, Nemorino returns, singing that he saw a "furtive tear running down her face" when Adina earlier discovered him among the other women. In the much admired aria and soliloquy, "Una furtiva lagrima," he admits that he wants only Adina. But he needs to hear her declare her love for him. She does appear and sings a passionate aria, apologizing for causing his

46 Music-Dramas, Evolutionary Biology, and Psychology

unhappiness, and she wants him … to … stay in the neighborhood, as she's bought back his military enlistment.

That's *it!* This is not the response he's been waiting for. "Since I'm not loved, I'll die a soldier's death!" cries the dashed Nemorino, and hearing this, Adina's resistance dissolves. Donizetti picks up the pace into a gallop; Adina confesses she does love him, after all, apologizes again, and their joy crests in an intense and happy musical climax. This enjoyable comedy ends with good humor and villager credulity as Dulcamara expresses his conviction that his elixir really is phenomenal, "for love, more potent than coffee."

That the chorus of villagers is enthusiastic about the happy ending, buys more of Dulcamara's magic elixirs, and sings his praises ("Viva il grande Dulcamara!!") provides some echoes of the role of the chorus and the origin of Greek comedy. The Greek chorus, made up of citizens, not professional entertainers,[22] often expressed what their counterparts in the audience might be reflecting on. The chorus sang and chanted and moved in place to underscore what they were singing or chanting.[23] Aristotle claimed that the chorus in a drama of the classical period was a descendent of the practice of men singing and dancing in rituals dedicated to Dionysus, a god of fertility and renewal, that had arisen in previous centuries.[24]

Aristotle said that while tragedy emerged from hymns of praise for the god,[25] comedy may have emerged from "phallic song,"[26] which were rather lewd processions with men drinking, brandishing giant decorated phalluses, and shouting insults. Thousands of paintings on vases, starting in the seventh century BCE, show these sorts of uninhibited processions, depicting sexual behavior, wine-drinking, and a general sense of frivolity and licentiousness.[27] The details of comedy may have changed, but its essence really has not. As the literary scholar Northrop Frye observed, comedy embodies the myth ("mythos") of Spring, new life, fertility, and renewal.[28] This has been the pattern of comedy for a long time, arguably because mating, first of all, is essential to the pattern of life itself. The renewal and continuity of life comes from progeny as it does from the return of Spring. "Is it not the singularity of life that terrifies us?" asked the novelist John Updike.[29] Tragedy denies its protagonist another chance, he saw; the great virtue of comedy is that it offers one.

L'Elisir is still commonly among the top dozen operas performed today.[30] As a romantic comedy, it features a young couple finally getting together through a somewhat torturous courtship. The outcome may seem magical. Adina had to change in her assessment of Nemorino, and it might appear that, superficially, Nemorino became an acceptable spouse because of his newfound riches. The riches changed the other village women's attraction to him, and that would be consistent with the cross-cultural modern research cited earlier that women value a prospective partner's ability to bring "resources" to a relationship.

But Nemorino's sudden wealth is not what changed Adina's feelings for him. That change occurred when she realized that Nemorino took a risk on his own life by joining the army to get some money, and then spent all the money in his continued hopes of winning her. She recognized that such behavior revealed a *commitment* to her ("So much love, and I was pitiless.").

While many modern surveys and studies[31] reflect that, across cultures, male commitment is a clear priority of women for long-term relationships, some, perhaps especially some men, would want to know why. Since commitment is the preference in societies that have very little if any contact with each other and less direct influence suggests looking for a cause more primary than diverse culture. Our species' biology would seem such a cause. We Sapiens have had essentially the same anatomy (have been "anatomically modern") for some 200,000 years.[32] Sexual reproduction, then and now, produces the next generation, and while both males and females are commonly motivated to produce progeny, their different biology entails both different sexual roles and the consequences of those roles.

For their part, evolutionary scientists would ask what persistent challenges in the remote past would a behavior have arisen to solve, and would that behavior have led to reproductive success and progeny, which would cause that behavior to have been selected for and inherited over the generations. Women bear the great biological risks and demands of pregnancy and the primary responsibility of childcare, if for no other reason than they know the child is theirs. Pregnancy takes months, and raising a child into independence takes many years, very different for humans than for other animals. Thus, for women, the main challenges of long-term mating would be identifying men who, first, have the ability or are willing to acquire and invest resources in her and her children[33] and, second, also offer protection to them, as needed.

Men, on the other hand, have a trivial investment in time in creating a pregnancy, but to commit to a long-term bond they first would need to identify women high in reproductive potential, so that they may have one or more surviving children.[34] Second, since fertilization happens inside the woman's body and out of sight, a man would want to be sure that he is the father before investing his time and resources in rearing a child not his.

So, an evolutionary argument would predict that predominant behaviors arose to address these challenges, which are based in biology. A great deal of observational data in scientific research support that view.[35] For long-term relationships, women do indeed look for men who either have or show the clear potential to acquire resources to benefit her and their children. And men will seek relatively young women as long-term mates, because childbearing years are comparatively short, and a younger woman may have more energy for childbearing and childraising than one who is older. In their selection strategy men also look for signs of physical quality that would

48 Music-Dramas, Evolutionary Biology, and Psychology

readily produce children who would be healthy and survive. From an evolutionary perspective, these well-established behaviors for long-term mating are considered "adaptations," that is, features of an organism shaped by evolutionary selection that promote reproductive success.

An evolutionary perspective would also predict that the stories people tell would support these sexual adaptations. *L'Elisir* does, as do many other stories in Western culture since at least the romances of the late Medieval period.[36] But perhaps that is just evidence of purely cultural influence, of a good story prompting others like it in the culture regardless of biological cause. Or maybe the similar stories are just limited to Western culture. One research study addressed these two alternate explanations and found them wanting.[37]

In 2004, Jonathan Gottschall led the study in which the mate preferences of characters in two different sources of literary data were analyzed. Multiple individuals "coded" more than 650 traditional folktales as well as plot and character summaries from 240 works considered representative of Western literature. The folktales came, in part, from tribal, preindustrial, and non-Western communities from 48 different culture areas. Findings supported the contemporary ethnographic research of Buss mentioned earlier, namely, that male characters were two-and-one-half times more likely to prize beauty than were female characters; and female characters three times more likely to prize wealth or status than males.

Sexual selection is more than a strictly rational process (as discussed in chapter 1), and men and women also prefer physical beauty, in part because it pleases them but also because they perceive that beauty indicates physical quality. A visibly deformed person may be a remarkable human being, but the deformity raises questions about that person's inherent physical quality and whether those features would be passed on to children. As a simple reminder of how well-established preferences for beauty are, and often how beauty seems a proxy for quality, note that opera companies are also more likely to cast attractive youthful people as Nemorino and Adina than singers who are not so.

With this explanatory turn, it is fair to ask if the audience viewing *L'Elisir* in 1832, 1932, or 2032 are supposed to be conscious of the courtship behaviors on display. From the evolutionary perspective, audiences don't need to analyze the drama that way; the adaptations were established long ago and part of who humans are.

Moreover, for individuals the appeal (or not) of the opera itself can have multiple causes. The recognition that people experience "transportation" into narrative worlds may have left the impression that the process is somehow automatic. It is not. Whether a person is "transported" into a narrative can initially be affected simply by whether the narrative presents content that is familiar to them.[38] One can imagine that a pre-teenager would have more difficulty being "transported" into the courtship focus of *L'Elisir* than would an adult, for example.

And then there's the music. How Donizetti's music pointed and enlivened the drama in several scenes has already been commented on, but the enduring popularity of *L'Elisir* must be due to something in the overall character of the music itself. During his lifetime, *L'Elisir* was the most frequently performed of Donizetti's 65 operas, and during the peak years of his career (1838–1848), his operas altogether were the most frequently performed in Italian opera houses.[39] Donizetti's operas were extremely popular then, and the musical causes seemed clear enough to some of his contemporaries, who ventured to explain them, as for example, "Donizetti is brilliant, pleasing, insinuating; he understands how to produce an effect ... With a plenitude of happy moments he knows how to beguile the ear and to divert the mind from serious pursuits."[40]

Brilliant, pleasing, and beguiling to the ear appear to be qualities with staying power. Indeed, why is it that *all* the operas most frequently performed today[41] were composed during an earlier period of about 140 years, between Mozart and Puccini,[42] which includes Donizetti? While a compelling dramatic subject is necessary, a second reason for the popularity of the "Mozart to Puccini" operas must be that most people prefer the *sound* of them. But why?

A proposed evolutionary explanation starts with the sounds a voice makes. When a singer sings the A above middle C on the English vowel sound "Ah," for example, air rising from the lungs puts pressure on the two somewhat-elastic vocal cords[43] in the voicebox[44] of the throat. The vibrations of the cords sends an acoustic wave up the throat, resonating there and in the head before coming out the mouth. That wave repeats with a "frequency," and the tone whose frequency is 440 times per second (known as 440 Hertz or 440 Hz) is that A the singer is producing.

In addition to the main tone that is heard—that A—the vibrating cords also make additional faint, higher "overtones" at predictable distances, or intervals, from the fundamental tone. These overtones are simply the result of the physical property of waves, which generate additional waves that are fractions of the originals: one-half, one-third, one-quarter, and so on. The smaller the fraction, the higher the frequency of the wave and the higher the pitch of the overtone. These overtones can be analyzed as a series of intervals, the first of which is the octave (a higher doubling of the original frequency), then the perfect fifth above, perfect fourth, major third, and minor third. These individual overtones of an "harmonic series" *may* sometimes just be heard faintly, but, as they occur simultaneously, the fundamental tone is mainly heard.

Here the basic physics and acoustics meet music. Music puts sounds together, most simply in pairs.[45] Research studies have been designed to find

50 Music-Dramas, Evolutionary Biology, and Psychology

out which pairs listeners find harmonious ("consonant") and which dissonant. In the studies, the pairs were made up of the same root note combined,
in turn, with each of the other 12 notes in the chromatic scale. The results,
across eight separate studies analyzed in 2017, showed the relative consonance of intervals.[46] The perfect fifth, a perfect fourth, a major third, and
then a major sixth were judged most consonant, while the major seventh and
finally minor second were the least.[47] Each of these dissonant ones is only an
apparently uncomfortable half-tone away from the baseline "tonic" (that is,
in the key of C, a leap up to B or a squeeze down to B or up to C#).

So, the musical intervals listeners judge as being harmonious are the same
ones present naturally in the overtone series. These findings about consonance may not be surprising, but they become even more interesting when
linked with other results. In sophisticated acoustic research a very large database of human speech utterance was examined.[48] The speech was diverse:
English, Mandarin, Farsi, and Tamil. Again, significantly, prominent intervals identified in the speech were the octave, major third, perfect fourth,
perfect fifth, and major sixth (which is the inverse of the minor third).[49] It
is one thing to note that a singer can generate overtones, making music, but
something much more to find the same "harmonious" intervals revealed in
natural human speech of many cultures.

One scientific interpretation is that humans have been listening to the
sounds of each other before there were words. Under the complex demands
of group living humans came to express themselves vocally,[50] as the vocal
tract itself evolved along with modifications of the human head and face,
those modifications themselves occurring over many tens of thousands of
years.[51] We are by nature and long evolutionary experience in human culture
attuned to detecting and interpreting various communication repertoires,
including gestures and bodily expressions as well as vocalizations of several kinds, such as grunts, clicks, growls, and hisses.[52] But also tones. The
evolutionary hypothesis is that humans' sense of tonality arose because of
the great value of recognizing the tones and their combinations that *other*
humans made, because they were routinely the most important sound-sig-
nals in their environment.[53]

The sounds we are suited to utter and to hear also appear to predict the
frequency range of human music and the instruments used to make it.[54] The
frequency range of human vowel sounds is about 50–5000 Hz, while the
wide-ranging piano, for example, makes tones of about 27–4100 Hz.

Music across the world and across time varies greatly, but a great many
people seem to naturally prefer music that orients itself around a familiar tonal structure, dominated by movements to the fifth (the "dominant"
interval) and the fourth (the "subdominant") and returning to the root, the
tonic. People rather expect that gratification; and those same musical intervals are more often used in musical composition than others across time

and cultures.[55] Opera listeners' preference for "Mozart to Puccini"—and Donizetti—follows suit with this scientific research. Why *L'Elisir* "beguiles the ear" is now clearer.

Notes

1 The description of this scene and aria and the translation are from Opera Zuid | Dutch National Touring Opera | Dutch National Opera, *L'Elisir d'Amore* by Gaetano Donizetti. YouTube video. May 23, 2021. http://youtu.be/TQdg1 HM_jzY

2 Proverbs 17.22, King James Bible: "A merry heart doeth good like a medicine ...."

3 Lee S. Berk et al., "Neuroendocrine and Stress Hormone Changes during Mirthful Laughter," *American Journal of the Medical Sciences* 298, no. 6 (1989): 390–396.

4 Marina Davila Ross, Michael J. Owren, and Elke Zimmermann, "The Evolution of Laughter in Great Apes and Humans," *Communicative & Integrative Biology* 3, no. 2 (2010): 191–194.

5 For modern evidence of the slipping-laughing connection see, "Make 'em laugh," in *Singin' in the Rain*, the popular 1952 musical film.

6 Episode is the "Black Adder Special," in Comic Relief: Red Nose Day, June 8, 2009, at 9:32. http://www.youtube.com/watch?v=_SXf9-Z3jwk

7 Delineated at several points in Northrop Frye, *Anatomy of Criticism*, paperback ed. (New York: Atheneum, 1966).

8 David M Buss and David P Schmitt, "Mate Preferences and Their Behavioral Manifestations," *Annual Review of Psychology* 70 (2019): 3.

9 My translation of the opening lines of the aria "Quanto è bella."

10 The first two of the seven characteristics of "romantic love" identified by Helen Harris (cited in Jonathan Gottschall, "Romantic Love: A Literary Universal?," in *Literature, Science, and a New Humanities* (Basingstoke, UK: Palgrave Macmillan, 2008), 454.

11 The libretto lists their characters as stated, and hers as "una ricca e capricciosa fittaiuola" — a rich and capricious tenant farmer. http://www.librettidopera.it/zpdf/eldam.pdf

12 Romani acknowledged that he largely imitated an earlier libretto by Eugène Scribe for Auber's *Le Philtre* (1831).

13 Naturally, this brief characterization cannot do justice to all the variants of a literary form much produced in Europe from the Middle Ages through the Renaissance. See C. H. Holman, W. F. Thrall, and A. Hibbard, *A Handbook to Literature* (Indianapolis: Odyssey Press, 1972), 459–461.

14 Harry Warren, Jack Brooks, songwriters, "That's Amore," lyrics © Famous Music LLC, Four Jays Music Publishing Company, 1953.

15 Susan M. Hughes and David A. Puts, "Vocal Modulation in Human Mating and Competition," *Philosophical Transactions of the Royal Society B: Biological Sciences* 376, no. 1840 (2021): 5.

16 A contemporary view within a framework of evolutionary psychology is Nathan Oesch and Igor Miklousic, "The Dating Mind: Evolutionary Psychology and the Emerging Science of Human Courtship," *Evolutionary Psychology* 10, no. 5 (2012): 899–909.

17 Nicholas M. Hobson et al., "The Psychology of Rituals: An Integrative Review and Process-Based Framework," *Personality and Social Psychology Review* 22, no. 3 (2017): 260–284.

18 Nancy Easterlin, "The Functions of Literature and the Evolution of Extended Mind," *New Literary History*, no. 44 (2013): 671.

52 Music-Dramas, Evolutionary Biology, and Psychology

19 Buss and Schmitt, "Mate Preferences and Their Behavioral Manifestations."
20 David M. Buss, "Sex Differences in Human Mate Preferences: Evolutionary Hypotheses Tested in 37 Cultures," *Behavioral and Brain Sciences* 12, no. 1 (1989): 1–14.
21 For example, several mentions are found in just the first volume of his collected correspondence. C. Darwin et al., *The Correspondence of Charles Darwin: Volume 1, 1821–1836* (Cambridge, UK: Cambridge University Press, 1985).
22 Eric Csapo and Margaret Christina Miller, "General Introduction," in *The Origins of Theater in Ancient Greece and Beyond : From Ritual to Drama*, ed. Eric Csapo and Margaret Christina Miller (Cambridge: Cambridge University Press, 2007), 5.
23 The choreography, like the melody, is not known in any detail for particular dramas, losses that are equally unfortunate.
24 The interpretation of Aristotle's writing on the origin of tragedy and comedy gets keen attention from David Depew, "From Hymn to Tragedy: Aristotle's Genealogy of Poetic Kinds," in *The Origins of Theater in Ancient Greece and Beyond*, ed. Eric Csapo and Margaret Christina Miller (Cambridge, UK: Cambridge University Press, 2007).
25 Modern scholarship substantiating this view is quoted in Depew, 2007: 130. See also Csapo and Miller, "General Introduction," 9.
26 Aristotle, *Poetics*, 1902, 3.
27 Painting on vases does not necessarily match what's going on in the streets, but scholars who have considered more than 2,000 vases from all over the ancient Greek world, which depict "energetic human male dancers, normally in large groups," confidently link such vases with the prehistory of drama. Csapo, "Introduction," 13.
28 Frye, *Anatomy of Criticism*, 44.
29 John Updike, *Self-Consciousness: A Memoir* (New York: Random House Publishing Group, 2012), 242.
30 By all composers. See Operabase for data: http://www.operabase.com/statistics/en
31 See Buss, "Mate Preferences," references.
32 Ian McDougall, Francis H. Brown, and John G. Fleagle, "Stratigraphic Placement and Age of Modern Humans from Kibish, Ethiopia," *Nature* 433, no. 7027 (2005): 733–736.
33 Buss, "Mate Preferences," 10.
34 Ibid.
35 Again, Buss, "Mate Preferences," cites the research and is itself the prime instance.
36 Irving Singer, *The Nature of Love*, Vol. 2, *Courtly and Romantic* (Chicago: University of Chicago Press, 1984).
37 Jonathan Gottschall et al., "Sex Differences in Mate Choice Criteria Are Reflected in Folktales from around the World and in Historical European Literature," *Evolution and Human Behavior* 25, no. 2 (2004): 102–112.
38 Melanie C. Green, "Transportation into Narrative Worlds," in *Entertainment-Education Behind the Scenes* (Cham, Switzerland: Palgrave Macmillan, 2021), 94.
39 William Ashbrook, "Popular Success, the Critics and Fame: The Early Careers of Lucia Di Lammermoor and Belisario," *Cambridge Opera Journal* 2, no. 1 (1990): 66.
40 Ibid., 73.The translation by Ashbrook is of an Italian commentary from 1837 about the opera *Torquato Tasso*.
41 "Operabase" tracks the data, online. http://www.operabase.com/statistics/en Select "20 most played titles" for 2004–2019 to see one instance.
42 Roughly from *Marriage of Figaro* (1786) to *Turandot* (1926).
43 ("vocal folds").

44 ("larynx").

45 Known as "dyads."

46 D. Purves, *Music as Biology* (Cambridge, MA: Harvard University Press, 2017), 60.

47 The octave interval, effectively a doubling of the root tone, was not tested on the presumption that given the similarity, it would be judged most consonant.

48 David A. Schwartz, Catherine Q. Howe, and Dale Purves, "The Statistical Structure of Human Speech Sounds Predicts Musical Universals," *Journal of Neuroscience* 23, no. 18 (2003): 7160–7168.

49 The researchers in this case analyzed the audio spectrum of the sounds of the speech. In simple terms they plotted the sounds' intensity against the intervals embedded in the sounds (technically their "amplitude" against their frequency ratios).

50 See R. I. M. Dunbar, "The Social Brain: Mind, Language, and Society in Evolutionary Perspective," *Annual Review of Anthropology* 32, no. 1 (2003): 163–181. Also A. Kendon, "Reflections on the "Gesture-First" Hypothesis of Language Origins," *Psychonomic Bulletin & Review* 24, no. 1 (2017): 165.

51 A. S. Wilkins, *Making Faces* (Cambridge, MA: Harvard University Press, 2017), 358.

52 Joseph Henrich, *The Secret of Our Success* (Princeton, NJ: Princeton University Press, 2016), 234.

53 Purves, *Music as Biology*, 52.

54 Ibid., 24.

55 K. Z. Gill and D. Purves, "A Biological Rationale for Musical Scales," *PLoS One* 4, no. 12 (2009): e8144.

4

LE NOZZE DI FIGARO

Marital Commitment and Challenges to It

As the coach jostled along the road to Prague, she sang a tune he had written. Slightly off-key, deliberately. But when she made up the words to a phrase, he cried, "Schlaba Pumfa!"

"Punk-i-tit-iti!" she shot back. They both giggled, and when he started to tickle her, she reached over to tickle their friend, the clarinetist, and when that good man began to protest, she lowered her voice and growled, "Natschi-binit-*schibi*!"

And so it went. On the road from Vienna in the second week of January 1787, the passengers in the coach broke up their three-day journey with song, funny stories, and absurd nicknames; and no one got a free pass, not even the family dog, who nonetheless answered as happily to "Schmanuzky" as to his given name, Gauckerl. They might not have remembered a week later exactly what they sang to pass the time, though "Punkititi" was well known for dashing off uninhibited vocal farces for the entertainment of his close friends, who sang along.[1]

Schlaba Pumfa would probably have teased her husband by singing little bits of his latest opera with her own impromptu elaborations, as she was a trained singer and musician. That opera, *Le Nozze di Figaro* (*The Marriage of Figaro*), was the occasion for their journey to Prague,[2] and they were all in high spirits because *Figaro* had recently premiered there and had been a great success. So Wolfgang Amadeus Mozart had been invited to give concerts and to be entertained by the music patrons of this cultured city.

Arriving, the good-humored couple Mozart ("Punk-") and Constanze ("Schlaba") were pleased to find that not just the patrons but also many everyday people had been captivated by *Figaro*. Café orchestras played popular arias; dances were created to arrangements of its melodies.

DOI: 10.4324/9781003254478-6

Le Nozze di Figaro **55**

"Nothing is played, sung, or whistled but 'Figaro,'" Mozart wrote. "A great honor for me."[3]

That January, at age 30, Wolfgang Amadeus Mozart was in the prime of life. He and Constanze had been married for four and a half years,[4] since she was 20 years old, and she had borne him three children (only one of whom was still alive in 1787, unfortunately). But the couple appeared committed to each other,[5] despite occasional speculations to the contrary (most published after his death).[6] As the documented Prague journey suggests, they knew how to laugh about themselves, each other, and their circumstances, generally good indicators of contentment with a marriage.[7]

As a musician, Mozart was a child prodigy who had composed his first symphonies by the time he was 10. By two decades later Mozart had composed 38 symphonies, 22 piano concertos, and 16 operas, to name just some of his creative production, which ultimately included more than 600 compositions. Regarding this astonishing river of creativity, physicist and violinist Albert Einstein observed that "Mozart's music is so pure and beautiful that I see it as a reflection of the inner beauty of the universe."[8] Einstein arguably had a clearer appreciation of the inner beauty of the universe than most other people. But at least the Austrian emperor in 1785 had had the good sense to commission the writing of the earthy *Marriage of Figaro*.

Figaro is a type of comic opera known as "buffa" that hearkened back to the characters and situations that began with the Italian *commedia dell'arte* hundreds of years before—stock characters including foolish older men, often attracted to pretty maids, and contending with clever or devious male servants.[9] In *Figaro* Mozart and his librettist, Lorenzo Da Ponte, play off these cultural types, which were as common on stage and as familiar to audiences then as the superhero and femme fatale are to today's mass entertainment. But *Figaro* will strike many who see it as a troubling comedy, quite different in emphasis from *L'Elisir D'Amore*, for example, in its presentation of mating. In *Figaro* the central characters, the Countess and Count Almaviva, are already married, but the Count shows that his commitment to his wife is dubious. A philandering aristocrat, as the opera opens he has schemed to "have his way" with a young servant in his employment. More than that, the Count wants to retain the old feudal "right" of having the first night of her marriage with this servant,[10] even though he courts praise for abolishing the practice.

The Marriage of Figaro, as its name might telegraph, is not partial to the Count, who thinks he is superior but becomes ensnared in the scheming of others, including the clever servants, Figaro and Figaro's even more clever betrothed, Susanna, the object of the Count's unwanted affections. Figaro and Susanna are themselves the targets of others' mating intentions. And that only begins to pull on a couple strings of a tightly woven plot that Mozart and Da Ponte delight in weaving. *Figaro*'s complicated plot—involving

56 Music-Dramas, Evolutionary Biology, and Psychology

11 characters, each one with distinct motivations and machinations that collide, succeed, or fail—challenges the audience to keep track of who's doing what to whom and for what reason. All these complications contribute to dramatic tension and its resolution, including some laughter.

But this comedy is much more than a laughing matter, despite that the Count thinks he can enjoy himself with any woman he wants.[11] Why the Count thinks he can get away with his behavior is that he is the lord and economic master of his domain of family, servants, and other dependents. As a "Grandee of Spain," he also acts as a judge under the authority of the king. But the Count's complacent power more than meets its match when Susanna understands his intentions. She wishes to protect her body and her choice of sexual partner.

Presenting challenges to the aristocracy in the 1780s initially put the original French playwright, Pierre Beaumarchais, afoul of King Louis XVI and his censors. Louis was adamant, exclaiming at a private reading of *Le Mariage de Figaro*, "It is detestable! It will never be played! ... [Beaumarchais] mocks everything that ought to be respected in government."[12] But Louis's wife, Marie-Antoinette, liked the play, overcame objections, and *Figaro* was permitted, in 1784.[13] The next year it became the vehicle for Mozart's opera, which premiered in Vienna, in 1786. (Three years after that, the French Revolution began, ending the government, and lives, of Louis and Marie-Antoinette.)

Beaumarchais, in his more overtly "political" drama, was keen on linking the Count's behavior to his status as a privileged aristocrat. But in Da Ponte and Mozart's *Figaro* that privilege just gives the Count the opportunity to demonstrate his underlying immaturity as an adult man. He had previously courted and selected a mate, Rosina (which is the story of Beaumarchais's earlier drama, and Rossini's later opera, *The Barber of Seville*). Courtship and mate choice in heterosexual humans, as discussed in the previous chapter, are usually secured by commitment, which women look for in men. In fact, commitments between mates is the foundation of security in marriages and have great consequences not only for them but also for children and other relations, and even the wider community who know the couple. A drama that explores marital commitment will have, by default, great potential interest for nearly all adults.

As the Count displays, men have differing biologically based motivations. A commitment to a single woman can have the benefit of offspring, which the man typically can be confident are his. But that benefit also has the distinct cost of the energy required for parenting and provisioning the family, as humans evolved to have childhoods that are comparatively very long, requiring the sustained support of parental figures.[14] For the male this energy, from an evolutionary (not an ethical) perspective might better go into pursuing and having children by other women. This could be called his Plan B.

European and Christian societies since at least the late Middle Ages have promoted monogamous mating,[15] as would have been the norm in Mozart's time. But it is a fact that polygamy has also long been a practice in various cultures and times. (Technically the topic here is "polygyny," in which a male mates with several females—a practice that approximately 80% of preindustrial societies permit.[16]) Count Almaviva is interested in pursuing sexual favors, but whether he is prepared for the consequences of a pregnancy, of Susanna, for example, is not in the purview of the drama. Children are not apparently at issue in *Figaro*. The Count and Countess do not have any. The drama does not tell whether this may be because one or both of them are prevented biologically or are specifically uninterested in having children together. But what is evident is the Count's interest in other young women and the effect that behavior has on Susanna and the Countess.

Before turning to them, a brief but important aside to reflect on the Countess and all the other individuals. They are, of course, not actually a Countess, Count, servants, etc., but imagined characters, and *Figaro* is a representation of life by creative artists, not a documentary account (as if one were watching a video shot by a marriage counselor at the request of someone having relationship difficulties). Viewers recognize that the characters of *Figaro,* as in other fictions, are the creation of actual real persons with all *their* human misunderstandings, personal biases, and creative selectivity mixed into their understanding and abilities. The Count and the others are their representations of living people and are being impersonated by performers who temporarily play these roles, saying or singing words that originate with the authors.

Nevertheless, many do empathize with fictional characters. This response, of having real emotions about a fictional person, is sometimes called a puzzling "paradox of fiction."[17] A common explanation of the paradox is the notion of a "suspension of disbelief," meaning that people temporarily ignore that the fiction is not reality in order to be engaged by it.[18] As appealing as that notion might be, it is at least incomplete. Plato and Aristotle debated long ago why audiences allowed themselves to be "deceived" by fictions, and an insight was that personalizing a universal concern through a story was the way to generate an emotional response and the potential for learning.[19]

Modern neuroscience research takes that a step further, finding that a reason an audience member might have "real emotions" about the fictional Susanna, say, is that the character's circumstances ring a personal bell, an individual memory that has relevance (such as, "I've been in that lousy situation myself"). "Self-engagement through personal memory recollection could be one of the processes responsible of our emotional engagement toward fiction," noted Marco Sperduti and colleagues based on their study of brain activation in response to short videos.[20]

58 Music-Dramas, Evolutionary Biology, and Psychology

An additional perspective on the "paradox" of treating fiction as real comes from psychologists who study the "parasocial" relationships some audience members establish with characters.[21] True, Susanna will not walk off the stage and resume her personal life in Seville as your acquaintance, but she is felt to be "real"—as the product of the real persons Mozart and Da Ponte; as enacted "live" by a real person, directed by real people, and finally filtered by the experience of the viewer, unequivocally a real person.[22] In fact, humans believe in the reality of, and attach important feelings to, other characters who are not "real," not even present to the senses—the gods. But that's another story.

Figaro takes place in a world and with characters in circumstances similar to our own, rather than one of mythic figures, gods, and legendary royalty, as with Monteverdi and Handel. In the pressing concern that Susanna has she enlists Figaro and conspires with him to expose the Count's philandering. As a potential prey in a power relation in which the predator has the distinct advantage, Susanna needs to be quick and wily, which, in her case, takes the form of being a persuasive and adroit storyteller. The stories she presents to the other characters instigate what happens; in a sense, she is the creative dramatist in *Figaro*.

At the very start of the opera, Figaro is measuring the new bedroom the Count has provided to him and Susanna, as they will be married that very night (they think). Figaro naively imagines these new quarters as a convenience for them, providing the servants ready access to the Count and Countess. Tentatively at first, Susanna divulges the background situation. She says that the Count has given up looking for sexual partners outside his castle and is now focused on her; and she sees that the closeness of the bedroom to the Count provides His Lordship ready access to *her* when Figaro happens to be called away for something. Figaro becomes incensed and vows (in his first aria) that if the Count wishes to "ballare" (to dance, but possibly with a sexual double-entendre), he, Figaro, intends to call the tune. Knowing the background, recognizing the Count's real intentions, improves Figaro's position.

A moment of discovery, of vital recognition, is a central feature of drama, as Aristotle had observed,[23] and it has continued to be so. But discovery's prevalence in stories strongly suggests an origin in long human experience, in which learning something from others previously unrecognized by oneself could improve or even save one's life. From the perspective of cultural evolution, that is exactly what happened. "Cultural evolution is smarter than we are," Joseph Henrich has summarized.[24] Early in our species ancestry those who would have acquired and used successful information from previous generations would have generally outcompeted those who ignored such information and expected to succeed on their own.

Susanna wants to inform and enlist the help of the Countess, but in the remainder of Act 1 she first needs to contend with an older, female rival,

Marcellina, whom the Count wants to marry off to Figaro, so that he can have access to Susanna. Marcellina gone, the teenage Cherubino arrives to tell Susanna how much in love with women he is, but he is forced to hide as the Count next appears to attempt to woo Susanna. The Count's discovery of Cherubino prompts him to question Susanna's virtue and, because the lad had heard him courting Susanna, the Count intends to get rid of him that day by commissioning Cherubino as a soldier in his regiment.

Act 2 introduces the Countess, a wife ignored and humiliated by her husband, but who still believes in married love. Susanna, then Figaro, arrive at the Countess's "magnificent" private room, where they quickly share their understanding of the Count's behavior. The Countess is not surprised to hear that her husband visited Susanna ("he wished to seduce you?"), but her servant replies that he had come then to offer her money for a dowry. Modern husbands are like this, the Countess observes:

> ... per sistema
> Infedeli, per genio capricciosi
> E per orgoglio poi tutti gelosi.[25]

> ... on principle
> Unfaithful, by nature fickle
> And by pride then all jealous.

Figaro offers the male perspective that what the Count wishes to do is "natural" and certainly possible, if Susanna were to consent ("Possibile è la cosa e naturale"). How striking these characters' observations are: all frank and all in line with an evolutionary understanding of male behavior.

Figaro, who, after all, as the clever barber of Seville, mentored the young Count in the plan to win Rosina, now presents his plan to trap and embarrass the Count, save Susanna, and restore the Countess. Cherubino will be dressed as Susanna, who will arrange a rendezvous with the Count that very night. The trap will be sprung when the Countess discovers the Count wooing "Susanna," exposing his improper behavior. The remainder of Acts 2 and 3 essentially proceed with this plan with, of course, twists and turns.

Cherubino arrives to be dressed for his part, declares his love for the Countess, his godmother, and both she and Susanna recognize the young man's charms. When the Count appears and believes that Cherubino has hidden in a locked closet because of improper behavior with his wife, the Count furiously condemns her (as she had predicted): "You are faithless, wanton and seek to disgrace me!" His hypocrisy is apparent, as is his very unequal power in their marriage. But so may be that evolutionary concern of males, to be sure of the fidelity of partners whom they support (not that that excuses the Count's hypocrisy).

60 Music-Dramas, Evolutionary Biology, and Psychology

But Susanna defuses the crisis by trading places with the teenager, who escapes before the Count returns to unlock the door and "kill" him. The Count then attempts to repair his relationship with his wife and enlist Susanna in doing so. But the women are not much taken in.

In Act 3, Susanna persuades the Countess that she should dress as Susanna and be the nighttime assignation decoy, as Cherubino is not reliable, and, in that way, the lady will directly observe her husband's improper behavior. Susanna will dress as the Countess. The Count is overjoyed when Susanna agrees to meet him for that tryst. The Countess, meanwhile, is distressed that she, a gentlewoman, must rely on her servant for assistance and that circumstances have come to the clothing deception. Her own soliloquy traverses a range of feelings, eloquently expressed in rhyming Italian:

Dove sono i bei momenti	Where are the lovely moments
Di dolcezza e di piacer?	Of sweetness and pleasure?
Dove andaro i giuramenti	Where have the promises gone
Di quel labbro menzogner?	That came from those lying lips?
Perchè mai, se in pianti e in pene	Why, if all is changed for me
Per me tutto si cangiò,	Into tears and pain,
La memoria di quel bene	Has the memory of that goodness
Dal mio sen non trapassò?	Not vanished from my breast?
Ah! se almen la mia costanza,	Ah! if only, at least, my faithfulness,
Nel languire amando ognor,	Which still loves amidst its suffering,
Mi portasse una speranza	Could bring me the hope
Di cangiar l'ingrato cor!	Of changing that ungrateful heart![26]

This aria is widely considered one of the finest in all of opera and merits several kinds of observations, the first about operatic language itself. These few lines are in poetic verse with the Italian rhyming at the ends and occasionally in the interior of lines. Such a sophisticated use of language is likely quite different from a disjointed outpouring that might happen in "real life." Speech in verse is common in opera, and while it may seem artificial, in performance the sound-echoing of rhyming and the concentration of language may actually aid listening comprehension.

As the first stanza, sung, would illustrate, the words in an operatic speech are often prolonged momentarily in music. Music also provides a harmonic structure that gives the speech a recognizable shape. These features of construction, of the purposeful prolongation of speech and the shaping of speech via musical form, are central to opera. Although they are routinely used by many composers, some listeners may not appreciate how significant they are.

A common observation is that music is "a kind of language." Indeed, music, like speech, embodies an expressive structure, a syntax, of units organized by recognized rules, the units being tones in music and words in speech. A musical statement, like a spoken sentence, for example, will have a shape to it, developing over a certain amount of time, such as a theme in a sonata, for example. However, and this is crucial, music lacks the semantics of language, lacks a literal meaning.[27] We hear the syntax, but, in itself, we don't know what the musical statement independently *means*.

Music enhances language on two different timescales. Moment-by-moment, music can complement, accentuate, and amplify the meaning of words and phrases through tones, rhythm, and volume of sound, for example.[28] And as just suggested, over the time of the whole verbal statement music can provide a structure to words that can shape and resolve them through melody, tempo, and harmonic progression, mainly. Often this structure appears superior to the syntax of the words themselves. This is how the marriage of music and words thrives.

Soliloquies like "Dove sono?" can be a strong draw for audience interests for a basic reason, even independent of drama. In social life people attempt to understand what others think as a guide to interpreting their behavior ("Why won't my brother turn to look at me when I speak?"). Such understanding has always been an essential task to accomplish the two main priorities of people as social animals, which have been succinctly described as "to get along" and "to get ahead."[29] Briefly, by getting along an individual may obtain assistance within a group of people, beneficial for survival. By getting ahead an individual may distinguish themselves and may also become more desirable to prospective mates. To accomplish either of these priority tasks, interpreting others' behavior is crucial.

Even when others, in daily life, tell us what they're thinking, we usually need to interpret that statement in light of our relationship, its history, and the present moment. But a character in a drama alone and talking to herself, as the Countess is here, is very likely to be accepted as credibly "transparent": we are seeing the true person (or at least what she believes herself to be in the moment).[30] Since this experience of transparency is surely desirable but nearly impossible in daily life, the fact that drama may provide it is distinctly appealing.

One could imagine the Countess's soliloquy being spoken to good effect, but with the singing voice and orchestral accompaniment, Mozart can offer considerably more. Opera composers, from Monteverdi on, routinely create melodies for various characters to sing that reflect, at least in a general way, feelings embodied in familiar speech patterns, as noted in chapter 2. In common descriptions of these songs or arias, the feelings are

62 Music-Dramas, Evolutionary Biology, and Psychology

often specified, such as angry "vengeance" arias (which, like the Count's in Act 3, often feature a loud, leaping, disturbing vocal line) and joyous love duets (which feature smooth, agreeable sonorities and close harmonies or unison singing). In the Countess's soliloquy, Mozart colors every phrase distinctly within an overall harmonic and tempo structure that supports the sentiments expressed in the text.

Formally, the aria's opening stanza is an andante "A" section, followed by the second stanza as contrasting "B"—"Why if all is changed for me into tears and pain" (Perchè mai ...). From C major, the melody moves quickly through a number of keys, descends and wraps around itself questioningly, and is accompanied by the plaintiff sound of an oboe and bassoon, on the way to touching on the key of G, the "dominant" key. The expository "A" returns ("Dove sono"), but Mozart breaks off a formal recapitulation as the Countess shifts from mourning to hope in the final stanza. This bravura, allegro conclusion is not only faster but also features a rising pitch, louder sound, and energetically returns to the home key of C major, as if solidifying her resolve.

Through this soliloquy Mozart has been developing a heroine—one who can both express her deep feelings and then act on them in a hopeful way.[31] Complementing the meaningful dynamism of the musical form, for some listeners the memory of a similar episode in their own lives, as noted before, may make the Countess's experience resonate with them.[32]

Turmoil in *Figaro* Act 3 comes to some resolution with the marriage of Susanna and Figaro (and also Marcellina and Bartolo, who turn out to be Figaro's parents from some long-forgotten fling). The arrival of the wedding party led by Figaro and Susanna provides a striking example of another of opera's dramatic means: dance. In contrast to the agitation, crosscurrents, and negativity from the Count for having failed to prevent the marriages, Mozart's processional music for the Count's servants and retainers is stately and measured, offering a calming effect.[33] No words are spoken or sung.

Underlying that dance pattern in *Figaro* is a simple and regular rhythm, a musical pulse that is calmly sustained over about 80 seconds of performance. Humans respond to a regular rhythm because we *are* such rhythm ourselves. Our heartbeats and breathing in and out set the subtle, organic relationship between sound and movement.

People moving in a pattern, synchronized to music, provides a distinct pleasure in viewing, as such patterned movement represents a coordinated activity of a group, with an evolutionary origin.[34] Human dancing requires abilities to imitate, to learn often complex sequences of actions, and to remember and enact that learning. Dancing, like making music, would have arisen to support social bonding, as evolutionary scientists have argued.[35] Likely important to the bonding effects of moving to a beat are certain brain

Le Nozze di Figaro **63**

chemicals. Endorphins are part of an opioid system within the body that generates a kind of euphoria during exercise, popularly called a "runner's high." Dancers know it, too, as these neurohormones are released by the synchronized movements of dancing.[36]

Act 4, out in the garden in the night's darkness, progresses to the climax that has long been building dramatically—and also musically, as Mozart structures the finale around specific harmonic keys with a logical progression.[37] However, the dramatic progression is marked by several confusions over the cross-dressing disguise of Susanna and the Countess. Not knowing the women's plan, Figaro has his own dark moment when he thinks that Susanna has betrayed her commitment to him and intends to have the assignation with the Count. Calling Susanna a "traitor" and on the very night of his wedding to her, he rails against her and all women in an aria advising men to open their eyes! ("Aprite un po quel ochi"). Then Cherubino, still at large and looking for Barbarina, finds who he thinks is Susanna, and begins a seduction of her instead. But it is the Countess who is alarmed that the Count should find her with Cherubino, and she repulses the teen. Later the Count finds "Susanna" (the Countess in her disguise) and begins to woo her, but he is interrupted and outraged by the sight of Figaro (who is then fully engaged with the women's scheme) apparently wooing the "Countess" (Susanna in the Countess's clothing). Apprehending them, the Count calls to all in shouting distance to witness his *wife's* supposed infidelity, adamantly refusing all their requests to pardon her and Figaro. "No. No. *No!*"

At that exact moment, the Countess herself appears. Everyone freezes, especially the Count, whose behavior has been exposed before all—his servants, the other people in his household, his wife. In an abrupt change of manner, he apologizes to the Countess in the simplest terms—"Perdono" (Pardon me)—which he repeats three times and ends on a unresolved upward note, as a request. It could well be a heartfelt change, one in which the Count appears in an instant to be transformed. But it might be only a new pose, as he may just feel shamed and embarrassed and that this time he sees that he cannot bluff his way out. No matter. It is the Countess's reply to him that musically and figuratively attempts to put their relationship in a new key, for rather than giving him his comeuppance she does, indeed, forgive him:

Più docile io sono,	I am more flexible [considerate/docile] than you
e dico di sì.	and I say "yes."

The dignity of her forgiveness is given by a poised, limpid melody that initially imitates his request but arches up to a higher interval. In it can be heard a new "voice" for the Countess,[38] whose previous statements lacked its calm authority and confidence. Mozart gives the moment much more

64 Music-Dramas, Evolutionary Biology, and Psychology

weight and development than the paltry text offers, and immediately following her forgiveness, all the characters take up the Countess's melody, responding to her manner and singing together, "Ah, tutti contenti saremo cosi" (Let us all be content). As the novelist Stendhal noted with only slight exaggeration, this "choral" moment sounds like "the finest church music one could expect."[39]

"Contento," usually translated as "happy," here has the added connotation of being content with one's commitments and circumstances.

In Beaumarchais's original stage play the Countess's moment of pardon transpires in some seconds of dialog, and then each of the assembled main characters offers, in turn, a statement of reconciliation with their circumstances.[40] But the cumulative effect in the play is not as great as in the opera, due to Mozart's handling of the musical opportunity. As the musician and musicologist Charles Rosen observed, Mozart ingeniously used the contrasting harmonies and tempos of sonata-form to develop the extended and contrasting movement of lengthy scenes like this garden one.[41] Here the chorale solidifies the dominant key of G major as the chorus of individuals not only say the same thing but also harmonize, which nicely fits the sentiments being expressed.

As with *Rodelinda*, *L'Elisir*, and many other operas, *Figaro* concludes with a chorus (with its plausible evolutionary echoes of group singing and bonding).[42] All the characters, on stage, end up-tempo singing "Lovers and friends, let's round things off in dancing and pleasure." Mozart vigorously asserts that rounding off in pleasure by concluding the opera in the tonic key (D major) with which *Figaro* began.

At the first performances of the opera in 1786, the audience's response was ecstatic, as one of them recollected: "I thought the audience would never have done applauding and calling for Mozart; almost every piece was encored."[43]

The enthusiasm for this opera and, in particular, the conclusion, reflects fundamental features in the human response to stories. Significant relationships and critical events in human life-history—often those involving marital relations—move people, as research has found.[44] But the power of story lies deeper.

As mentioned, the earliest stories likely treated survival in the natural world[45]; for example, what local plants were safe to eat, which animals were dangerous, even more fundamentally, how to recognize patterns in the environment.[46] But gradually, as humans banded together in larger and larger groups, stories would have also concerned themselves with the human environment, the social setting, the challenges posed by other people. Stories can have a distinct advantage in presenting how other people act in difficulties and dangers[47] that arise from our common, evolved concerns for survival and progeny.[48]

Le Nozze di Figaro **65**

"Fiction projects us into intense simulations of problems that run parallel to those we face in reality," evolutionary literary scholar Jonathan Gottschall has argued.[49]

And like [learning to fly a plane by training on] a flight simulator, the main virtue of fiction is that we have a rich experience and don't die in the end ... Nature designed us to enjoy stories so we would get the benefit of practice.

Consider, as a thought experiment, how difficult life would be if we had no stories—*none*—of how other people addressed the common challenges of living. Again, from the cultural-evolution perspective, stories would be one manifestation of that essential character of humans as a cultural species. People may think of themselves as smart, but the collective intelligence of humanity is vastly superior to that of individual intelligence.[50] That said, not all stories told provide an advantage. Some can include fatal errors, such as encouraging beliefs that are demonstrably false and thereby have maladaptive consequences.[51]

But the story of *The Marriage of Figaro* continues to engage audiences because, at root, it is all about a number of challenges to marriage, one of life's crucial decisions, biological investments, and potentially significant changes in social status. Love, emotional stability or maturity, and a dependable character are today ranked the highest among traits preferred in a mate by *both* men and women,[52] and evolutionary psychology finds reasons those preferences would have arisen long ago.[53] *Figaro* is a comedy, finally, as the pairing commitments of marriage appear restored.

Nonetheless, many stories about marriage have not had the staying power of Mozart's, whose musical articulation of the drama has seemed unexcelled for more than two centuries and may well remain so. As the evolutionary humanist Brett Cooke succinctly observed about the opera's essence, "Like other great artists, Mozart reveals to us things about ourselves."[54] As Johannes Brahms wrote a century after its composition, "Every number in Mozart's *Figaro* is a miracle to me; I find it absolutely incomprehensible how someone can create something so absolutely perfect; nothing like it has ever been done again."[55]

Notes

1 Such multilingual nonsense lyrics as "Caro mio Schluck und Druck, ti lasso, oh Dio! Kugelrund" ("My beloved Sip-and-Squeeze, I leave you, oh God, my Butterball!") gives the flavor. *Wolfgang Amadeus Mozarts Werke, Serie XXIV: Supplemente, Bd.2, No.50* Leipzig: Breitkopf & Härtel, 1885, 82–83. Plate W.A.M. Anh.5.

2 For the travel and arrival: Piero Melograni, *Wolfgang Amadeus Mozart: A Biography*, trans. Lydia G. Cochrane (Chicago: University of Chicago Press, 2007), 200–201.

66 Music-Dramas, Evolutionary Biology, and Psychology

3 Melograni, *Mozart*, 201.
4 Their marriage was August 4, 1782.
5 "Whoever gets a wife like Constanze will certainly be a happy man," Mozart to his father, July 27, 1782. Cited by A. Selby, *Constanze, Mozart's Beloved* (Vienna: Hollitzer Wissenschaftsverlag, 2013), n.p.
6 See Selby, *Constanze, Mozart's Beloved.*
7 C.C. Weisfeld et al., *The Psychology of Marriage: An Evolutionary and Cross-Cultural View* (Lanham, MD: Lexington Books, 2017), 247.
8 Albert Einstein, *The Ultimate Quotable Einstein*, ed. Alice Calaprice (Princeton, NJ: Princeton University Press, 2010).
9 The stock characters mentioned here are Pantalone, Colombina, and Arlecchino.
10 While present in the opera, how widespread that specific "right" was in society is not certain. Richard Andrews, "From Beaumarchais to Da Ponte: A New View of the Sexual Politics of 'Figaro,'" *Music & Letters* 82, no. 2 (2001): 214–233.
11 Susanna mentions others in 1.1. "Il signor Conte"ff. Barbarina says he's often kissed and embraced her. 3.12 "Eccellenza" ff. References are to act, scene, and first words of relevant speech.
12 Linda Lister, "Beaumarchais, Figaro, Paisiello, and Mozart: Sociopolitical Criticism and Censor in Eighteenth-Century Opera," *Opera Journal* 45, no. 1 (2012): 17.
13 Ibid., 18.
14 Peter J. Richerson and Robert Boyd, "The Human Life History Is Adapted to Exploit the Adaptive Advantages of Culture," *Philosophical Transactions of the Royal Society B* 375, no. 1803 (2020): 6.
15 Kevin MacDonald, "The Establishment and Maintenance of Socially Imposed Monogamy in Western Europe," *Politics and the Life Sciences* 14, no. 1 (1995).
16 J. Cartwright, *Evolution and Human Behaviour: Darwinian Perspectives on the Human Condition* (Basingstoke, UK: Palgrave Macmillan, 2016), 51. Also J. Henrich, R. Boyd, and P. J. Richerson, "The Puzzle of Monogamous Marriage," *Philosophical Transactions of the Royal Society London B Biological sciences* 367, no. 1589 (2012): 657.
17 Eva-Maria Konrad, Thomas Petraschka, and Christiana Werner, "The Paradox of Fiction: A Brief Introduction," *Journal of Literary Theory* 12.2 (2018): 193–203, http://www.jltonline.de/index.php/articles/article/view/970/2269.
18 However, the poet Coleridge, who coined the modern "suspension" phrase did not mean it with respect to all fictional characters, rather only supernatural ones. For a philosophical discussion, see Peter Kivy, *Once-Told Tales: An Essay in Literary Aesthetics* (Malden, MA: Wiley, 2011), 100ff.
19 See Paul Woodruff, "Aristotle on Mimesis," in *Essays on Aristotle's Poetics*, ed. Amelie Rorty (Princeton, NJ: Princeton University Press, 2012), 88.
20 M. Sperduti et al., "The Paradox of Fiction: Emotional Response toward Fiction and the Modulatory Role of Self-Relevance," *Acta Psychol (Amst)* 165 (2016): 58. The videos were identified as showing "real" and fictional scenes. Emotions in response to the fictional scenes were "robust" and "genuine," arousing physiological reactions comparable to those set off by the "real" video scenes.
21 Olivia A. Gonzalez, "Real Characters: The Psychology of Parasocial Relationships with Media Characters," *International Journal of Communication* (Online) (2021).
22 See Karen E. Shackleford, "Constellation of Psychological Experiences Involved in Our Connection with Fictional Characters and Actors," in *Real Characters: The Psychology of Parasocial Relationships with Media Characters*, ed. Karen E. Shackleford (Santa Barbara, CA: Fielding University Press, 2020).
23 Aristotle: "anagnoresis."

24 Joseph Henrich, *The Secret of Our Success* (Princeton, NJ: Princeton University Press, 2016), 116.
25 W. A. Mozart, *Le Nozze di Figaro*, libretto by Lorenzo Da Ponte, English translation by Jane Bishop, http://www.aria-database.com/translations/nozze19_dove.txt.
26 Ibid.
27 Nina Penner, *Storytelling in Opera and Musical Theater* (Bloomington: Indiana University Press, 2020), 18.
28 For a thorough development of these ideas: Peter Kivy, *Osmin's Rage: Philosophical Reflections on Opera, Drama, and Text* (Princeton, NJ: Princeton University Press, 1988).
29 D. P. McAdams, "From Actor to Agent to Author," in *Darwin's Bridge: Uniting the Humanities and Sciences* (New York: Oxford University Press, 2016).
30 For more on soliloquy: Lisa Zunshine, "Culture of Greedy Mindreaders," in *Getting Inside Your Head: What Cognitive Science Can Tell Us about Popular Culture* (Baltimore, MD: Johns Hopkins University Press, 2012), 130–131.
31 This conclusion is shared by a feminist critic: Susan McClary, "Towards a Feminist Criticism of Music," *Canadian University Music Review / Revue de musique des universités canadiennes* 10, no. 2 (1990) : 9–18. http://doi.org/10.7202/1014882ar: 10.
32 P. N. Juslin, L. Harmat, and T. Eerola, "What Makes Music Emotionally Significant? Exploring the Underlying Mechanisms," *Psychology of Music* 42, no. 4 (2013): 599–623.
33 The simple, measured pace also befits its miscellaneous actor-performers on stage.
34 An argument developed by K. Laland, C. Wilkins, and N. Clayton, "The Evolution of Dance," *Current Biology* 26, no. 1 (2016): R5–R9.
35 Summary: Patrick E. Savage et al., "Music as a Coevolved System for Social Bonding," *Behavioral and Brain Sciences*. 44. (2021). Also Robin Dunbar, "On the Evolutionary Function of Song and Dance," in *Music, Language, and Human Evolution*, ed. Nicholas Bannan (Oxford: Oxford University Press, 2012).
36 B. Tarr, J. Launay, and R. I. Dunbar, "Music and Social Bonding: "Self-Other" Merging and Neurohormonal Mechanisms," *Frontiers in Psychology* 5 (2014).
37 John Platoff, "Tonal Organization in 'Buffo' Finales and the Act 2 Finale of 'Le Nozze Di Figaro,'" *Music & Letters* 72, no. 3 (1991): 401.
38 This argument is consistent with claims in Carolyn Abbate, *Unsung Voices: Opera and Musical Narrative in the Nineteenth Century* (Princeton, NJ: Princeton University Press, 1991).
39 Henry Pleasants, *The Great Singers: From the Dawn of Opera to Our Own Time* (New York: Simon and Schuster, 1966), 70.
40 A period English translation is online: *The Follies of a Day; or, the Marriage of Figaro; A Comedy*, as it is now performing at the Theatre-Royal, Covent-Garden. From the French of M. de Beaumarchais by Thomas Holcroft (London: G. G. and J. J. Robinson, 1785), https://oll.libertyfund.org/titles/beaumarchais-the-marriage-of-figaro-or-the-follies-of-a-day
41 In revealing detail in "Comic Opera" in Charles Rosen, *The Classical Style: Haydn, Mozart, Beethoven*, expanded ed. ed. (New York: New York: W.W. Norton, 1997).
42 Ellen Dissanayake, "If Music Is the Food of Love, What about Survival and Reproductive Success?" *Musicae scientiae* 12, no. 1_suppl (2008): 182.
43 M. Kelly, *Reminiscences of Michael Kelly of the King's Theatre, and Theatre Royal Drury Lane, Including a Period of Nearly Half a Century: With Original*

68 Music-Dramas, Evolutionary Biology, and Psychology

Anecdotes of Many Distinguished Persons, Political, Literary and Musical (Colburn, 1826), 261.

44 W. Menninghaus et al., "Towards a Psychological Construct of Being Moved," *PLoS One* 10, no. 6 (2015): 24–33.

45 B. Boyd, *On the Origin of Stories: Evolution, Cognition, and Fiction* (Cambridge, MA: Harvard University Press, 2010).

46 Argued by Brian Boyd, "The Art of Literature and the Science of Literature," *American Scholar* 77, no. 2 (2008): 118–127.

47 See Dan P. McAdams, "First We Invented Stories, Then They Changed Us: The Evolution of Narrative Identity," *Evolutionary Studies in Imaginative Culture* 3 (2019).

48 Denis Dutton, "The Uses of Fiction," in *Darwin's Bridge: Uniting the Humanities and Sciences*, ed. Joseph Carroll (New York: Oxford University Press, 2016), 191.

49 Jonathan Gottschall, *The Storytelling Animal: How Stories Make Us Human* (Boston: Houghton Mifflin Harcourt, 2012), 58.

50 R. Boyd, P. J. Richerson, and J. Henrich, "The Cultural Niche: Why Social Learning Is Essential for Human Adaptation," *Proceedings of the National Academy of Sciences of the United States of America* 108 Suppl 2 (2011): 10918–10925.

51 Such as religious beliefs that gods will inevitably support the survival of their people.

52 David M. Buss, "Sex Differences in Human Mate Preferences: Evolutionary Hypotheses Tested in 37 Cultures," *Behavioral and Brain Sciences* 12, no. 1 (1989): 1–14.

53 David M. Buss and David P. Schmitt, "Mate Preferences and Their Behavioral Manifestations," *Annual Review of Psychology* 70 (2019): 77–110.

54 Brett Cooke, "Instinctual Humanity and Rational Humanism in Mozart's 'Le Nozze Di Figaro,'" in *Reasoning Beasts: Evolution, Cognition, and Culture, 1720–1820*, ed. Kathryn Duncan and Michael Austin (New York: AMS Press, 2017), 166.

55 Peter Gay, *Mozart* (New York: Lipper/Viking Book, 1999), 131. Brahms's letter to a friend was written in 1881.

5

DON GIOVANNI, WOZZECK

Assessing Adult Character

His loose-fitting ruffled shirt is open to his chest, pulled and crumpled by her as she grabs at him, crying out, "Unless you kill me, don't hope I'll ever let you escape!"[1]

In the darkness she apparently does not know who the masked man is, but she knows what he did to her, or tried to do, there in her bedroom stealing in during the night. Watching her does not tell exactly, but her own clothes are amiss, her hair undone, and she's clinging and gasping out, "Men ... Servants" ... "—the betrayer!"

Why exactly she is not letting him go, and why he is not just going are questions only forming when suddenly Anna's father appears, rushing to aid her. He's a military commander, a "Commendatore," so he rushes in with his sword drawn and barks out an order, "Let her go, villain!" and challenges the intruder to a duel. The intruder at first declines to fight an old man—whether out of prudence, a sense of honor, or mere disdain, is also not clear. But at the father's insistence to fight him, the intruder's emotions get the better of him; and with his sword he quickly mortally wounds the old man. The agitated music that began the scene, the frantic, yet musically parallel, lines the intruder and Anna press on each other; the thrusting accompaniment to the sword fight: all this energy finally dissipates in a mordant hush. The killer leans over Anna's father and removes the mask covering his features so that the dying man can recognize him; and the Commendatore expires.

The servant Leporello, who has been in watchful hiding, comments in recitative on his master's actions: "Two pretty exploits: rape the daughter, then kill her father." Don Giovanni replies, "It is what he wanted"; and Leporello, "And Donna Anna, is it what she wanted?"

DOI: 10.4324/9781003254478-7

70 Music-Dramas, Evolutionary Biology, and Psychology

"Silence!—don't provoke me, unless," Giovanni responds quickly, "you also want something for yourself."[2]

Completed about seventeen months after *The Marriage of Figaro*, *Don Giovanni* finds Mozart and librettist Da Ponte presenting a lead character who exists far outside the behavioral sideboards of *Figaro*. The Don, a nobleman, is not a sly philanderer like Count Almaviva. He is apparently an extraordinary force of nature, at least according to a list of 2,065 women's names that Leporello keeps in a book of Giovanni's "conquests." In the opera Giovanni clearly intends to keep right at it. *Don Giovanni* is not about marriage; it is about sexual desire, that persistent force in human life. Although the full title of Mozart's opera is *Il Dissoluto Punito, ossia il Don Giovanni* (*The Rake Punished, or Don Giovanni*), the opera's presentation of the rake and his punishment appears ambivalent. On the one hand, the drama of *Don Giovanni* portrays vividly the conflict between individual licentiousness and societal restraint, permitting or demanding a negative judgment of Giovanni. On the other hand, the music of the opera often seems captivated by Giovanni. The music-drama, melodious, sometimes violent, unsettling in its tensions, seems to be able to be read two ways, which is not to say they are equal. *Don Giovanni* still routinely ranks among the top dozen operas performed.

To start with the drama, it takes place in a heterosexual world. A lengthy digression is surely not needed to observe that the main sexual "orientation" of the most-performed operas is heterosexual. Male and female is simply the mode of human reproductive pairing and a widespread cultural norm—not that sex or love are so limited, on the stage or elsewhere. Nor does heterosexual behavior merit approval by default, obviously. Following the rape or seduction of Donna Anna and the killing of her father, Anna and Don Ottavio, her fiancé, swear vengeance on the disguised perpetrator, whoever he was. In short order Donna Elvira abruptly appears on the scene, having come from a neighboring city where she was seduced and abandoned by Giovanni after he promised to marry her. "If I find the traitor and he will not return to me, I'll kill him and tear his heart out,"[3] she swears, in an agitated, vehement aria that introduces her, although perhaps too vehement by half, the music suggests.

Giovanni overhears her and decides to "console" the damsel, not realizing that it's Elvira. When he approaches, she confronts him—but does *not* kill him. She's flustered, and Giovanni saunters off, leaving Leporello to mollify her. Giovanni's behavior is now well established with the repetitive elements of this scene and the first one. He appears, looking for women, and disappears when it suits him, without explanation, like a wind blowing through the social world.

Leporello is left holding the bag, or book in this case, to explain things. In his aria ("Madamina, il catalogo è questo") he tells Elvira she's not the only one.[4] Not only are there the more than 2,000 others in his "catalogue," allegedly, but Leporello assures her that Giovanni is indiscriminate in his seductions: women of "every size, rank, and age ... Even the elderly he courts for the pleasure of adding them to the list." As if that would console her.

However exaggerated the catalog may be, from any societal perspective Giovanni's behavior is beyond the pale, indicating obsession and misogyny. Many, perhaps most, of his conquests must be rapes, which is totally unacceptable from a feminist point of view but also from probably every rational, cultural view. Musicologist and teacher Liane Curtis advocated that

> students today will have encountered issues such as date rape and will see the situations of the opera as relevant to their own lives. I suggest that the strengths of the female roles should be central to the teaching of the work.[5]

Leporello's catalog, boisterously, obnoxiously presented, serves to cue the audience that, in any event, Giovanni is certainly a human exception, an exaggeration. Next we see the Don, he has crashed a party of peasants and fixed on the pretty bride-to-be, Zerlina. She seems, indeed, quite taken by his charming manner and his promise of marriage, but Donna Elvira interrupts, singing another impassioned aria, advising Zerlina to learn from her example with him, and then hustling the bride-to-be away, protecting her.

The very next scenes are pivotal in judging the Don.[6] Giovanni enters lamenting that his "pleasant plans" seem all to be going awry, when Donna Anna and Don Ottavio suddenly appear. They ask him as a gentleman for his help—and though they are interrupted before they can specify with what—they, Giovanni, and the audience all know that the help is to find her father's killer. Anna and Ottavio are trying to solve a murder mystery, but Giovanni runs his own narrative. Of course, he will help them—even his "blood and possessions are at their service."

"But why are you weeping, Donna Anna?" Giovanni asks.

His question provides another useful example of the perennial value people can receive from attending to stories. Giovanni puts out a favorable account of himself, despite his last remark, which can seem either sadistic or disengaged, depending on which "reading" of the character one makes. He appears to be acting agreeable and conscientious, two personality traits that humans routinely pay attention to. The other three traits identified in contemporary personality psychology—the so-called "big five" traits[7]—are openness, extraversion, and neuroticism. But an individual in society or in the theater audience habitually compares traits to actions, the social performance of others as "actors."[8]

Evolutionary psychologists argue that our evolved nature makes us alert to social performance, as this permits success in groups, which are necessary

72 Music-Dramas, Evolutionary Biology, and Psychology

to survival; and being successful in groups often confers resources, including food for energy and mates for progeny.[9] Studies of many languages throughout the world have shown that the "big five" are common descriptors of social performance.[10] Paying attention to social performance of the big five traits can provide answers to important questions such as "Will person O be curious, flexible, help me solve problems?" (Openness); "Can I depend on person C?" (Conscientiousness); "Will person E help me gain social resources?" (Extraversion); "Can I trust person A?" (Agreeableness); "Is person N emotionally stable?" (Neuroticism).[11] We ask these questions not only of different people (O, A, etc.) but also of all of them for the same individual. (The real-life relevance of such questions can be checked by considering one's own perception of personal friends or public figures.)

Giovanni appears to be faking his agreeable concern and conscientiousness and is not to be trusted; the audience knows that from observing his previous actions. Such observation of other people and our own selves leads to a conviction that others have beliefs and desires in their minds just as we do, and experience teaches to be alert to cues in their actions and behavior that may suggest those concealed beliefs and desires.[12] Where this cognitive capacity to infer the mental states of others came from is that it evolved, neuroscientists claim, in ancestral hominins in concert with the ability to recognize one's own mental states.[13] As a result humans theorize, developing what has come to be called a "theory of mind"[14] from reading the other's external cues. We habitually guess what's happening inside another's head.

Observing Giovanni, Anna and Ottavio would be developing a theory of his mind. Exactly at this point Elvira enters the scene, which seems a bit coincidental unless Da Ponte puts her there for a reason. As Susanna warned Figaro about the Count in *Figaro*, Elvira provides the rest of the story here. Giovanni tries to suppress her story and support his, saying she's crazy.

"I begin to have doubts" about him, Anna and Ottavio say. Developing their "theory," they quickly check it against what they observe in the interaction between Elvira and Giovanni when he pulls her aside and quietly tries to get her to "be more discreet." She responds loudly:

> Don't place your hopes there, villain,
> I have lost my sense of modesty!
> Your guilt and my situation
> shall be known to all.[15]

Anna and Ottavio observe (*aside, watching Giovanni*):

> Those whispered undertones,
> that constant blushing,

are all too clear an indication
and banish all my doubts.

Elvira leaves, Giovanni follows her, and Anna quickly reflects on what's been happening. Anna could be doing here what anyone might do with any mysteries in life (and fiction)—running through different explanations for observed behavior, looking for the best fit that puts the puzzle pieces together. But suddenly Anna focuses on Giovanni's voice, telling Ottavio that that voice made her recall vividly her intruder and killer of her father.[16] She demands again that Ottavio revenge her, in the adamant aria, "Or sai chi l'onore/ rapper a me volse" (Now you know who tried to steal my honor).[17]

In these scenes, *Don Giovanni* gives clear examples of some psychological processes people have to assess the character of others. As "processes" they may run without our being aware of them in detail, as generating a "theory" of someone else's mind and intention appears to be.[18] Also, Anna's identification of Giovanni, linking his voice to the intruder and killer, would have occurred because the intense emotions of almost being raped would have caused those memories to have prominence.[19] One more psychological mechanism is evident with Anna. As she progresses quickly (in Act 1, scene 13) from describing the circumstances on that fateful night to demanding vengeance on Giovanni, Anna herself makes moral judgments, of having been wronged and responding to that wrong. She presents these moral beliefs very rapidly and apparently without any detailed thinking.

Why moral beliefs would arise this way was suggested by the philosopher David Hume in 1777, who wrote that they come from "sentiments ... founded entirely on the particular fabric and constitution of the human species."[20]

In recent years Jonathan Haidt and colleagues have expanded on Hume's suggested linkage between moral beliefs and feelings ("sentiments") grounded in the nature ("constitution") of our species. Haidt and others have developed the hypothesis that moral judgments are fundamentally intuitive, and, like Anna's here in the real-time of the opera, made very quickly, a "sudden appearance in consciousness, or at the fringe of consciousness, of an evaluative feeling (like-dislike, good-bad) about the character or actions of a person."[21]

This making of a good-for-me or bad-for-me "feeling" appears part and parcel of the continual scanning the mind is doing, described by the Nobel Prize–winning psychologist Daniel Kahneman in *Thinking, Fast and Slow*, as the "fast" System 1, which "operates automatically and quickly, with little or no effort and no sense of voluntary control."[22] By contrast, the mind's System 2 devotes attention to mental activities that require effort, using "slow thinking." Haidt's "social intuitionist model" of moral judgment agrees that so-called System 1 thinking happens first, generally, and

74 Music-Dramas, Evolutionary Biology, and Psychology

drives System 2 thinking, "particularly when a person needs to invent a justification that can be shared with others."[23] Anna knew from the start that the attempted rape was "bad for her," and in the aria she adds her father's murder to the wrongs which she demands that Ottavio avenge ("vendetta ti chiedo").

The audience of *Don Giovanni* is very likely making its own moral review. "In most works of any significance," the literary scholar Wayne C. Booth observed, "we are made to admire or detest, to love or hate, or simply to approve or disapprove of a least one main character."[24] The most significant and lasting dramas stimulate the moral judgment that audiences may make on one or more characters, loving or hating them, approving or disapproving. According to the moral foundations theory of Haidt and colleagues, in judging the morality of Giovanni viewers would be considering five "foundations," each listed with a positive/negative identity: care/harm; fairness/cheating; loyalty/betrayal; authority/subversion; purity/degradation.[25]

These moral psychologists claim that human evolution prepared the mind for sensitivity to these foundations.[26] Whether another person cares for or harms others has obvious consequences for survival, for example, as does whether another treats fairly or cheats, or betrays others in their group. From this moral perspective, Giovanni harms, cheats, and betrays.

Because assessing character traits and social performance is such a routine and habitual human activity, having the opportunity to do it in a concentrated way with the characters of a story is one reason stories are compelling. *Don Giovanni* does not disappoint. For much of the opera, Anna, Elvira, Ottavio, and Masetto (the fiancé of Zerlina) commit themselves to public retribution for being wronged by Giovanni. That moment finally arrives, although not according to their plans. In a churchyard Giovanni had invited the funerary statue of the dead Commendatore to dinner, thinking the invitation absurd. But later, during dinner, the statue suddenly does appear at Giovanni's door.

What follows is the most powerful scene in the opera. While librettist Da Ponte gave Mozart a workmanlike finale of speech and action, the composer turned it into something much greater. The dead Commendatore's words of accepting the invitation Mozart makes ominous, first simply by the use of sound. As the statue enters, Mozart gets Giovanni's and Leporello's attention by an audio equivalent of the visual surprise that occurs onstage—loud, crashing chords. The sudden appearance of something large and loud— think a large bear stepping out into a forest clearing and rising up, roaring—automatically gets the attention of a human, a comparatively small and weak mammal. Humans evolved to react to sudden disturbances in order to survive.[27]

But Mozart applies not just any sounds: the chords are dissonant ones that are both disturbing and hearken back to the opera's overture, resolving

Don Giovanni, Wozzeck **75**

to its home key of D minor. In his first two lines, the "Stone Guest" sings loudly and fiercely, tracing the fundamental chord of that key. *You thought you were getting away? No, we're back where we started* is the music's subliminal message. Leporello cowers, awestruck. When suddenly threatened, humans often are momentarily stunned or "freeze up." The hair on anyone's neck would quite likely stand up at seeing the dead walking.

For a moment Giovanni has no words, but he quickly collects himself, singing "I would never have believed it, but I'll do the best I can," which musically alternates between the tones of F and A while the orchestra inserts irritating G#s in between. That eerie accompaniment was also first heard several times in the overture, priming the audience's ear, as the interval Mozart exploits is notably unstable (the "tritone") and doesn't sound at all comfortable to most listeners. The musical discomfort continues as Giovanni orders Leporello to bring food for the ghost of the Commendatore, who refuses it but invites Giovanni to have dinner with *him*.

Leporello immediately sees this is going nowhere good, even though he has no explicit prior experience. His fast "System 1" thinking can put the cues together instantly, without deliberation, as survival is at stake. But Giovanni, over his servant's protests, defiantly says he is not afraid and accepts the counter-invitation.

These exchanges are all sung, but the Commendatore is setting the tune, a loud, imperious traversal step by step up the musical scale, accompanied by agitated, swirling, chromatic passages punctuated sharply by the orchestra. When Giovanni gives the Commendatore his hand in pledge to come to his dinner, the horror increases. The dead man won't let go of his hand and orders Giovanni to repent, who, again, defiantly refuses, as the music's tempo and intensity increase even more. "There's *no more* time!" the dead man thunders, and a chorus of hellish figures drags Giovanni downward into flames, as they loudly proclaim, "No doom is too great for your sins! Worse awaits you below." Mozart's orchestra could not sound more agitated as chords of D minor and major, one note different, rapidly whip a final tension that resolves emphatically with three loud exclamation points—into the major.

With Giovanni burned out of the picture, the other soloists return to the stage and conclude by singing together the smug moral DaPonte provided: "This is the end which befalls evildoers. And in this life scoundrels always receive their just desserts!"[28]

Maybe. But the characters touting that end did not make it happen.

Da Ponte labeled *Giovanni* a "dramma giocoso," a term for comic operas with serious elements.[29] The ending, where the norms of society apparently prevail over the immoral behavior of an individual, could justify calling Da Ponte's *Giovanni* a serious comedy. But Mozart's *Giovanni* is not so pat,

76 Music-Dramas, Evolutionary Biology, and Psychology

or flat. Normally heard today is that moralizing ending, as originally written for the premiere in Prague. For the second premiere, in Vienna in 1788, Mozart made a few changes.[30] Most importantly, the Vienna libretto omits that final sextet, and Mozart's score shows deletions suggesting the opera would end with Giovanni's fiery demise and without the final comments of the other characters. Although it is not completely clear that the opera was performed this way, the changes to text and music again suggest ambivalence about which ending Mozart preferred—the independent individual or the conventional social order.

From the perspective of biology and evolution, Giovanni is "just" a male going about the countryside having sex with as many females as possible. Still, Mozart does make him beguiling. When Giovanni focuses on what he wants Mozart gives him music of great energy, even abandon. Then in the final scenes the music gangs up on Giovanni, but he stays true to his own self whatever the cost; and the cost is total. For some, this defiance may appear "heroic," but does it negate the rest of his "anti-heroic" behavior?

For two and half centuries *Don Giovanni* has been an interpretive puzzle and challenge, exerting a kind of magnetic attraction on philosophers, poets, musicologists, filmmakers, as well as audiences.[31] One of the most provocative and early interpretations was written in 1843 by the Danish philosopher Søren Kierkegaard, in a lengthy essay on the opera, "The Immediate Stages of the Erotic, or the Musical Erotic." Kierkegaard posits that *Don Giovanni is* that "immediate" and "musical erotic" and exists beyond simple and exclusionary moral categories, which to this philosopher appear to depend upon reflection in time. Rather, the opera is about "sensuous love [which is] a disappearance in time, [and] the medium which exactly expresses this is music."[32]

As a medium for communication, Kierkegaard writes, music is more sensuous than language, since it stresses sound over sense; and music revels in immediacy. Giovanni is the ideal impersonation of these qualities of music. Giovanni

> simply does not fall under ethical categories. ... his life is as effervescent as the wine with which he stimulates himself ... He requires no preparation, no plan, no time, for he is always prepared. Energy is always in him and also desire ... This force, this omnipotence, this animation, only music can express ... [Giovanni] does not have a stable existence at all ... precisely like music.[33]

While philosopher Peter Kivy in 1988 mocked the "well-nigh cosmic depth of character that Kierkegaard sees in Don Giovanni,"[34] the Danish philosopher in 1843 is arguably trying to specify what is different about the opera. He does not exonerate Giovanni, and he identifies that the ambivalence of the opera, and about the opera, has to do with the body and "sensuousness." But his understanding of biology has the limitations of his time. Giovanni is, in part, the representative, victim, and victimizer of our biological inheritance of powerful unconscious forces, hormonal pushes to procreate. That's evolution.

But unrestrained Giovannis cannot be accommodated in a monogamous society, as espoused in the Europe of Mozart's time. As noted previously, women may not want them, because sex without commitment puts them at risk, and other men can't tolerate Giovannis, if they prefer a social order in which paternity is clear and women are solitary possessions.[35] Social ordering into more-or-less monogamous coupling was favored by cultural evolution in Christian Europe[36] and became the norm, it is reasoned, because of the benefits to the social group.[37]

Social norms are extremely powerful in human societies because, it is argued, cultural evolution made them so, long ago. Competition between human groups gradually and naturally selected for certain behaviors that would have strengthened the group, like being loyal friends, attentive parents, and upstanding members of the community adhering to its rules of conduct. Following social rules would have "domesticated" humans, Joseph Henrich claims,[38] so *un*domesticated individuals like Don Giovanni inevitably would have been expelled. Indeed, evolutionary anthropologists argue that the increasing brain size of hominins and the ultimate development of language arose to keep track of behaviors in society, and to share observations.[39] Once our *Homo sapiens* ancestors had language, by about 70,000 years ago, gossip would have served a critical social function[40] of detecting those who don't follow the rules in a group, such as those who harm and cheat, like Giovanni.

The intended regulation of individual behavior and the confirmation of the norms and values of the community are common functions of imaginative stories, and these functions argue for them as an adaptation, as the internalizing by their auditors of their messages would have helped individuals and groups to thrive.[41] As a leader of evolutionary humanities, Joseph Carroll, observed, "the most advanced and adequate concept in [this field] is the idea that humans evolved the capacity to create imaginative virtual worlds and use those worlds to guide human behavior."[42] Carroll's observation appears in much-elaborated form in the writing of historian Yuval Noah Harari, who argues in *Sapiens* that humans' cognitive ability to imagine all kinds of fictive entities—including "gods, nations and corporations,"[43] for example—and live believing in them, guides individual and, more importantly, collective behavior. Money, democracy, human rights, religion are all kinds of imagined realities in this view, and "as long as a communal belief in them persists, the imagined reality exerts force in the world."[44] Our lives, not only our arts, are bound up with such "fictions" as humans have created.

78 Music-Dramas, Evolutionary Biology, and Psychology

The imaginative virtual world that Alban Berg created in his opera *Wozzeck* was in part a sober reflection of his own world, of World War I and its aftermath. In it is presented another disturbing lead character, a murderer like Don Giovanni. But for many the assessment of soldier Wozzeck's character may be different.

Berg was 30 years old in 1915 when inducted into the Austrian army. Although he did not see combat, Berg's experience in World War I affected him sharply.[45] Initial military training was apparently too rigorous for his asthmatic condition, and he had a physical breakdown, was hospitalized, and diagnosed as suitable only for guard duties. This also proved too challenging for his fragile health, and he was transferred ultimately to a desk job in the War Ministry in Vienna in 1916, where he served out the remainder of the war. His correspondence to family and friends describing his wartime experience decries the "injustice" to him[46] and his "imprisonment."[47] "All of these years I suffered as a corporal, humiliated, not a single note composed," he complained in 1919 to a fellow composer, concluding, "I don't think you'll find such a fierce anti-militarist as I!"[48]

Earlier, Berg initially expressed a radical belief that the war might "act as a cathartic," cleansing German and Austro-Hungarian society of "hypocrisy," "selfishness," and other vices he perceived.[49] He had begun working on his opera before the war, in 1914, after having been impressed by initial performances of its source play, *Woyzeck*. Although written some 76 years before, the play had not been produced, as the playwright had died before putting the scenes of the drama into a final form. The drama by Georg Büchner was based on a real-life event in which a common soldier murdered his mistress over infidelity, pleaded insanity in his defence, was convicted nonetheless, and executed in public. Büchner's drama sympathizes with Woyzeck, showing the indifference and hostility of others in his limited social world as a kind of contributing madness, itself.

The disturbing experience of a poor, troubled soldier apparently attracted Berg even before the war, and after his own wartime experience it meant more to him. "There is a little bit of me in his character," he had written his wife in 1918, "since I have been spending these war years just as dependent on people I hate, have been in chains, sick, captive, resigned, in fact, humiliated."[50] As in the later 1919 letter, "humiliated" would appear to be Berg's particular sensitivity.

In trimming and organizing the scenes of Büchner's drama Berg emphasized its two main elements, the main character's difficulty coping in the world and how the people in his world were unable or unwilling to help, or even actively hostile. The characters with more social status than Wozzeck[51]—notably his Captain and a medical Doctor who is using him for experiments—are malign.[52]

The first scene of the opera thrusts the audience directly into this disturbed world. Wozzeck is at his army duty, shaving his Captain with a straight razor. From his chair, the Captain takes the opportunity to lecture Wozzeck about the speed at which he works, which segues into the officer's free-floating anxiety about time and eternity ("It makes me afraid for the world, to think about eternity"). This one statement covers four measures of music, with the Captain starting on middle-C, lurching angularly through flats and sharps to an extremely high B-natural nearly two octaves above, ending *pianissimo* on the first syllable of the word "eternity" (ewigkeit), then falling disjointedly. The sheer difficulty of singing such a vocal line can only accentuate the Captain's very odd, self-absorbed personality.

As the Captain rambles on, Wozzeck is obliged to agree with his ravings, then endure his superior saying that he "looks so harassed"! But when the Captain chides him for having had a child out of wedlock, one "not blessed by the Church," Wozzeck responds, saying that God won't spurn the child because "Amen" wasn't spoken at his conception. Wozzeck continues:

Poor folk like us! You see, Captain, money, money! If you have no money! Just try to bring people like us into the world in a moral way! …Yeah, if I were a gentleman, and had a hat, and a watch, and a monocle, and could talk genteelly, I would be virtuous, too! It must be a beautiful thing, virtue … People like us are cursed in this and the other world![53]

It is perhaps Wozzeck's most sympathetic moment in the drama, defending himself with a cogent social critique against persistent humiliation. Berg's vocal line is gingerly responsive to Wozzeck's tone and argument, and the orchestral accompaniment could be described as in sync and supportive of him.

Berg's development of an appropriate musical language for the intense, often extreme, sometimes violent drama is, finally, the reason that *Wozzeck* is still frequently performed a century after its premiere. The music is usually chromatic and dissonant, often serial and atonal but sometimes not, making it jarring to many listeners, especially on first hearing. "I had the sensation of coming out of an insane asylum," one reviewer wrote after the 1925 Berlin premiere. "I regard Alban Berg as a musician … dangerous to the community."[54]

But Berg's music communicates the disjointed, repugnant world of the play, which is both an aesthetic accomplishment and a choice. By contrast, Mozart never makes Giovanni musically repugnant; and he had a compositional theory for that choice. Music "must never offend the ear, but must please the hearer, or in other words must never cease to be music,"[55] Mozart explained to his father, in discussing how he presented the anger of

80 Music-Dramas, Evolutionary Biology, and Psychology

a character. With his musical means and aesthetic choice, Mozart defines a certain decorum with respect to his characters, which, in turn, causes some modern directors to strenuously remove that decorum, presumably to reveal a character like Giovanni for who, or what, he "really" is. That approach in practice is open to question if the staging and direction undercut what Mozart created, unless, of course, that is the director's purpose.

With Berg, musical analysts note how he appropriated various classical forms—sonata, rondo, fugue, and others—to create some structure within and between the successive scenes of the opera, which are separated by interludes of various lengths and manners. But Berg himself was modest about the theatrical significance of his use of these classical forms. "No one in the audience pays any attention [to them]," he wrote, approvingly.[56] "No one gives heed to anything but the vast social implications of the work which by far transcend the personal destiny of Wozzeck. This, I believe, is my achievement."[57]

The music of *Wozzeck* can be heard as illuminating a bleak tragedy of a modern kind, in which the institutions of society—military, medical, economic, political—are hostile to the individual. Worse, these institutions appear hypocritical, pretending to be good but preying on individuals' cognitive and emotional weaknesses. The principal characters in *Wozzeck*, different from those in prior mainstream operas, possess very limited abilities, self-awareness, and coherence of action. Compared with the lower-class servants Figaro and Susanna, for example, Wozzeck and Marie are barely competent in the world. Marie attempts to care for their young child, but Wozzeck, often delusional, can scarcely take care of himself. Such incompetence is very hard to watch since the extended care of children is so critical a part of human life history.[58]

Berg's "vast social implications" recalls his critique of Austria before and during the war, which he clearly saw as abnormal and wanted to do something about. Although his own city of Vienna was not in a combat zone, the Viennese certainly suffered during the war, as more and more of them became victims of wartime malnutrition and disease.[59] Much worse off was Germany, where even finding the bodies of soldiers, recognizing and burying them properly, was a horrible problem.[60] War is hell for individuals, and hell does not end when a war stops, as the 1920s, 1930s, and 1940s would all too grievously show.

Perhaps not too much should be made of the single instances of operas composed, on the one hand, before the French Revolution, which upended European societies, and, on the other, after the cataclysm of a world war, which caused so much personal suffering. But in *Don Giovanni* the wayward individual appears the enemy of society, while in *Wozzeck* society is the enemy of the wayward individual. Adult character has its biological bases, but clearly, for us social animals, the society of particular cultural moments influences how character is expressed, and how received.

When *Don Giovanni* premiered in Prague in 1787 one reviewer reported an unusually large audience, which demonstrated "unanimous approval," cheering Mozart three times, but noting, particularly, that "connoisseurs and musicians say that Prague had never heard anything like it."[61] When *Wozzeck* had its Prague premiere in 1926, the occasion ignited a firestorm of controversy between those who approved of its musical and social avant-gardeism and those who detested it—including by stopping with noise the third performance while underway.[62] One of the music-drama's opponents was a conservative reviewer who complained that "the [vocal] parts are either only spoken ... or 'sung,' but move in the most impossible intervals, such that the listener has the impression that he were in front of alcoholics erupting into desperate, delirious shrieks."[63] A drama interpreted as a stage full of alcoholics, or, as in Berlin, an "insane asylum" is telling. The individual antihero appears a controllable aberration in 1787 but a society of anti-heroes appears a very uncomfortable symptom in 1926.

Notes

1 This interpretation of the scene is drawn from a 2009 production starring Ildebrando D'Arcangelo as Giovanni, staged at the Macerata Opera Festival.
2 W. A. Mozart, *Don Giovanni*, libretto by Lorenzo Da Ponte, English translation by William Murray, 1961, accompanying recording Angel 3605 D/L (Calif.: Angel, 1961). The Italian-English libretto available online at DM's opera site: http://www.murashev.com/opera/Don_Giovanni_libretto_Italian_English.
3 Mozart, *Giovanni*, tr. Murray, 1.5 All further translations from this source.
4 Ibid.
5 Liane Curtis, "The Sexual Politics of Teaching Mozart's 'Don Giovanni,'" *NWSA Journal* (2000): 119.
6 *Giovanni*, 1.11–13.
7 Oliver P. John and Sanjay Srivastava, "The Big-Five Trait Taxonomy: History, Measurement, and Theoretical Perspectives," in *Handbook of Personality: Theory and Research*, ed. L. A. Pervin and O. P. John (New York: Guilford Press, 1999). N.B. More recently these traits have been questioned as applicable mainly to educated Western societies. See J. Henrich, *The WEIRDest People in the World: How the West Became Psychologically Peculiar and Particularly Prosperous* (New York: Farrar, Straus and Giroux, 2020).
8 See D. P. McAdams, "From Actor to Agent to Author," in *Darwin's Bridge: Uniting the Humanities and Sciences* (New York: Oxford University Press, 2016).
9 Ibid., 151.
10 Ibid.
11 The mnemonic device OCEAN may help in recalling the traits as listed in the footnoted sentence.
12 Henry M. Wellman, "Theory of Mind: The State of the Art," *European Journal of Developmental Psychology* 15, no. 6 (2018): 734.
13 See Elisabeth A. Murray et al., "The Story of Your Life: Memories All Your Own," in *The Evolutionary Road to Human Memory* (Oxford: Oxford University Press, 2019), 167.

14 R. I. M. Dunbar, "The Social Brain: Mind, Language, and Society in Evolutionary Perspective," *Annual Review of Anthropology* 32, no. 1 (2003): 169. Also: Wellman, "Theory of Mind: The State of the Art."

15 *Giovanni*, tr. W. Murray, 1.12.

16 "richiamar nel cor mio."

17 *Giovanni*, tr. W. Murray, 1.13.

18 Important questions relating to ToM research: François Quesque and Yves Rossetti, "What Do Theory-of-Mind Tasks Actually Measure? Theory and Practice," *Perspectives on Psychological Science* 15, no. 2 (2020): 384–396.

19 Tony W. Buchanan, "Retrieval of Emotional Memories," *Psychological Bulletin* 133, no. 5 (2007).

20 Hume's 1777 *Enquiry Concerning the Principles of Morals* is cited and glossed in Jonathan Haidt and Fredrik Bjorklund, "Social Intuitionists Answer Six Questions about Morality," in *Moral Psychology*, Vol. 2, *The Cognitive Science of Morality*, ed. W. Sinnott-Armstrong (Cambridge, MA: MIT Press, 2007), 185.

21 Haidt, "Social Intuitionists," 181.

22 Daniel Kahneman, *Thinking, Fast and Slow* (New York: Farrar, Straus and Giroux, 2011), 20.

23 Jesse Graham et al., "Moral Foundations Theory," in *Atlas of Moral Psychology*, ed. Kurt Gray and Jesse Graham (New York: Guilford Press, 2018).

24 Wayne C. Booth, *The Rhetoric of Fiction*, first ed. (Chicago: University of Chicago Press, 1961), 133.

25 Graham, "Moral Foundations Theory," 212–213.

26 Haidt, "Social Intuitionists," 201.

27 Joseph E. LeDoux, "Feelings: What Are They & How Does the Brain Make Them?" *Daedalus* 144, no. 1 (2015): 102.

28 *Giovanni*, tr. W. Murray, final scene.

29 Oxford Reference, s.v. "dramma giocoso," http://www.oxfordreference.com/view/10.1093/oi/authority.20110803095730252.

30 For details, see Brian Soucek, "Giovanni auf Naxos" in *The Don Giovanni Moment*, Lydia Goehr, Daniel Herwitz, eds. (New York: Columbia University Press, 2006), 196.

31 L. Goehr and D. Herwitz, *The Don Giovanni Moment: Essays on the Legacy of an Opera* (New York: Columbia University Press, 2006).

32 S. Kierkegaard, *Either/ Or*, trans. David F. Swenson and Lillian Marvin Swenson, Vol. 1 (New York: Anchor Books, 1959), 94.

33 Ibid. As Kierkegaard has an informal, repetitious manner in the essay and is prone to stringing insights across multiple pages, it does not seem amiss to assemble these comments from pages 97, 99, 100, 101.

34 Peter Kivy, *Osmin's Rage: Philosophical Reflections on Opera, Drama, and Text* (Princeton, NJ: Princeton University Press, 1988), 269.

35 David C. Geary, "Evolution of Paternal Investment," in *The Handbook of Evolutionary Psychology*, Wiley Online Books (2015), 499.

36 See Henrich, *WEIRDest People*.

37 J. Henrich, R. Boyd, and P. J. Richerson, "The Puzzle of Monogamous Marriage," *Philosophical Transactions of the Royal Society London B Biological Sciences* 67, no. 1589 (2012).

38 Joseph Henrich, *The Secret of Our Success* (Princeton, NJ: Princeton University Press, 2016), 318.

39 See Dunbar, "Social Brain," for substantial presentation of these ideas.

40 R. Dunbar, "Gossip in Evolutionary Perspective," *Review of General Psychology* 8 (2004).

Don Giovanni, Wozzeck **83**

41 Nevertheless, the debate over story as an adaptation or not so, seems not settled.

42 Joseph Carroll, "Dutton, Davies, and Imaginative Virtual Worlds," *Aisthesis* 6, no. 2 (2013): 82.

43 Yuval Noah Harari, *Sapiens* (New York: HarperCollins, 2015), 32.

44 Ibid.

45 His war career is treated in a chapter in Karen Monson, *Alban Berg* (Boston: Houghton Mifflin Co., 1979).

46 A letter December 25, 1915. Willi Reich, *The Life and Work of Alban Berg.* Translated by Cornelius Cardew (New York: Da Capo Press, 1981), 43.

47 Monson, *Berg*, 138.

48 Ibid., 140. The letter was not truthful, at least about "not a single note composed."

49 Ibid., 131.

50 Glenn Watkins, *Proof Through the Night: Music and the Great War* (University of California Press, 2002), 235.

51 Berg's spelling.

52 This exploration of disturbed social psychology would have had some currency in Vienna, home to Sigmund Freud (who Berg had known since 1908, when the doctor treated him during a severe asthmatic attack).

53 A. Berg, *Wozzeck*, libretto by the composer, 1922. English translation, uncredited. Naxos Records, Catalogue No: 8.660390-91, 2017.; http://www. naxos .com /sungtext /pdf /8 .660390 -91 sungtext .pdf

54 Anonymous reviewer cited in George B, Stauffer, "Alban Berg's Dissonances," review of *Berg* by Bryan Simms and Charlotte Erwin, *New York Review of Books*, June 23, 2022.

55 Cited in the publisher's description introducing Kivy, *Osmin's Rage: Philosophical Reflections on Opera, Drama, and Text.*

56 The letter was published in 1927 after the first two years of performances. Douglas Jarman, *Alban Berg: Wozzeck* (Cambridge, UK: Cambridge University Press, 1989), 153.

57 Jarman, *Wozzeck*, 11.

58 Hillard S. Kaplan and Steven W. Gangestad, "Life History Theory and Evolutionary Psychology," *The Handbook of Evolutionary Psychology*. (Wiley Online Books, 2015), http://doi.org/10.1002/9780470939376.ch2.

59 "Vienna in the First World War – How the City Changed," The World of the Habsburgs, accessed September 2, 2021, http://ww1.habsburger.net/en/stories/vienna-first-world-war-how-city-changed

60 See Robert Weldon Whalen, "War Losses (Germany)," *International Encyclopedia of the First World War*, Daniel Ute et al., eds. (2017).

61 Otto Erich Deutsch, *Mozart, a Documentary Biography* (Stanford, CA: Stanford University Press, 1966), 303.

62 All covered in rich detail in Brian S. Locke, "The 'Wozzeck Affair': Modernism and the Crisis of Audience in Prague," *Journal of Musicological Research* 27, no. 1 (2008).

63 Ibid., 72. The reviewer was Antonín Šilhan.

6

DIE WALKÜRE, SIMON BOCCANEGRA

Parenting, Power, and Posterity

For several minutes the valkyries have been arriving to the summit of a rocky mountain, confidently flying in on horses, dressed in armor, calling out their wild song, "Hoyotoho! *Hoyotoho!*" They carry astride their horses the bodies of dead warriors, destined to become their father's immortal defenders in Valhalla, the mighty hall of the gods in the sky. But the eight valkyrie sisters are astonished and troubled when they see their last sister, Brünnhilde, fly in, carrying a living woman.

"Protect me from our father's wrath," she cries, "for I have disobeyed him and saved this woman's life!"[1] The other sisters fear their father's anger, watching menacing storm clouds roll in toward the mountain top heralding his arrival. The music roils, the valkyries interject their anxieties. None of them dares to help Brünnhilde.

Many adults become parents, but all people have been children. Operas that focus on the interactions between parents and children presumably will have a large and likely interested audience, and this opening scene of the final act of Richard Wagner's *Die Walküre (The Valkyrie)* is clearly meant to provoke that interest.

Of course, every child will have their own personal experiences, which will have some effect on their interest and reception. And yet evolution will set a framework for that reception. Humans take a comparatively long time becoming adults; and parents, as noted before, typically spend years in the role of supporting children through adolescence into adulthood. *Homo sapiens* evolved to have comparatively big heads to house our unusually big brains; and current understanding is that the brains evolved larger in response to the needs and opportunities of life[2] as cooperative and competitive social animals.[3] One consequence of our big heads, however, was

DOI: 10.4324/9781003254478-8

to make childbirth hazardous for both Sapiens mother and child. A consequence of our big brain is that, at birth, the brain itself is not fully developed. The slow development of the brain[4] (and especially its frontal cortex, whose functions contribute most to making us human[5]) requires the sustained support of others. Parents are primarily responsible, though grandparents and others in the social group may play important parts[6] (as in "It takes a village to raise a child" [7]).

Although parenting demands usually lessen over time, concerns often continue for the remainder of the parents' life. All this allocation of energy to parenting comes at the cost of other survival and reproductive activities, which might have been undertaken instead, including other mating;[8] and often parents perceive that cost as a valuable permanent investment (which may sound like a cold calculation right out of behavioral economics).[9] But from an evolutionary perspective the child is a genetic investment, and, from a cultural perspective, the child is recognized to have value worth protecting. Costs and losses human minds understand very differently;[10] and parents often view the loss of a child through death as incalculable.

These observations about parenting and children are perhaps not controversial, but dramas thrive on the particular and the controversial, as does Wagner's *Die Walküre*. It is the second of four music-dramas in Wagner's epic *Ring of the Nibelung*. An elaborate tale of the Norse gods, dwarfs, giants, and humans, the *Ring* revolves around a magical ring, which affords the power to dominate the world, but, in doing so, the ring undoes its bearer. The four *Ring* music-dramas performed in sequence take about 15 hours, over four nights. The plot of *Walküre* inevitably connects to the other dramas in complicated ways. Still, plots are not what dramas are ultimately "about" but rather the occasion for the examination of character and relationships. *Walküre* can be somewhat briefly summarized regarding the family relationships.

Wotan, king of the gods, has great power in the cosmos. He exerts his will and ingenuity to succeed in his domain, but the moral compromises he makes threaten to undo what he has put together. Similarly, his powerful desires bring him children outside of his marriage, but to him, these children are mainly extensions of himself and, if they stand in the way of his plans for them, it appears they must bend to his will.

Years earlier, his son and daughter, Siegmund and Sieglinde, twins born of a mortal woman, were abandoned during their adolescence by Wotan. In Act 1, both children, now adults, are in desperate circumstances and initially unrecognized by the other, but they are reunited and escape those circumstances, becoming lovers as they do so. In Act 2, Hunding, the husband of Sieglinde, determines to get her back and kill Siegmund, which Fricka, Wotan's wife and goddess of marriage, tells Wotan he must enable to show his respect for her, "your eternal spouse" (deiner ew'gen Gattin) by avenging

86 Music-Dramas, Evolutionary Biology, and Psychology

the incestuous elopement of his illegitimate children. Wotan, telling her she does not understand his entire purpose in permitting the liaison, nevertheless bitterly agrees to let Siegmund be killed in the upcoming battle with Hunding. He sends his trusted daughter (by another goddess), Brünnhilde, to announce his fate to Siegmund. But she disobeys and tries to protect her half-brother in battle, believing her father actually wanted him protected. In Act 3, Wotan severely punishes Brünnhilde for her disobedience, although ultimately conceding to her last wish.

While Wagner titled the music-drama for one of Wotan's children, the title is not Brünnhilde's name but her role, a "warrior maiden," an immortal in service to her father. While the meaning of that title deflection is not obvious, it should not obscure a more fundamental and prior question about the drama. Parent-child relations may be the core of *Walküre*, but what is one to make of dramatic characters who are gods? Wagner does depict Wotan and Brünnhilde as gods who are different from humans at least in having supernatural powers, such as the ability to fly through the air.

Probably no opera composer has had more written about the music and the imaginative worlds he created than Wagner, including by the often-verbose composer himself; and much ink has been spilled interpreting the *Ring of the Nibelung*. But perhaps something useful can be said coming from a different analytical position.

How the audience is to understand the presence of the gods in *Walküre* seems to have three possible answers.

First, one may accept that they are as "real" as any other character in a dramatic work. Stories about gods are not anything unusual; all religions have them, and gods are a commonplace of human thinking, for psychological reasons provocatively explained by evolutionary psychologists[11] and those who study "error management theory"[12] (which would, however, cause too long a digression here). However, for those who reject belief in gods outright, this literalist view that they are "real" may well present a barrier to understanding the drama or accepting it as other than fantasy.

Second, one may ignore whether gods are real or not, and consider *Walküre* and the rest of the *Ring* an allegory about human society, perhaps from a political perspective, for example a socialist one. Playwright George Bernard Shaw did just that in his *The Perfect Wagnerite*, addressed to readers wanting to understand the *Ring*:

> The danger is that you will jump to the conclusion that the gods, at least, are a higher order than the human order. On the contrary, the world is waiting for Man to redeem it from the lame and cramped government of the gods. Once grasp that; and the allegory becomes simple enough. Really, of course, the dwarfs, giants, and gods are dramatizations of the three main orders of men: to wit, the instinctive, predatory, lustful, greedy

Die Walküre, Simon Boccanegra **87**

people; the patient, toiling, stupid, respectful, money-worshiping people; and the intellectual, moral, talented people who devise and administer States and Churches. History shows us only one order higher than the highest of these: namely, the order of Heroes.[13]

The Ring "gods," despite their supernatural abilities, are no better than humans; in fact, they are properly overthrown later by the heroes Siegfried and Brünnhilde.

Since Wagner personally wrote the libretto and the entire *Ring* story, one would expect his biases and blindspots on display in a socio-political allegory. He was alert to repressive social norms, having had to flee his home in Dresden at a warrant for his arrest after a failed left-wing uprising in 1849, in which he'd play a role.[14] Completing *Walküre* in 1856, he showed his disdain for aspects of conventional society in his depiction of Hunding and of marriage as a matter of property. (Perhaps not coincidentally, the married Wagner appears to have been infatuated with another, married woman at the time of writing *Walküre*.[15])

Finally, third, one may understand the gods only in psychological terms as expressions of evolved adult behavioral priorities. Fricka is the belittled wife who still believes in marriage and insists on its bond. Wotan is the spouse much more interested in social power than in family obligations, and he has a will to dominate, as many men and fathers continue to do, unless or until challenged. Brünnhilde expresses that challenge, personifying that to become an adult means to separate from the father's dominance and become ready to mate with another, ultimately becoming a parent oneself.

Brünnhilde disobeys Wotan when she sees Siegmund's commitment to Sieglinde, a love against all odds; and she tries to help her half-brother in battle. Nevertheless, Wotan intervenes and smashes Siegmund's sword, allowing Hunding to kill him. In a cold rage Wotan then kills Hunding and races off to find Brünnhilde, who has escaped with Sieglinde (who is pregnant with Siegfried). In Act 3 Wotan confronts Brünnhilde for her disobedience, but in a lengthy argument she counters that she had done only what she perceived he had himself truly wished for, to save the child he loved. Bitterly, since he had agreed to renounce that love and, worse, had been the cause of the son's death, Wotan tells her that since she is now captivated by love, their paths must forever part. He will strip off her godhead and put her asleep on a high rock where the first man to arrive can claim her for "love."

This unimaginable fall from paternal grace leaves Brünnhilde stunned, alarmed; and the music-drama takes on a breathless rapid pulse. As she searches for what can be said to sway her father, she falls to her knees and asks for one concession, that it won't be just any man but someone bold and fearless who will claim her.

88 Music-Dramas, Evolutionary Biology, and Psychology

Wotan's having none of that either, for "you chose in rapture the power of love ... From Wotan you turned away; your conqueror I cannot choose." So Brünnhilde grabs him around the knees, desperately—and goes right to the edge. "Kill me at once," she cries—and she has seen that he is quite capable of doing that with his children, so it is no naive gambit—"but cast not this shame /this cruel disgrace on me."[16] Then, "*with wild inspiration*," as Wagner's stage direction says, she boldly, loudly gives an ultimatum: Light a magic fire ring around me, so that only a hero would dare come through it. Or kill me.

As previously discussed, evolutionary psychologists see that women evolved to be choosy, to not just accept the first man who might come calling, and Wagner presents Wotan as ultimately a decent father who will give his daughter the chance for a better mate (which would also serve his genetic, and perhaps other more immediate, purposes).

In this lengthy confrontation scene Wagner gives a psychological depth to his characters that previous opera had rarely if ever plumbed; the particular dynamism of his music makes this intense scene of family relationship even more so. Wagner had reimagined the relationship of music and drama, starting with essays written before the *Ring* compositions. Wagner saw set pieces, such as solo arias, duets, and so on, conventional in previous opera, as interruptions on the flow of the drama, which is continually unfolding. Responding to the drama, the music should also continually unfold without interruption.[17] In these views Wagner was arguably taking the next step in an evolution of the form of opera, extending the reforms championed by Gluck, for instance. To achieve a greater dramatic continuity and verisimilitude, Wagner also advanced a different kind of musical structure, what he called "melodic moments," also known as themes, and later, by others, as "leitmotifs."

"These Melodic Moments," he wrote, "will be made by the orchestra into a kind of guides-to-Feeling through the whole labyrinthine building of the drama."[18] Typically, the melodic themes would be associated with a particular person, place, or thing. That theme could then be reused and modified repeatedly as an individual drama or even successive *Ring* dramas unfolded, subtly changing in duration, tempo, and the notes themselves and their relationship (such as from a major to a minor key). But once heard, listeners make an association of musical theme to "the magic fire," for example, and they become like Pavlov's dog, salivating when it hears the theme even though the associated object may not be visibly present.

In his 1850 essay, "The Art-Work of the Future," Wagner envisioned an "associate work" of many arts, and music-drama alone uniting them, bringing them to their own perfection in the unity, and in that unity creating something new and valuable to its listeners, "a living, breathing, moving drama."[19] In such drama, music must be a means, and drama the ends, not the other way around, as he vilified most Italian and French opera for doing. Music as a "means" and, thus, an equal, not a dominant, partner in the drama is on full display in the final scenes of *Walküre*.

Ever since the moment when Wotan determines to punish Brünnhilde the music has been gathering in volume and intensity as several of the melodic themes rapidly and flexibly arise, are asserted, and dissolve. Listeners hear, among others, themes associated with Wotan and Brünnhilde, of course, and Valhalla, the home of the gods, now forbidden to her. More subtly are heard the magic fire theme and the as yet unvoiced response of Wotan to her plea *before* those themes are presented as onstage developments in the drama. This swirling, urgent undercurrent creates a peak at the decisive moment when Wotan might kill her, and the music surges with Brünnhilde to a crescendo. Wotan is won over, "overcome and deeply moved" (in Wagner's own stage direction).

As a father, Wotan then sings a long, emotional farewell to his daughter, conceding that he loves her. Kissing her godhead away, he says that she, now to be human, is freer than he is, a god. This factor will become crucial in the later *Ring* dramas.

As discussion of other operas has emphasized, evolutionary theory of storytelling predicts that people are motivated to attend to stories that illuminate significant issues, and often conflicts, in one or more of the major phases in human life (life-history).[20] Dramatic stories often hold interest because they can help people learn from the dangers, troubles, and mistakes presented in them,[21] and *Walküre* provides many learning opportunities about human relationships. The powerful, sonorous conclusion of the music-drama, when Wotan summons a magic ring of fire around Brünnhilde to protect her, leaves the audience to sort out this complex father and king, struggling between those two roles and their conflicted consequences.

For his part, Wagner professed that his story of the old Norse gods and heroes would reanimate Germanic culture and peoples and music-drama, finding a model in classical Greece,[22] as Monteverdi and Gluck had also done. In "The Art-Work of the Future,"[23] Wagner asserted that Athenian tragedy emerged from a "tribal fellowship"[24] that (somehow, Wagner is not clear) spawned "religious ideas" expressed in rituals and myth, which he referred to as a "primaeval, anonymous folk poem." In myths, "conventional" human relations disappear, Wagner wrote, replaced by "that which is eternally comprehensible and purely human."[25]

While Wagner may have been hoping for the timeless and hoping to refresh the German "folk"[26] by drawing on the ancient sagas, the *Ring* cannot really escape its own time or its interpretation in later times. Wagner's intention to refresh (or revolutionize) the German folk has been linked to his antisemitism.[27] Later, Adolf Hitler loved and promoted Wagner's works as consistent with his own antisemitic, racist ideology and ambitions for

90 Music-Dramas, Evolutionary Biology, and Psychology

Germany, with the gravest consequences. More recently, the modern critic Bernard Zelechow deflated *the Ring* as "ultimately a suburban drama of the acquisitive newly rich who are driven by infinite yearning and insatiable desire."[28]

Wagner had considerable influence on other composers and writers[29] in many European countries. Even so, another great composer, working in his own tradition, had equally important music-dramas to offer in his own time, and they have proved more broadly popular down to today.

Giuseppe Verdi's operas routinely receive more performances and theatrical productions per year than those of any other composer.[30] His dramas explore intensely the primary relationships, of husbands and wives, of lovers, of parents and children. Consider one of his last operas, *Simon Boccanegra*, first written in 1857 and revised in 1881.[31]

The drama, set in fourteenth-century Genoa, begins in a Prologue with the unseen death of Maria, a young noblewoman who has borne an illegitimate child, a girl, to a commoner, Simon Boccanegra. He is a corsair, or privateer, who has defended coastal Genoa from pirates. Because of the hatred her patrician father, Fiesco, has for Boccanegra, the corsair has previously stolen away the infant girl and hidden her with an old woman to look after her. Boccanegra arrives outside Fiesco's palace intending to ask him for permission to marry Maria, not knowing that she has just died. Fiesco demands to see his granddaughter, but the child (named Maria after her mother) has subsequently disappeared, Boccanegra explains. No forgiveness is possible from Fiesco, and, as the Prologue ends, the old man has neither daughter nor granddaughter. Boccanegra has neither daughter nor her beloved mother, for he then enters the palace to find her dead.

Twenty-five years have passed as Act 1 begins, and Boccanegra, still the Doge, makes a visit to the home of a patrician family. He does a favor for the young Amelia Grimaldi by pardoning exiled Grimaldis, who had been Boccanegra's adversaries for years. Amelia is touched by his unexpected kindness, and she confesses to Boccanegra that she is actually *not* a Grimaldi. She lives there as the ward of an older man named Andrea (whom she does not know is actually Fiesco).

Amelia reveals hesitantly to Boccanegra that, before she was adopted as a child, she remembers living with an old peasant woman, who cared for her and loved her. Starting with this revelation, Boccanegra comes to recognize that "Amelia" is his long-lost daughter Maria. The musical pitch, volume, and tempo of their questions and answers increase with each confidence, culminating when they show each other small portrait lockets that each wears. It pictures the elder Maria, his dead wife, and her mother. The gathering expectancy comes to a dramatic and musical climax as Boccanegra declares:

"Embrace me, my daughter!"
"Father! ... Hold me!"[32]

Die Walküre, Simon Boccanegra **91**

The power of this scene is based on the love of father and child, which needs no more elaboration regarding its essential nature in human life and thus its appeal to most audience members. The surprise and joy of mutual discovery elevates the emotional response. The music itself comes to an energetic but melodious peak at the moment of discovery, a peak that is sustained for about ten seconds as the chord reluctantly diminishes. Then a rapturous duet begins in which the voices twine around each other and eventually merge. "'Daughter'—at that name I tremble as if heaven had opened to me … a world of utter bliss," sings Boccanegra, "Your loving father will create a paradise for you." "I will wipe away your tears," replies Maria, "I will be the dove of peace at your palace."

Unlike the relationship of Wotan and Brünnhilde, which is mostly about the father's dominance, Boccanegra wants nothing more than to reclaim his daughter and protect her, and assuage their suffering. Such care supports the daughter claiming or at least obtaining an appropriate mate. In the drama, the very next thing Boccanegra does is tell his supporter, Paolo, to give up hope of ever marrying "Amelia"—whom Paolo is interested in because he would become linked to the Grimaldi fortune. Instead, Boccanegra will support Maria's own choice in a mate, despite that her choice, the patrician Gabriele Adorno, is initially opposed, violently, to Boccanegra.

Boccanegra's support of his daughter has consequences for all his relationships in the remainder of the opera. For Paolo, the Doge's peremptory decision against him is pivotal, for he originally engineered Boccanegra's rise to government power and will vengefully bring about Boccanegra's downfall. Maria does defend her father, and he her, just as they promised to do, while maintaining her public identity as "Amelia Grimaldi" rather than Maria Boccanegra. She prevents him from being killed, twice, but is unable to stop Paolo from poisoning Boccanegra.

In the final act of the opera, the dying Boccanegra encounters Fiesco, his political rival, personal enemy, and the guardian of the foundling "Amelia" when she was growing up. The encounter begins with Fiesco suddenly appearing in the Doge's apartment within the palace. A brief battle between the patrician forces allied with Fiesco and the plebeians allied with Boccanegra has ended, and Fiesco has lost, but the older man, at first concealing his identity, enters declaring that like a ghost he has come to avenge an ancient outrage ("Come fantasima, Fiesco t'appar, antico oltraggio a vendicar!"). His adamant vocal line is accompanied at first by a swirling orchestration, suggesting a phantasm, and ends with individually emphasized chords played *fortissimo*, rather like Mozart's accompaniment to the frightening, ghostly "Stone Guest" in *Don Giovanni*.

But the sudden tension quickly evaporates once Fiesco reveals who he is, for then Boccanegra reveals to him, in an expansive melody, that Amelia/Maria is his long-lost granddaughter. Verdi instantly changes the entire

92 Music-Dramas, Evolutionary Biology, and Psychology

mood. Stunned, Fiesco weeps and is grateful, and Boccanegra calls for the two to embrace and ask for the other's pardon. In the pulsing contours of their slow, conversational duet, the low voices of Fiesco, a bass, and Boccanegra, a baritone, readily convey a grieving about how life turned out, and yet a dignity, even a magnanimity in their reconciliation. Its elevated quality depends on Verdi's treatment of what is, to begin with, again, one of opera's extraordinary advantages, that more than one person can speak at the same time and be understood.

In this instance, fittingly, Fiesco and Boccanegra at first sing separately, expressing their individual perspectives, and then sing together, in harmony. But it is the same basic melody they develop. And it is also one of those elegiac Verdi melodies that, through its expansion and contraction, maintains its poise, expressing but not exaggerating their feelings. This effect of recognition and revelation (of Aristotelian "anagnorisis") brings to mind similar scenes of understanding the true identity of another in Shakespeare,[33] whom Verdi greatly admired, and also other ones in opera, including that of the Count when the Countess appears at the end of *Figaro* and, indeed, the mutual discovery of father and daughter earlier in *Boccanegra*.

Boccanegra's magnanimity here with Fiesco cements multiple impressions of his character observed earlier in the drama.[34] His moral foundation would appear to rest on care for others. One feature that is both compelling and comparatively rare about this opera is that many major concerns in adult life are presented: courtship, mating and parenting, maturity and social responsibilities, and dying. Maturity and an engaging in the wellbeing of others are prominently on display in Boccanegra himself.

These qualities are expressed by Boccanegra as Doge in a great scene in the grand Council Chamber of Genoa.[35] Early in the scene Boccanegra urges the councilors, half of whom are patricians, half commoners, to make peace with rival Venice—which they appear to reject, when a mob of their own citizens storms the chamber. And Boccanegra, saying he does not fear them, orders them to be let in. The commoners have swept up the patrician Andrea/Fiesco and Gabriele Adorno for having killed the commoner Lorenzino, but Adorno did so because Lorenzino was one of three men who abducted Amelia.

Believing that Boccanegra is responsible for the abduction, Gabriele is about to strike him when Amelia appears and puts herself between them, stopping Gabriele. Boccanegra has him disarmed but left unhurt, and now asks her to tell everyone how she was abducted, which she does. But when she declines to name the ringleader even though she "stares at Paolo," the commoners and patricians are ready to attack each other as the perpetrating group. At this, Boccanegra makes a powerful plea to all to stop their internal conflict in a moving aria that concludes, "I call to you for peace; I call for love."[36]

Die Walküre, Simon Boccanegra **93**

Healing divisions is what most people expect their leaders to do, as a shared peace in which to live is so valuable for social life. From an evolutionary perspective, leadership—the organizing of collective effort to meet common goals—is a basic feature of human social evolution.[37] For a species like ourselves, cooperation within a population is often vital to survival. Evolutionary psychologists have argued that supporting kin is the basis of cooperation, as doing so will likely promote the continuation of one's interests as well as one's genes. The cooperation of Amelia/Maria, Boccanegra, Gabriele, and even Andrea/Fiesco shows this motivation.

From the perspective of cultural evolution, such "kin selection" is a necessary but not sufficient reason for broad cooperation, as is also "reciprocity," another evolved social behavior ("I'll scratch your back if you scratch mine"). Kin and reciprocity are arguably not strong enough for larger groups with unrelated or distantly related participants.[38]

Instead, agreed-upon social norms, shared beliefs and values solidify cooperation.[39] If the (imagined) society of fourteenth-century Genoa, for example, depends on every adult conforming to the norm that the abduction (rape) of young women is intolerable, then those who break that norm are shunned and cannot expect to have the cooperation of their peers. This is exactly what happens to Paolo, as Boccanegra perceives that his estranged ally is the lead abductor. Before all those gathered in the chambers, the Doge, here as enforcer of community values, calls upon Paolo to condemn the unnamed norm-violator. Paolo speaks the malediction ("sia maledetto!") on himself with unconcealed horror; and everyone repeats it.[40]

The scene shows Boccanegra displaying two characteristics of leadership probably established during human evolution because of their effectiveness.[41] The first is male dominance, directing others by the force of personality, most apparent with this demand that Paolo, in effect, condemn himself. This is an overwhelming demand, and notable is how Verdi scores Boccanegra's vocalization: it is not soft and suggestive but loud and insistent, and the pitch is lower than the Doge had recently used. These vocal manners will get the attention of listeners, both on the stage and in the audience, as Verdi is imitating the vocal habit of dominators—a loud, insistent growl—again very likely with an evolutionary origin.[42]

The second characteristic of leadership is, here and elsewhere, more prominent with Boccanegra; he has prestige. He acts out of concern for the future of his community, has been a champion of the people, a corsair, and elected leader, and the success of these behaviors have made many people defer to him and follow him willingly. His supporters will win the civil war.

Before then, in the next Act, he again pardons Gabriele when he attempts to stab him (although again Maria intervenes). Gabriele had falsely believed that Maria may be Boccanegra's mistress; and he also blamed Boccanegra for the death of his father in the internecine struggles in Genoa. In

94 Music-Dramas, Evolutionary Biology, and Psychology

pardoning Gabriele, Boccanegra thinks out loud, "There must be peace in Italy, even over my grave." In turn, when Gabriele understands the truth about Boccanegra and his daughter, he switches sides to support the Doge in the imminent battle between patricians and commoners, and Boccanegra responds by approving his marriage to Maria.

His concern for his own family and posterity is how the opera concludes. In the opera's final scene, poisoned and dying, Boccanegra reunites Maria with her grandfather, Fiesco. Then, as Doge, on his throne, he gathers his daughter and Gabriele to his side to bless them and appoint his son-in-law as his successor. Maria pleads, "No, you shall not die, for love/conquers the coldness of death/Heaven will respond in pity to my sorrow."

Her tenderness and desperation are elaborated by others in a concerted section, with individuals and a chorus commenting: "All pleasure on earth is a lie and illusion …" / "How swiftly joy passes" / "We all weep, sorrowful creatures; we clothe our human nature in sorrow."[43]

But Boccanegra does die, his last word "Maria," the name of both beloved daughter and wife.

In several of Verdi's 26 operas a parent is not able or fails to protect a child. Prominent examples are fathers in *Macbeth, Giovanna d'Arco, Luisa Miller, Rigoletto,* and *Aida.* A listener to the father-child scenes in these operas and in *Simon Boccanegra* would very likely be struck by not only their musical but also their emotional intensity, even a disproportionate intensity and focus in the opera, overall. In addition, in nearly all his operas lovers or close family members die, frequently leaving another loved one alone and distraught (this happens, for example, in *Ernani, Lombardi, Battaglia di Legnano, Traviata, Trovatore, Rigoletto, Boccanegra, Forza del Destino,* and *Otello*). Young women frequently die (in *Giovanna d'Arco* (Joan of Arc), *Corsaro, Luisa Miller, Rigoletto, Traviata, Forza, Aida,* and *Otello,* to again name just a few). These indicators suggest the possibility of some personal reasons for such pessimism on Verdi's part.

Alternatively, an explanation could be that, as a savvy man of the theater, and a person driven to succeed financially, Verdi was just taking dramatic materials provided to him that he thought would be popular, indeed, already were, via their previous incarnations as stage plays. After all, unlike Wagner, for instance, Verdi did not write the stories of his operas. Nor was he the librettist, although these generalizations miss the important details. In nearly all his operas, Verdi was highly selective about the story and how it should be shaped. Moreover, with certainly his major operas routinely performed today, Verdi was very closely—in fact often fiercely—involved with the text, both for its linguistic value but also for its dramatic and musical purpose. He was a notorious taskmaster with his librettists, often specifying the language he wanted to set. So, the notion that Verdi's operas might be some sort of disinterested work-for-hire is superficial.

But the philosopher Peter Kivy is among those who strongly caution against making claims about "what an opera might tell us about a composer," denying the possibility of what he calls, dismissively, "symptomatic revelation" of "truths about the composer."[44] With reference to individual works, this caution is persuasive: Verdi's tragic *Boccanegra* and comic *Falstaff* would together, taken apart from his others, make it very difficult to discern singular "truths" about Verdi.

On the other hand, with Verdi there is a body of major work composed over five decades, the 26 operas as well as the equally "dramatic" Manzoni *Requiem*, which invite a consideration of the meaning of the consistent relationship patterns they display. These dramatic works, in their selection and particularity, were made by one individual, out of all his individual ability, experience, and mind. Is there nothing to be gained by looking at Verdi himself?

When Verdi was between 24 and 26 years old and a young husband and father, his two young children, a son and a daughter, and then his wife, all died. They all died in a two-year period, one after the other. If that has not happened to the person learning of it, it may be difficult to comprehend the potential consequences of such losses for a sensitive individual. By his own account, Verdi plunged into a deep despair at these deaths and stopped composing anything new. Years later, he wrote, "With my soul torn apart by my family tragedies ... I decided never to compose again."[45] After some months, and needing to support himself, he decided to resume—generating all the "pessimistic" output just described. One interpretation of that creative effort could be that he may have been, at least in part, repeatedly examining and expressing his own lingering grief and shock.[46] People return to subjects for a reason; the repetition suggests a lack of resolution.[47]

Almost all Verdi's operas focus on the loss of loving relationships, the loss of progeny, and the uncertainties of posterity. Perhaps in the aggregate they reveal no "truths about the composer" and have whatever power they possess because they dwell on such evolutionary concerns. But, at least, for the untold millions who have admired Verdi's operas, the great benefit is that these concerns were personalized and made vivid in his art.

Notes

1 This statement and the description of the scene to this point are drawn from Wagner's own libretto and stage direction but condensed from a staging that lasts about ten minutes.
2 Probably critical among those needs and opportunities was environmental variability. See Peter J. Richerson and Robert Boyd, "The Human Life History Is Adapted to Exploit the Adaptive Advantages of Culture," *Philosophical Transactions of the Royal Society B* 375, no. 1803 (2020): 6.

96 Music-Dramas, Evolutionary Biology, and Psychology

3 An accessible, "popular" book on cultural evolution by a recognized expert (and referenced in other chapters here) is Joseph Henrich, *The Secret of Our Success* (Princeton, NJ: Princeton University Press, 2016).

4 A brief account from a reliable "popular" source is Psychology Today Staff, "How the Brain Develops," *Psychology Today*, Sussex Publishers, LLC, 2023. http://www.psychologytoday.com/us/basics/neuroscience/how-the-brain-develops

5 R. M. El-Baba, and M. P. Schury, "Neuroanatomy, Frontal Cortex," [Updated June 5, 2022]. In: StatPearls [Internet]. Treasure Island (FL): StatPearls Publishing; 2022 Jan. Available from: http://www.ncbi.nlm.nih.gov/books/NBK554483/

6 A summary about the evolution of the brain, which informs this paragraph is S. Condemi and F. Savatier, *A Pocket History of Human Evolution: How We Became Sapiens*, trans. Emma Ramadan (New York: The Experiment, LLC, 2019), 21–31.

7 Said to be an African proverb: A. Reupert et al., "It Takes a Village to Raise a Child: Understanding and Expanding the Concept of the 'Village,'" *Front Public Health* 10 (2022): 2.

8 Parenting or mating is "one of three fundamental trade-offs" recognized in life-history theory. Hillard S. Kaplan and Steven W. Gangestad, "Life History Theory and Evolutionary Psychology," *The Handbook of Evolutionary Psychology*. (Wiley Online Books, 2015), http://doi.org/10.1002/9780470939376.ch2. 69.

9 The "endowment effect" (Richard Thaler (1980)) describes that people are very reluctant to part with assets in their endowment. Daniel Kahneman, *Thinking, Fast and Slow* (New York: Farrar, Straus and Giroux, 2011), 444.

10 Ibid., 364.

11 See S. Atran, "Evolution and Religion," in *Science, Religion, and Society : An Encyclopedia of History, Culture, and Controversy*, ed. Arri Eisen and Gary Laderman (Armonk, NY: M.E. Sharpe, 2007). Also: Satoshi Kanazawa, "Where Do Gods Come From?" *Psychology of Religion and Spirituality* 7, no. 4 (2015).

12 See Martie G. Haselton and David M. Buss, "Error Management Theory and the Evolution of Misbeliefs," *Behavioral and Brain Sciences* 32, no. 6 (2009). Note this qualification, Dominic D. P. Johnson, "The Error of God: Error Management Theory, Religion, and the Evolution of Cooperation," in *Games, Groups, and the Global Good*, ed. Simon A. Levin (Berlin, Heidelberg: Springer Berlin Heidelberg, 2009).

13 See "Wagner as Revolutionist" in Bernard Shaw, "The Perfect Wagnerite: A Commentary on the Niblung's Ring, " (Project Guttenberg, 1998/1907), http://www.gutenberg.org/cache/epub/1487/pg1487-images.html.

14 The complexities of Wagner's revolutionary experience, its relation to his thinking about Germany, and his antagonism towards Jews are discussed in detail in P. L. Rose, *Wagner: Race and Revolution* (New Haven, CT: Yale University Press, 1992), 59ff.

15 The other woman was Mathilde Wesendonck. Exact timing details relative to the composition of *Walküre* are unclear, however. Extended discussion in J. Köhler and S. Spencer, *Richard Wagner: The Last of the Titans* (New Haven, CT: Yale University Press, 2004).

16 R. Wagner and A. Porter, *The Ring of the Nibelung* (New York: W.W. Norton, 1977), Includes English transation of "*Die Walküre*," 148–150. Andrew Porter's English translation is more available than most, but he claims it is not a "straight, literal crib."

17 While set pieces do occur in Wagner's mature works, more common is an ongoing declamatory style of singing without assertive vocal melodies.

18 Richard Wagner, *Opera and Drama*, trans. William Ashton Ellis, Vol. 2, *Richard Wagner's Prose Works* (1893), 172.

19 Wagner, "The Art-Work of the Future," 81. See note 23 below.

20 To summarize, "Life history theory" describes these as "birth, extended infant dependency, extended childhood, pair-bonded dual parenting combined with cooperative male coalitions, cooperative child care, post-reproductive longevity, and death." Joseph Carroll, "Evolutionary Literary Theory," in *A Companion to Literary Theory*, ed. David H. Richter (Chichester, UK: John Wiley & Sons, 2018), 428.

21 A main theme in Jonathan Gottschall, *The Storytelling Animal: How Stories Make Us Human* (Boston: Houghton Mifflin Harcourt, 2012).

22 See Glenn Stanley, "*Parsifal*: Redemption and *Kunstreligion*," in Thomas S. Grey, *The Cambridge Companion to Wagner* (Cambridge, UK: Cambridge University Press, 2008), 155.

23 Richard Wagner, *The Art-Work of the Future*, trans. William Ashton Ellis, The Wagner Library ed., Vol. 1, *Richard Wagner's Prose Works* (1895), 64–65. The essay was written in 1850.

24 Ibid. Wagner means the "circle of all those who claimed descent from a common ancestor."

25 Quotes are from Wagner's essay, "Zukunftsmusik" (1861), translated by and cited in Mark Berry, "Richard Wagner and the Politics of Music-Drama," *The Historical Journal* 47, no. 3 (2004): 674.

26 A word ("Volk"), which he uses repeatedly and emphatically.

27 Wagner's personal views about Jews or their implied presence (or absence) in his operas have been much discussed. For one critique, see Rose, *Wagner*, 1992. For those wanting only a summary, this may suffice: http://www.britannica.com/biography/Richard-Wagner-German-composer/Wagners-anti-Semitism

28 Bernard Zelechow, "The Opera: The Meeting of Popular and Elite Culture in the Nineteenth Century," *History of European Ideas* 16, nos. 1–3 (1993): 96.

29 See J. L. DiGaetani, *Richard Wagner and the Modern British Novel* (Rutherford, NJ: Fairleigh Dickinson University Press, 1978), 12. Also: Bryan Magee, *Aspects of Wagner* (Oxford: Oxford University Press, 1988), 56.

30 As of 2020. See Operabase statistics: http://www.operabase.com/statistics/en.

31 The revised version is discussed in this chapter. For acute comparison of the two versions, see J. Budden, *The Operas of Verdi* (Oxford: Oxford University Press, 1978).

32 G. Verdi, *Simon Boccanegra*, libretto by F. M. Piave and Arrigo Boito, 1881; English translation by Mary Ellis Peltz (New York: G. Schirmer, 1964).

33 One tragic example would be Othello's discovery that Desdemona is innocent of the claims made by Iago.

34 Boccanegra had previously had Fiesco freed after the battle, although not knowing who he was. Intricate plot.

35 Act 1, scene 2 is an addition to the 1881 revision by librettist Arrigo Boito.

36 Aria begins "*Fratricidi!*"

37 For one summary, see Joseph Carroll, "Evolutionary Literary Theory," in *A Companion to Literary Theory*, ed. David H. Richter (Chichester, UK: John Wiley & Sons, 2018), 429.

38 Henrich, *Success*, 142.

39 Ibid., 144.

40 Some similar points are made in "Verdi's fathers and daughters" in Paul A. Robinson, *Opera, Sex, and Other Vital Matters* (Chicago: University of Chicago Press, 2002).

98 Music-Dramas, Evolutionary Biology, and Psychology

41 Maciej Chudek and Joseph Henrich, "Culture–Gene Coevolution, Norm-Psychology and the Emergence of Human Prosociality," *Trends in Cognitive Sciences* 15, no. 5 (2011): 218–226. Also: Henrich, *Success*, 117–124.
42 See a review of relevant literature in Susan M. Hughes and David A. Puts, "Vocal Modulation in Human Mating and Competition," *Philosophical Transactions of the Royal Society B: Biological Sciences* 376, no. 1840 (2021): 3–4.
43 *Boccanegra*, tr. Peltz, 19.
44 Peter Kivy, *Osmin's Rage: Philosophical Reflections on Opera, Drama, and Text* (Princeton, NJ: Princeton University Press, 1988), 275.
45 Arthur Pougin, *Giuseppe Verdi: Vita Aneddotica* (in Italian) (Milan: Ricordi, 1881), 43. English translation by Mary-Jane Phillips-Matz.
46 See Joseph Cone, *Verdi's Dream* (Corvallis, OR: Text & Context, 2012).
47 For a psychobiographer's perspective, see William Todd Schultz, "How to Strike Psychological Paydirt," in *Handbook of Psychobiography*, ed. William Todd Schultz (New York: Oxford, 2005), 43–44.

7

THE TEMPEST, LEAR, FALSTAFF

Aging and Wisdom

At the end, Prospero brings all the courtiers together whom he had shipwrecked in *The Tempest* on his isle, to be merciful to them, despite that he had greatly suffered previously at their hands. He restores to the King of Naples his son Ferdinand, whom the king had thought dead in the shipwreck; and Prospero introduces his daughter, Miranda, to whom Ferdinand is now wed. The king falls to his knees before the young couple, pleading their forgiveness, since his previous deviousness had long before caused Miranda and Prospero to have been shipwrecked themselves on the remote island.

Now all sing of their good fortune, Miranda, Ferdinand, the King; and Prospero, aside, more quietly reflects, "Now my work is at an end / I can mar and I can mend."[1] Making it a harmonious vocal quintet is Gonzalo, a courtier who had helped Prospero when his brother, Antonio, had usurped Prospero's position as Duke of Milan. Gonzalo sings "Now the wild despair is past / Reconciled and healed at last."

Prospero, in reclaiming his title, forgives his brother for having stolen the dukedom years before. But Antonio rejects him, and, not reconciled to his loss, he walks away, which his brother observes sadly. Finally, in recognizing his age, Prospero prepares to return to Milan to rule and, as he says, to die. To become only, and fully human again, he breaks his powerful, magical staff. The music, previously animated and melodious with the vocal quintet, becomes somber and spare as Prospero takes his leave.

This last scene of the opera[2] composed in 2003 by Thomas Adès to Shakespeare's final play dramatizes the performance of wisdom, that rare and valuable asset of individuals and societies. The libretto of Meredith Oakes is succinct in presenting Prospero's wise behavior here, from mending

DOI: 10.4324/9781003254478-9

100 Music-Dramas, Evolutionary Biology, and Psychology

relations to forgiving enemies to accepting mortality and letting go of his special power, each of which are changes for him that he grows into in the course of *The Tempest*. A minority of operas focus on aging and the development and expression of wise behavior. But those that do may go deeply into human life.

As discussed previously, the distinctive feature of our species is that humans learn from others and carry that information forward over time (which, of course, does not assure its prudent use). Cultural learning itself was established probably about a million years ago in our evolutionary lineage.[3] Many tens of thousands of years ago, that advantage of holding and carrying forward information and knowledge apparently led to the phenomenon of advanced human age, age past childbearing years.[4] Because the aged possessed accumulated information that could be passed on to the next generation, they also presumably acquired a degree of value in those capacities. In addition to whatever loyalties would have accrued from their contributions to the physical care of younger generations, support for them in their inevitable physical decline may have also been merited by that value.

Not always, but with some individuals, the knowledge that others would have gained would have been more than instrumental but would have included the interpersonal—how to behave successfully as a member of a group of humans. As a result of being part of a group and observing others over many years, reflecting on which behaviors were successful in supporting the group, some older individuals would have acquired a measure of wisdom to offer.

Western psychology recognizes several components of wisdom. One contemporary review of wisdom research identified "knowledge of life," which provides the ability to act skilfully and to give good advice, as a clearly essential component.[5] Others were sociable ("prosocial") attitudes, including empathy and a sense of fairness; self-understanding; emotional balance; and effective coping with the uncertainties of life. Tolerance, openness, and spirituality were also cited within the two dozen psychological studies reviewed, as was an appropriate "sense of humor," perhaps especially about one's own sureties.

In historic times, wisdom is recognized as not being dependent on old age as such, for people who are not aged can certainly act wisely, and many who are old do not.[6] Instead, wisdom depends on a deep understanding of people and the world but also on being attuned to other people's concerns and values while being able to control oneself.[7] Finally, though, what matters is not "wisdom" as an abstract potential, but wise behavior, a certain kind of moral conduct, a transcendence of the self in relating to others.[8]

Humans are not born acting wisely, and one feature of Adès' *Tempest* is that it shows Prospero coming to temper the tempest in himself. His daughter, Miranda, plays a crucial role in his transformation. The opera begins with the shipwreck which Prospero's "art" inflicts on his enemies, and in the scene immediately following, Miranda confronts her father, having watched others being killed: "Their ship is torn apart / Their cry harrows my heart / Father / Is this your art? / Woe the day."[9] Prospero then recounts to Miranda the circumstances of their own expulsion from Milan, his brother's wrong-doing, ending in their own shipwreck on this remote island: "I flew trans-porting you / To where we could await / A better fate."

To which Miranda replies, "What you have told me / Means nothing to me / Words full of fury / Distant and strange." She asks why Prospero has killed the others, which leads directly to his telling his servant Ariel to retrieve the shipwrecked, unharmed. Prospero does cause Ariel to separate Ferdinand, the son of the King of Naples, from his father on the island, so that they both may feel the pain of loss. But it is again Miranda who brings about a transformation of this revenge, as she falls in love with Ferdinand, and he her. It is abundantly clear even before that point how devoted to Miranda Prospero is, for when Caliban, whom Prospero considers an unworthy subhuman, indicates he has sexual designs on Miranda, Prospero flies into an outrage. His powerful vocal response dominating the unworthy suitor is worthy of Simon Boccanegra condemning Paolo; and for largely the same evolutionary reasons. The father has a stake in the future of the child and the grandchildren.

When Miranda discovers Ferdinand, they two immediately become enraptured with each other like young lovers in a naive Romance ("You're handsome / Are you human?" … "I never saw/Your like before").[10] Initially Prospero will have none of Ferdinand for his daughter, because he is the son of the "odious father" who helped overthrow Prospero and is "unworthy" of her. Prospero puts a spell on the young prince, binding him in place. But the romantic spell Ferdinand has put on Miranda ultimately proves stronger.

In the pivotal scene that ends Act 2, Miranda returns to the bound Ferdinand, the two express their love for each other, and she frees him from her father's magical binds. Their rapturous duet ends with their expression of contentment with exactly where they are and who they see in the other. Observing their happy departure together and the power of love, or hopeful desire, Prospero recognizes the limitations of his own powers, the power over others, and specifically the generational authority that he had assumed. He is the process of accepting his own age, his own mortality, and his own limits, which reach their wise conclusion in that restoration scene at the end of the opera.[11]

It should not be neglected that in their telling of the *Tempest*, Adès and librettist Oakes repeatedly place the struggles of humans over their griev-ances and redress of grievance into an extra-human frame. The spirit Ariel chides Prospero ("These mortals and their woe bow-wow/When will they let me go bow-wow"); and Caliban, also the captive of Prospero's magic, is

102 Music-Dramas, Evolutionary Biology, and Psychology

happy to see the humans depart in the very last moments of the opera and return the island to its natural, non-human state: "They were human seeming / I was dreaming." Adès ends with the Caliban singing lyrically, and Ariel, out of sight, singing stratospherically, freely, as the orchestra repeats quietly some of the sonorous, ascending music associated with the natural world heard earlier.[12]

"Shakespeare had the gift for seeing deep into human nature and finding language adequate to what he saw," observed Joseph Carroll, the evolutionary literary scholar.[13] That language and those circumstances are never more painful in Shakespeare than in *King Lear*. The extremity of the drama is emphasized in *Lear*, a 1978 opera by Aribert Reimann, which has claims to be another successful modern opera based on Shakespeare with a foothold in the repertory of opera companies. Wisdom, and its lack, are again this opera's focus.

The story of King Lear related by Shakespeare is particular, but the starting circumstances are common, and now will be familiar. In general, human parents seek to support the survival and welfare of their biological children in part because their offspring carry their genes forward to their progeny (what evolutionary biologists call the parent's "fitness"). Among individuals with material assets, parental distribution of those assets to children can support that genetic objective along with other objectives. An aging parent, like Lear, often divides property among children if there is more than one. Complications can bedevil the making and receiving of an inheritance, as not only property obtained over a lifetime but also the relationships between parent and children and among the children are involved.

Ultimately what is at stake with material inheritance are not only possessions and responsibility but also love and respect in the present as well as advantage for the future. A son or daughter who receives a generous inheritance may well feel and, in fact, be set up to prosper. In turn, a final bequest can also signify the dying of a parent, which entails its own distinct, often fraught response.

The succession of lives and their individual successes likely engage the attention of audiences, as these patterns have shaped human experience for a very long time. Shakespeare's *King Lear* and Reimann's *Lear*[14] shred any illusion that the dynamics of succession will be determined by reason and impartiality, let alone wisdom.

Different from most experiences of family succession, the drama shows what can happen to a particular parent and the children while the former is still alive and has made his bequest of property. Lear begins blinded by his own appraisal of his worth and power as king, and his vanity causes him to believe the oily blandishments of his two older daughters as they vie for his

The Tempest, Lear, Falstaff **103**

affection and provision of lands. His younger daughter, Cordelia, loves but refuses to dishonestly flatter him, saying (in *King Lear*), "You have begot me, bred me, lov'd me; I / Return those duties back as are right fit … Why have my sisters husbands, if they say / They love you all?"[15] Cordelia recognizes the appropriate obligations of offspring as children and as married adults in the human life cycle. Her sense of propriety couldn't be simpler or better grounded. But despite protests from a trusted counselor, Lear angrily disowns Cordelia. His kingdom, its responsibilities, and his care Lear divides between the false-hearted daughters Goneril and Regan, thereby setting in motion the grinding tragedy that follows.

Reimann's music is sometimes loud and strident although also occasionally calmer when the drama is. Arguably, however, the music of *Lear* sounds very appropriate to its extreme subjects, never more so than when Lear, turned away from his daughters' castles and wandering at night on a heath, is subject to lightning, thunder, and rain. The crashing percussion, whistling woodwinds, screeching strings, snarling horns, separately and together supply a tumult of an accompaniment to Lear's mad, defiant soliloquy, which begins in Shakespeare, "Blow winds, and crack your cheeks!"[16] (Blast, Winde, sprengt die Backen! in *Lear*).

In the opera, Lear, defying the storm, largely declaims rather than sings, although the listener does hear movement of pitches and rhythmic changes to match and point the text. The overall impression is of a man crying out to be heard against the overwhelming indifference of nature and his errors in judgment. He mistook his relationship with his older daughters, very unwisely. They turned on him and banned his retinue of followers when drunkenness seemed to be his men's routine for spending time together. Lear cannot tolerate his daughters contravening him, and just as he had disowned and cursed Cordelia he had cursed Goneril in the most extreme way, putting a curse on her to become sterile. And when Regan too orders him out, Lear, powerless, vows revenge on both daughters. This is all a crazy, sad mess. The extreme family hostility makes no biological sense.

"Thou shouldst not have been old till thou hadst been wise," Shakespeare's Fool tells Lear early in the play.[17] "O, he that has and a little wit / must make content with his fortune fit," Reimann's Fool tells Lear as they are getting soaked and cold out on the heath. [18]

The character who most attempts to act wisely, and certainly compassionately, is the disowned daughter, Cordelia. The King of France had taken her as his queen even though Lear disowned her, and, later, in the civil war that Lear's faithless daughters start in England, Cordelia and the French arrive to take the side of those who resist and to rescue her father. Cordelia discovers her father, exhausted and asleep after his ordeal on the heath. While she simply holds him, treble woodwinds and then sweet and high violins attempt to hold their sound against a constant low snarling of percussive

104 Music-Dramas, Evolutionary Biology, and Psychology

instruments. Cordelia softly begins: "My dearest father! May nature's balm lie in this kiss, and soothe the violence of your grief."

Composer Reimann said that the opera's "music is like a cage from which Lear cannot escape."[19] Cordelia's aria pushes against the bounds and corners of that cage, leaping, soaring to ethereal high pitches—at the word "kiss," for example—and also testing the lowest floor ("grief") as she recognizes that Lear no longer is "in perfect mind." Her aria is the most touching in the opera, eerily beautiful, and also extraordinarily challenging for the soprano.

Despite Cordelia's tenderness and their shared hopes for "contentment," the reconciliation of father and daughter and the hope for succession of generations is quickly dashed, as foreshadowed by that grating thrumming behind her solo and their duet. Cordelia and the French are defeated; Cordelia is murdered at her sister Goneril's request. Goneril and sister Regan vie for the affection of Edmund, and Goneril poisons Regan; and when the Machiavellian Edmund is slain by his virtuous brother, Edgar, in single combat, Goneril kills herself. At the end Lear dies of grief, his family destroyed.

In 2019 a large, international group of wisdom researchers discussed and evaluated the body of prior studies in the sciences about wisdom. Their refined "common wisdom model" described "morally-grounded excellence" in a certain kind of mental processing, which they shorthanded as "social-cognitive processing."[20] What they meant was that people who are wise have the "metacognitive" capacity to think clearly about their thinking, having the ability to consider diverse perspectives, balance different interests, and retain a humility about their own intellect and understanding.[21] And those who are wise pursue truth and orient themselves "toward shared humanity."[22]

"Even if you were not my sisters' father, your white hair would demand pity," Cordelia sings. She understands how morally out of bounds her sisters are. But Cordelia's behavioral "excellence" involves empathy and a sense of fairness to her father, being balanced and self-effacing despite his own treatment of her. She attempts to effectively cope with the great uncertainties and dangers of life for her father and herself. But to no avail.

Which raises an honest question: why would anyone want to expose themselves to this violent tragedy? Stepping back to see, it does possess three fundamental features in common with most compelling stories. First, it is grounded in and develops from a key event in adult human life, the retirement and care of parents. Second, because of this, what this particular story reveals can be of value to an observer. Third, those who give the drama's expression their full attention may be rewarded with feelings and insights that it can uniquely give. More than what is done, or what is merely said, is how Shakespeare, or Reimann in turn, expresses the human drama. Indeed, the sharing of insights would have been a value of the accounts of human

The Tempest, Lear, Falstaff **105**

behavior that older individuals would have presented to their family and tribe in Sapiens's ancestral past. Over time, those accounts of cause and effect would become stories; and the best stories might be expected, by those in the community who heard them, to still offer glimpses of wisdom.

Suffering is common to every human life, and a condition, in the foreground or background, of every opera and story. Suffering is physical and mental pain, of course, but human ignorance also makes suffering. Unlike some tragic dramas where the impulse is to begin to move to a better future and express some hope, Reimann's *Lear* does not. It is comfortless,[23] not part of a belief system of forgiveness or transcendence. Instead, *Lear* is the sort of tragedy that literary critic Richard Sewall described as recalling "the original terror, harking back to a world that antedates the conceptions of philosophy, the consolations of the later religions, and whatever constructions the human mind has devised to persuade itself that its universe is secure."[24]

At the harsh conclusion of *Lear*, dramatic catharsis is lacking. Audience members may well be scared and upset. Unfortunately, not too much research has been conducted after performances with audiences of operas (or even other theater) to understand how they made meaning of what they experienced.[25] Existing research does offer some fundamental insights, however.[26]

One is that audiences seek knowledge and believability ("authenticity") in performances, as two prime qualities.[27] Another research insight is that even with stark tragedies like *Lear* the human circumstances portrayed must also, as discussed previously, "transport" the audience out of their present moment. Usefully, in the context of *Lear*, researcher Melanie Green and her colleagues observe that "transportation" is not identical with enjoyment, as "transportation is thought to leave the experiencer's beliefs and perceptions changed in some measurable way, ... [and] can sometimes be downright scary."[28]

"I love your Majesty/ According to my bond; no more nor less," Cordelia said at the outset of the drama.[29] The audience may reflect on what extreme events may happen when normal bonds—moral ones based on biological ones—are broken.

Not merely "larger than life," wrote literary critic Harold Bloom describing Shakespeare's two greatest "personalities." Not merely larger, Prince Hamlet and Sir John Falstaff, but "life's largeness."[30]

Falstaff, in the enthusiasm of his way of life and his genius of self-expression, plays the role of surrogate father to the rebellious young Prince Hal in the two *Henry IV* historical dramas. But Falstaff, separately, still full of life but without the quasi-parental role and its stature, is the central "personality" of another Shakespeare play, the *Merry Wives of Windsor*.[31]

It is the comic plot of *Merry Wives* that Giuseppe Verdi and his librettist Arrigo Boito seized on for the composer's final opera, the first comedy

106 Music-Dramas, Evolutionary Biology, and Psychology

Verdi had written since the failure of *Un Giorno di Regno* (*King for A Day*) 53 years before. Boito had to persuade the 76-year-old Verdi to even take it on, suggesting that writing a comic opera would fittingly end Verdi's illustrious career with an "immense outburst of hilarity."[32] Boito had earned Verdi's confidence through his work with him as a librettist for the revision of *Simon Boccanegra* in 1881 and the masterful rendition of Shakespeare's *Othello* into *Otello* of 1887. Both Verdi and Boito greatly admired Shakespeare, with Boito incorporating his translation of some of Shakespeare's language, with its extraordinary eloquence. Verdi entertained himself (mostly) with the work, and *Falstaff* premiered in 1893 when the composer was almost 80 years old.

Again, as with Prospero and Lear, the role of Falstaff is sung by a baritone, the vocal range both commonly given to older men and to fathers in operatic leading roles, and also the natural range that adult men most often possess in speaking. That said, the vocal writing for Prospero and Lear is often to the extremes of the baritone's range and rife with discordant intervals, reflecting the frequent extremity of the characters in trying circumstances. Verdi's Falstaff, on the other hand, presents the baritone with almost no such vocal challenges, in what is a largely self-satisfied character.

In Shakespeare's *Henry IV* plays, Falstaff, who has no children, gives himself a generic satisfaction of parenting, as he cannot have the genetic. In those dramas, the old knight speaks with such quick wit and particular insight that he breaks conventional notions, including those of wisdom. Falstaff does show a deep understanding of people and the world and can be attuned to other people's concerns and values, though maintaining a sense of humor and an insight about others' motivations and the assumptions society makes about how people should behave. What he lacks is self-control. Falstaff's behavior is routinely self-indulgent and, at times, disreputable, usually around money.

Falstaff's self-protecting and convention challenging wit is crystallized when, before a battle, he tells Prince Hal that he'd rather not be there but that "honour pricks me on." And then Shakespeare does that unprecedented thing in drama (up until that time), of exposing the instantaneous thinking process of a character. Alone Falstaff reflects:

> Yea, but how if honour prick me off when I come on? how then? … Can honour set to a leg? — no: or an arm? — no: or take away the grief of a wound? — no. Honour hath no skill in surgery, then? — no. What is honour? — a word. What is in that word honour? what is that honour? — air … I'll none of it.

Here Falstaff applies his wit to a serious question, whether he should be guided by a conventional notion of "honour" to throw himself into combat

The Tempest, Lear, Falstaff **107**

and take on its deadly risks. Part of this same speech Boito grafted into *Falstaff*:

Che onor! ? Che onor?	What honour? What honour?
...	...
Può l'onor rimettervi uno stinco?	Can honour put back a broken shin?
Non puo.	It cannot.
Né_ un piede? No. Né_ un dito?	Or mend a foot? No. Or a finger?
No. Né_ un capello? No.	No. Or a hair? No.
L'onor non è_ chirurgo.	Honour is not a surgeon.
Ch'_è dunque? Una parola.	What is it, then? A word.
Che c'_ in questa parola?	What is there in this word?
C'_è dell'aria che vola ...	There's some air, which floats away.[33]

But in *Falstaff*, the comedy, this speech about honor does not arise from skepticism about warfare. Instead, it arises from Falstaff's irritation that his hangers-on, Bardolph and Pistol, declare that it is their "honour" that prevents them from agreeing to deliver two devious letters for Falstaff. Those letters are to two married women whom Falstaff intends to try to seduce, in part for his vanity and in part because their current husbands are wealthy and he, penniless old Sir John, would like to replace those men. Either one of them. He wants their money.

In the opera, the "honour" speech suggests that Falstaff is not as wise as he thinks himself, but rather foolish and, like his portly girth, too full of himself. There is another, biological, dimension to Falstaff's illusion about his amorous project. He may think of himself as still young enough to promote a sexual interest with these younger married women; a man in his sixties may still harbor such passions and even capabilities. But his targets are unlikely to stand for it, particularly if they have a dependable partner, security in their marriages, and children in their care.[34] Falstaff, here rather fatuous, should have known this.

A great accomplishment of Verdi's musical-dramatic style in *Falstaff* is the nimble musical gesturing the composer supplies frequently to whatever may be said. Falstaff's entire "honour speech" slips between a kind of parlando argumentation and a slightly more expansive, sung arioso; but take just the one central point to Falstaff's heresy. As merely a word, "honour" is just a thing of air "which floats away" (aria che vola), and so Verdi has the baritone's vocal line leap to a delicate high note while the orchestral accompaniment, swirling like little winds, flies up and away.

Such quicksilver orchestral gesturing sometimes supports the text, as in this instance, and sometimes the musical exaggeration winks at it or deflates it; the result—comic, satiric, or ironic—adding to the wit of the whole. There may be more to Verdi's wit worth reflecting on, but inasmuch as doing so involves

108 Music-Dramas, Evolutionary Biology, and Psychology

stealing from the opera, it is best to observe what Boito's Falstaff himself cautions about art: "Art lies in this rule: 'Steal with grace and at the right time.'"[35]

So, to a summary of the comic action. In Act 1 when Alice Ford and Meg Page receive and compare Falstaff's identical letters to them, requesting assignations, they ridicule his silly effrontery but quickly hatch a plan to teach the "fat knight" a lesson. In Act 2, their friend, Mistress Quickly, invites Falstaff to a scheduled tryst with Alice Ford, which he accepts, feels great about himself, dresses up for, and when he arrives at Ford's home, a series of misadventures, some planned by the women, cause him to hide in a large laundry basket, which ultimately gets dumped into the Thames River, Falstaff and all. That comeuppance could be the end of the comedy, but Boito and Verdi contrive for Act 3 to have Falstaff accept a second invitation to meet Alice Ford at midnight in Windsor Forest.

Act 3 touches on aging and wisdom not heavily but lightly, as appropriate to them and a comedy. The first scene of the act finds Falstaff soaked from the Thames, decrying the indignity he just suffered and denying his own role: "Evil world. There's no virtue any more. Everything is declining."[36]

However, despite his recent experience and momentary assessment of it, Falstaff allows himself to be persuaded by Quickly to attempt that second rendezvous with Alice, planned by her. Imagined sex and the comforts of wealth are illusions that evolution has made hard to resist. While others involved in the plot listen in and comment, out of view—Alice, her husband, their daughter, Nannetta, her boyfriend Fenton, Dr Cajus, and Meg—Alice summarizes, "We will pummel Falstaff until he confesses his perversity."

The final scene, out in the night forest, is a setting made for concealment and revelation, and Alice acts as the playwright of this play within a play. The fat knight enters at midnight, ridiculously attired as Alice requested and crowned with stag horns—horns being the usual symbol of a hapless cuckold—but Falstaff imagines quite the virile opposite, singing "Love metamorphoses a man into an animal." When the costumed townsfolk, wearing masks, appear later, they set about poking, pinching, needling, and stinging Falstaff with nettles. He cries out frequently as they deride him repeatedly about his weight, his drinking, and his intended licentiousness, much of it in rather pointed, vulgar terms. Their attacks on a defenseless old man begin to seem cruel—a common problem with repudiations when past motivations overrun present conditions.

Finally, Sir John contritely admits that "I was an ass." But he also saves face a bit by pointing out that his "cleverness" was the cause of all the rest of them becoming clever, which everyone seems to acknowledge: "Ma bravo!" Then Ford proposes to cap the evening by marrying off his daughter, Nannetta, to the groom he intends, the boring Dr. Cajus. But the merry wives have costumed Bardolph as Cajus's bride under cover of night and gathered the costumed Nannetta and Fenton as another couple who wish to be married. To

The Tempest, Lear, Falstaff **109**

a dignified wedding procession that sounds as if it might have been written by Mozart (or by the old-fashioned thinking of Ford), the two couples arrive, and Ford grandly proclaims the double marriage. With the masks off, it is clear that Alice has outsmarted her husband with the match she preferred. She tells Ford, "Man often falls into the nets woven by his own malice."

The fixed self-interests of Ford, Cajus, and Falstaff led them to act unwisely and fail. They bring to mind Lear and Edmund, Goneril, and Regan, with the distinct difference that the *Falstaff* trio can acknowledge the error of their ways. Ford states the lesson in general terms, "If you can't avoid your own annoyance, you should accept it with good humor," and then he blesses his daughter and Fenton. In a spirit of reconciliation Ford calls for them all, men and women, to go together—*where else in the wee hours?*—to dine with "Sir John Falstaff."

The resilience of human communities depends on how unexpected stressors—rogue elements like Falstaff, for example—are responded to, and ultimately a kind of group or collective wisdom can come into play.[37] Such wisdom dethrones the notion that acting in a wise way is solely the attainment of individuals, as wisdom is finally about the relationships between people, and learning from those relationships. The best wise crowd, psychological research suggests, is one in which the judgments of well-informed individuals are as completely different from each other as possible.[38] The supper conversation might prove interesting in this way.

But before their supper, Falstaff says they should sing a chorus to end the scene. And so they all—main characters and townsfolk: soloists and chorus—sing out the drama's summation to the audience in the theater, implicating them as well. As a character, Alice Ford has coordinated the moments of revelation in this final scene, but it is Verdi who has orchestrated it all, giving those revelations their point and measure. And it is Verdi who provides an ideal structure for the final comic insight, the gist being that we are all fools and everything in life may be considered a jest at our expense if we cannot finally laugh at ourselves and our plans.

That musical structure is a fugue, normally very formal, but Verdi, the old, wise one, has observed Falstaff's maxim about art. He has gracefully stolen a serious form at the right time, and made it laugh:

Tutto nel mondo è burla.	All the world's a prank [jest];
L'uom _è nato burlone,	Man is born a prankster [clown].
nel suo cervello ciurla	In his head his reason
sempre la sua ragione.	is always churning
Tutti gabbati! Irride	We all are fools! Each man
l'un l'altro ogni mortal,	laughs at the other [s' folly].
ma ride ben chi ride	But he laughs best who has
la risata final.	the last laugh.[39]

Notes

1 Thomas Adès, *The Tempest*, libretto by Meredith Oakes, 3.4. Also for other quotes from this last scene.
2 Nearly the last moments, but note discussion of Caliban below in text.
3 R. Boyd, P. J. Richerson, and J. Henrich, "The Cultural Niche: Why Social Learning Is Essential for Human Adaptation," *Proceedings of the National Academy of Sciences of the United States of America* 108, Suppl 2 (2011). Also: Joseph Henrich, *The Secret of Our Success* (Princeton, NJ: Princeton University Press, 2016), 3.
4 Henrich, *Success*, 133. Also: R. Caspari and S. H. Lee, "Older Age Becomes Common Late in Human Evolution," *Proceedings of the National Academy of Sciences of the United States of America* 101, no. 30 (2004).
5 K. J. Bangen, T. W. Meeks, and D. V. Jeste, "Defining and Assessing Wisdom: A Review of the Literature," *American Journal of Geriatric Psychiatry* 21, no. 12 (2013): 1254–1266.
6 For a review, see Igor Grossmann et al., "The Science of Wisdom in a Polarized World: Knowns and Unknowns," *Psychological Inquiry* 31, no. 2 (2020): 27.
7 Howard Nusbaum, "Wisdom Develops from Experiences That Transcend the Self," in *Self-Transcendence and Virtue: Perspectives from Philosophy, Psychology, and Theology*, ed. Candace Vogler Jennifer A. Frey (New York: Routledge, 2018).
8 Ibid.
9 Adès, *The Tempest*, libretto by Meredith Oakes, for all line quotes.
10 Shakespeare's play is routinely categorized as a Romance.
11 I do not agree with the interpretation of Prospero at the end as being "nihilistic," and Adès perhaps being influenced by the theatre of the absurd, cf. Michael Ewans, "Thomas Adès and Meredith Oakes: The Tempest," *Studies in Musical Theatre* 9 (2015): 243.
12 As with the love duet of Miranda and Ferdinand, "High on the Headland." A similar point about the natural world is made by Ewans, "The Tempest," 245.
13 Joseph Carroll, "The Truth about Fiction: Biological Reality and Imaginary Lives," *Style* 46 (2012): 137. Also: Joseph Carroll, "An Evolutionary Approach to Shakespeare's *King Lear*," in *Critical Insights: Family*, ed. John Knapp (Ipswich, MA: EBSCO: 2012).
14 *Lear* derives mainly from an eighteenth-century German prose translation by Johann Joachim Eschenburg.
15 *King Lear*, 5.1. 99–103 [act, scene, lines] http://www.opensourceshakespeare .org/views/plays/playmenu.php?WorkID=kinglear
16 *King Lear*, 3.2.1678.
17 *King Lear*, 1.5.917.
18 English translation: Desmond Clayton in Aribert Reimann, Claus H. Henneberg, and Desmond Clayton, *Lear: Opera in Two Parts after William Shakespeare* (Mainz: B. Schott's Sohne, 1978). All line quotes from this version.
19 Simon Hatab and Emmanuelle Josse, "The man who tamed a king: An interview with composer Aribert Reimann," Opera de Paris, October 24, 2019, https:// www.operadeparis.fr/en/magazine/the-man-who-tamed-a-king.
20 Grossmann, "Science of Wisdom," 43.
21 Ibid., 11.
22 Ibid., 43.
23 Writing about the Athenians of the fifth century BCE and Greek tragedy, the poet and translator Anne Carson observed that they "do not come to the theater

for comfort." Anne Carson et al., *An Oresteia*, 1st ed. (New York: Faber and Faber, 2009), 83.

24 Richard B. Sewall, *The Vision of Tragedy* (New Haven, CT: Yale University Press, 1970), 5–6.

25 But see further discussion of audiences and related research in Part 2.

26 Jennifer Radbourne, Hilary Glow, and Katya Johanson, "Hidden Stories: Listening to the Audience at the Live Performance," *Double Dialogues* 13, no. Summer (2010): 4.

27 See the evaluation in Wing Tung Au, Glos Ho, and Kenson Wing Chuen Chan, "An Empirical Investigation of the Arts Audience Experience Index," *Empirical Studies of the Arts* 35, no. 1 (2017).

28 Melanie C. Green, Timothy C. Brock, and Geoff F. Kaufman, "Understanding Media Enjoyment: The Role of Transportation into Narrative Worlds," *Communication Theory* 14, no. 4 (2004): 313.

29 *King Lear*, 5.1., 94–95.

30 Harold Bloom, *Shakespeare: The Invention of the Human* (New York: Riverhead Books, 1999), 4.

31 The *Henry IV* plays were probably written 1596–1598 and *Merry Wives* 1597–1601. "Timeline of Shakespeare's Plays," Royal Shakespeare Co., accessed September 20, 2021, http://www.rsc.org.uk/shakespeares-plays/timeline.

32 Letter, July 9, 1889 to Verdi. Giuseppe Verdi and Arrigo Boito, *The Verdi-Boito Correspondence*, ed. Marcello Conati and Mario Medici, trans. William Weaver (Chicago: University of Chicago Press, 1994), 142.

33 G. Verdi, *Falstaff*, libretto by A. Boito, 1893. English translation Vincent Sheean, accompanying recording, cond. A. Toscanini (RCA Victor, 1950). Sheean's translation used below except where noted.

34 David M. Buss, "Sex Differences in Human Mate Preferences: Evolutionary Hypotheses Tested in 37 Cultures," *Behavioral and Brain Sciences* 12, no. 1 (1989): 1–14.

35 "L'arte sta in quest massima. ..."

36 My translation.

37 A. Briskin and S. Erickson, *The Power of Collective Wisdom and the Trap of Collective Folly* (San Francisco: Berrett-Koehler Publishers, 2009).

38 Clintin P. Davis-Stober, David V. Budescu, Jason Dana, and Stephen B. Broomell, "When Is a Crowd Wise?" *Decision* 1, no. 2 (2014): 79.

39 My translation.

PART 2

Cultural Considerations Regarding Opera

Included in Part 2:

Introduction: What is Meant by "Culture"
8. Attracting Audiences: *War and Peace, Omar, Song from the Uproar*
9. Origins and Innovations: Before and After *La Bohème* (the movie)
10. Affording Extraordinary Experiences: *Les Troyens, Akhnaten*

DOI: 10.4324/9781003254478-10

PART 2 INTRODUCTION

What is meant by "Culture"

The following chapters will examine three important "cultural" concerns that face opera as its presenters want to see this performing art continue and thrive. Both opera's presenters and its patrons may well be concerned about attracting audiences, about using innovations in technology to present this art, and about offering audiences some distinctive value not so available elsewhere. Theatrical forms do fade and disappear. In the first quarter of the twenty-first century, for example, vaudeville is essentially extinct, and yet in the first quarter of the twentieth-century vaudeville brought very sizable audiences in many American locations to these "variety shows."[1] Competition from other and newer forms, such as cinema, occurred then, and they do now.

As with the previous chapters, the following ones will consider these matters through an examination of particular operas. While the book's first part featured a complex "biological" perspective, this part features a cultural one. But that renews questions presented in the first introduction. What is meant by "culture"? How did it arise originally; what affects it now? In understanding a cultural phenomenon such as an opera, is it sufficient to consider proposed causes that are historically recent?

While "culture" has been defined in various ways, this book has generally favored an understanding first expressed in 1984 by scientists Peter J. Richerson and Robert Boyd that said culture is "information acquired by imitating or learning from other individuals and able to affect an individual's phenotype [observable characteristics], usually behavior."[2] Culture evolves, and to recap a leading view of cultural evolution,[3] discussed previously, Sapiens became a "cultural species"[4] to accommodate the learning

DOI: 10.4324/9781003254478-11

116 Cultural Considerations Regarding Opera

needed to survive and thrive in ancestral environments. Obtaining information from others became crucial because learning from and imitating others is more effective and efficient than what anyone can independently learn in one lifetime.[5] Those who preferred accumulated information endorsed by the group would have had a survival advantage over those who preferred to go it alone, according to this line of reasoning.[6] In addition, cultural evolution may occur not only through the sharing of information about the physical environment, but also through the sharing of beliefs and practices about what, as Harari argues in *Sapiens*,[7] humans have come to imagine into existence, such as money, democracy, and codes of behavior, the latter as reflected in laws. social norms, and imaginative stories.

Such views of culture may not be widely understood by the public, nor would they be shared by all scholars.

The Introduction to Part 1 highlighted the results of a survey of 600 English-speaking scholars[8] who broadly represented the "two cultures"[9] in higher education: the humanities and the sciences, in the latter case some of the social sciences. Disciplines in the humanities included drama and theater, music, literary studies, and history. In contrast to these, the sciences in the study included psychology, philosophy, evolutionary social sciences, and political science.[10] The 2017 report of the survey concluded, through detailed statistical analyses, that the two groups understood culture very differently. Broadly, the humanities group favored the view that "culture operates in largely autonomous ways, overwhelming biological constraints," while the evolutionary social sciences group understood "culture as essentially constrained and channeled by genes,"[11] – or as one of the latter group commented:

"Cultural conventions don't come out of thin air; our capacities to be attuned to culture are rooted in genetically-evolved cultural learning."[12]

As dramas set to music, understanding opera tends to be guided by dominant current views held by academics in the humanities, including history, literature, and music. Since the 1970s, the underlying assumption of most such analysis appears to be that historically recent forces alone,[13] or primarily, shape human minds and behavior. This view arises in various critical perspectives, or "theories," including feminist, psychoanalytical, deconstructionist, Marxist, "new historicist," post-colonial, and "queer."[14] All these, associated with "post-structuralism" or "postmodernism," argue against a previous "modern" view that did not take them into account. One modern view, prominent after World War II in literary studies and teaching in the United States, was "New Criticism," which focused reader attention on explicating a text *in itself*, one ideally considered whole and independent of social and historical influences and the presumed intentions of the author.[15] By contrast, "postmodern" perspectives regard a text as dependent and contingent on many forces external to it and focuses reader attention on those forces.

Regarding opera itself, a leading publisher has established an innovative "interdisciplinary" series, arguing that "the course of [opera] study has developed significantly, going beyond traditional musicological approaches to reflect new perspectives from literary criticism and comparative literature, cultural history, philosophy, art history, theatre history, gender studies, film studies, political science, philology, psycho-analysis, and medicine."[16] These perspectives can all reveal aspects of cultural products, such as opera, that had been overlooked.

Since theory ideally guides research, however, what "theory" refers to deserves attention. "Theory" and "discourse" have become watchwords in the humanities in the past half-century, as its participants know. (Although space does not permit a review here, those with an appetite or curiosity can find some hundreds of pages of related essays in one major compendium.[17]) In a book of lectures that seeks to explain feminist, Marxist, and the other perspectives, a professor of English, Paul H. Fry, wrote that "Theory can be a purely speculative undertaking. It's a hypothesis about something [and] whatever the object of theory might be, if it even has one, theory itself requires . . . a large measure of internal coherence."[18]

"A purely speculative undertaking," plausibly without an "object" to it, and offering no more than "a large measure" of coherence in it, while perhaps agreeably modest as a set of standards, would, however, not meet the standards for established "theory" as usually defined in the sciences. For example, the U.S. National Academies of Science defines theory as "a well-substantiated explanation of some aspect of the natural world that can incorporate facts, laws, inferences, and tested hypotheses. . . . [T]heories are *the end points of science*. They are understandings that develop from extensive observation, experimentation, and creative reflection."[19]

For now, the disciplinary background and commitments that scholars have, and their comparative unfamiliarity with other knowledge and perspectives, means that what constitutes valid knowledge regarding "culture" may well continue to be disputed. Acknowledging that divisive reality does not mean that the quest to understand a topic and reach some degree of mutual understanding, in this case about opera and culture, should not be pursued.

As shown in Part 1, scholars not only in the sciences but also in literary studies[20] have been developing research that understands biology and culture together, as represented by biocultural theory and cultural-evolution theory. The latter already had an academic history in music from a century ago.

"The concept of cultural evolution was fundamental to the foundation of academic musicology in the late nineteenth century," musicologist Patrick Savage has observed.[21] But then cultural evolution passed out of favor in the twentieth century, in part because of "persistent misconceptions about

118 Cultural Considerations Regarding Opera

the roles of genes and progress in musical evolution." New scientific understanding of cultural evolution can allay those misconceptions, according to Savage.

Encouraging that development of understanding, in 2015 a new professional organization, the Cultural Evolution Society, was launched, attracting the interest of more than 1600 people representing more than 30 disciplines from over 50 nations.[22] More than 600 became founding members, and in a report of the "grand challenges" facing their field, the leaders observed that "the scientific study of culture is currently undergoing a theoretical synthesis."[23]

Two proposed theories of culture and its evolution have been most prominent to date. To simplify, the first and earlier, treats cultural evolution mainly as *analogous* to biological evolution, while the second frames cultural evolution as *integrated* with biological evolution.

The earlier, advanced by evolutionary biologist Richard Dawkins in the 1970s and 1980s, introduced the concept of "memes," the name he gave for the unit of inheritance in culture, similar to the gene in biological life. "Examples of memes are tunes, ideas, catch-phrases, clothes fashions, ways of making pots or of building arches," Dawkins wrote.[24] Even though some scholars early criticized the idea of memes as "oversimplification" of cultural change,[25] the term and concept have certainly caught on in contemporary society. Google "Trends" tracks Internet use of search terms, and starting in 2009 "meme" became rapidly popular, reaching peak popularity worldwide about April 2020.

Moreover, Internet culture itself, and particularly "social media," thrive on memes, which may be pictures, words, or both together. They often rapidly arise and disappear as the many millions of people who use these media platforms follow various trends. The long-term effect on culture of such evanescent "memes" is open to question. However, there should be little doubt about the potential power of "catch-phrases" taken up by social media that proliferate virally and have real-world effects. One notable American example was "Stop the Steal," the phrase U.S. ex-president Donald Trump[26] coined to claim that the 2020 presidential election had been stolen from him, despite *no* evidence supporting the claim. As a meme, "Stop the Steal" unleashed a torrent of conspiracy theories and increasingly strident calls for action to overturn the election results,[27] ultimately resulting in a Trump-provoked militant insurrection storming the U.S. Capitol,[28] which in turn led to legal action against many participants. Memes can have serious consequences.

The primary insight of Dawkins's meme concept was affirmed by the Cultural Evolution Society leaders in 2015: "Much like genes, many elements of culture (e.g., technology, language, religion) appear to change

Part 2 Introduction **119**

through descent with modification."[29] The media for commercial distribution of music gives an illustration of that descent.

The first recordings that tenor Enrico Caruso made, in 1902,[30] were generated acoustically, not electrically, with the sound waves produced by his voice activating the recording apparatus. These recordings were distributed on the innovation of flat "gramophone" discs,[31] which were poised to replace earlier "phonograph" cylinders, small, fragile tubes slipped over a revolving metal cylinder and "reproduced" with a needle. Those same 1902 recordings are available a century and some decades later, distributed as intangible digital audio files playable on handheld devices. From then to now those Caruso recordings were first recorded on shellac discs rotating at 78 revolutions per minute (rpm), later at 33 rpm, and by the 1960s on "stereophonic" long-playing (LP) recordings pressed on vinyl. These physical media, produced by analog copying, were succeeded in the 1980s by compact discs (CD), which presented a new disc medium containing digitized audio files. More recently, physical distribution media are vanishing, superseded by those standalone files that one can listen to but not touch and are sometimes not even resident with the user but rather housed somewhere in the Internet "cloud."

As with biological evolution, that cultural unrolling of forms was not preordained; the forms emerged in response to conditions in the human environment, including consumer preferences, technological innovations, and product marketing. The happy result for opera lovers, though, is that the recordings Caruso made in Milan in April 1902, with a very limited and expensive initial distribution, live on and are available to many millions of people on music apps on their smartphones—and who knows by what means and recording format in the future. One should not infer, however, that because the forms of distribution changed and became more convenient and accessible over time that the quality of sound of the recording inevitably improved. Anyone who has heard the 1902 recording played on an original machine has a very striking reference point to compare with sometimes inferior transfers later.[32]

This cultural evolution of media to distribute music is similar to biological evolution by natural selection, which, to recap, involves variations of a heritable trait within a population of organisms exposed to a particular environment; a "natural" (or "sexual") selection of the organisms with the trait better suited to that environment; and the differential survival and reproduction of the organisms carrying that trait.[33] By analogy the recording of Caruso is the organism and the "heritable traits" are the various recording formats in competition, from wax cylinders onward. The "environment" is diverse human consumer culture; and the human "selection" (most like a "sexual" or preferential one) is based on the ability of the format to "reproduce" the original sound in a desirable way.

120 Cultural Considerations Regarding Opera

"Descent with modification" can be seen to have happened with this element of culture, and could probably also be used to describe the evolution of Italian opera, for example. Consider the essential heritable trait, "song." Clearly, the form and style of song has changed considerably from Monteverdi to the present. Diverse selective pressures at various historical moments in opera's environment would have favored particular song characteristics, including the accumulated creative inheritance and individual abilities of composers from one generation to the next; external constraints on composers, such as those arising from funders; and audience preferences and proclivities.

This is no more than a simple sketch for one evolutionary framework; and arguably a rigorous Darwinian construct may not be needed. Some current cultural evolution theorists, for example, reframe "evolution" more broadly to refer to any "process that is cumulative, adaptive, and openended,"[34] as music surely is. At present, the potential value of evolutionary studies of music[35] intrigues scholars of diverse backgroundss and is being discovered through research.[36]

Returning to the proposed meme theory of cultural evolution, it has been criticized as limited[37] in that it specifies and concentrates on a mechanism while not fully explaining how the mechanism came to exist in the first place. This the Cultural Evolution Society described in a second theory of cultural evolution: "in many cases, genetic and cultural evolution interact in both developmental and evolutionary time."

The classic example often cited for the interaction of genes and culture is the evolution of lactose tolerance in humans.[38] Over the tens of thousands of years when survival depended on hunting and gathering, humans, after weaning, had effectively no regular access to the milk of mammals, and adults did not produce the enzyme that digests lactose. But then, with the domestication of cows, sheep, and goats some 10,000 years ago, this change in human culture led to the genetic mutation that allowed for the tolerance of milk in human adulthood and its strong natural selection. Fast forward to the present, and in many places in the world that genetic tolerance has culturally evolved into a huge amount of human activity, in production and consumption of dairy products, often benefiting health and even survival.

But biological evolution of genes is very slow, orders of magnitude slower than decadal or annual cultural evolution—or the daily or hourly evolution of memes. Because of that difference in speed, cultural evolution is seen by some to be the driving force in all *human* evolution in contemporary life now.[39] Still, for understanding how elements of culture came to exist in the first place, biological-cultural interaction affords a better understanding.

Part 2 Introduction **121**

The coming chapters use perspectives from postmodern cultural theories and cultural evolution theories to help understand opera audiences, innovations, and experiences. The theories and their usefulness to the purpose will be compared and contrasted at points.

Notes

1 A. Slide, *The Encyclopedia of Vaudeville* (Jackson: University Press of Mississippi, 2012), xiii–xv.
2 Peter J, Richerson and Robert Boyd, "Natural Selection and Culture," *Bioscience* (1984): 430.
3 R. Boyd, P. J. Richerson, and J. Henrich, "The Cultural Niche: Why Social Learning Is Essential for Human Adaptation," *Proceedings of the National Academy of Sciences of the United States of America* 108 Suppl 2 (2011).
4 Ibid., 10924; Also: Joseph Henrich, *The Secret of Our Success* (Princeton, NJ: Princeton University Press, 2016), 3.
5 Henrich, 112.
6 Henrich, 116.
7 Yuval Noah Harari, *Sapiens* (New York: HarperCollins, 2015).
8 Joseph Carroll et al., "A Cross-Disciplinary Survey of Beliefs about Human Nature, Culture, and Science," *Evolutionary Studies in Imaginative Culture* 1 (2017).
9 Recognized as such at least since the period following World War II and the publication of the book of that title by C. P. Snow.
10 Carroll, "Survey," 3.
11 Ibid., 21.
12 Ibid., 20–22 for the quotes.
13 Apparently that documented in the last centuries or few millennia.
14 See these discussed by chapter in Paul H. Fry, *Theory of Literature* (New Haven, CT: Yale University Press, 2012).
15 For a review of New Criticism, see David H. Richter, *The Critical Tradition: Classic Texts and Contemporary Trends*, ed. David H. Richter, 2nd ed. (Boston: Bedford Books, 1998), 703–708.
16 Ashgate Interdisciplinary Studies in Opera, "About the Series," http://www.routledge.com/Ashgate-Interdisciplinary-Studies-in-Opera/book-series/AISO#.
17 See Part 2, sections 2–9, in David H. Richter, *The Critical Tradition: Classic Texts and Contemporary Trends*, ed. David H. Richter, 2nd ed. (Boston: Bedford Books, 1998). A newer edition is also available.
18 Fry, *Theory*, 1–2.
19 My emphasis added. National Academies of Sciences, Engineering, and Medicine, *Science and Creationism: A View from the National Academy of Sciences*, 2d edition (Washington, DC: The National Academies Press, 1999). http://doi.org/10.17226/6024. http://nap.nationalacademies.org/read/6024/chapter/2.
20 Examples: J. C. Carroll, "Biocultural Theory and the Study of Literature," *Comparative Literature* 67, no. 1 (2015). Also: Catherine Salmon, "Evolutionary Perspectives on Popular Culture: State of the Art," *Evolutionary Studies in Imaginative Culture* 2 (2018).
21 Patrick E. Savage, "Cultural Evolution of Music," *Palgrave Communications* 5, no. 1 (2019/02/12 2019): 16.
22 J. Brewer et al., "Grand Challenges for the Study of Cultural Evolution," *Nature Ecology & Evolution* 1, no. 3 (2017): 3.

122 Cultural Considerations Regarding Opera

23 Ibid., 2.
24 R. Dawkins, *The Selfish Gene* (Oxford: Oxford University Press, 1989), 249.
25 Robert Boyd and Peter J. Richerson, "Meme Theory Oversimplifies Cultural Change," *Scientific American* 283, no. 4 (2000).
26 Trump fomented the insurrection against the government he presided over.
27 Emily Dreyfuss, Joan Donovan, and Brian Friedberg, "How Memes Led to an Insurrection," *The Atlantic* (2022).
28 A Congressional report of the January 6, 2021, insurrection is available in print and online: http://january6th.house.gov/sites/democrats.january6th.house.gov/files/Report_FinalReport_Jan6SelectCommittee.pdf.
29 Brewer, "Cultural Evolution," 2.
30 See http://en.wikipedia.org/wiki/Enrico_Caruso_discography.
31 Ken Steiglitz, "When Caruso's Voice Became Immortal," Princeton University Press,http://press.princeton.edu/ideas/ken-steiglitz-when-carusos-voice-became-immortal.
32 A sampling of those 1902 recordings, expertly restored, can be heard on the Naxos CD, Enrico Caruso: Complete Recordings, Vol. 1 (1902–1903). http://www.naxos.com/CatalogueDetail/?id=8.110703. Accessed Feb. 14, 2023.
33 A handy pictorial account: http://evolution.berkeley.edu/evolution-101/mechanisms-the-processes-of-evolution/natural-selection/.
34 See Cameron M. Smith, Liane Gabora, and William Gardner-O'Kearny, "The Extended Evolutionary Synthesis Paves the Way for a Theory of Cultural Evolution," *Cliodynamics: The Journal of Theoretical & Mathematical History* 9, no. 2 (2018): 91.
35 Patrick E Savage and Steven Brown, "Toward a New Comparative Musicology," *Analytical Approaches To World Music* 2.2 (2013).
36 Two examples, see Savage, "Cultural Evolution"; also C. Weiß, et al., "Investigating style evolution of Western classical music: A computational approach," *Musicae Scientiae*, 23(4) (2019), 486–507. http://doi.org/10.1177/1029864918757595
37 Boyd, "Meme Theory."
38 A good summary with additional references: N. Creanza, O. Kolodny, and M. W. Feldman, "Cultural Evolutionary Theory: How Culture Evolves and Why It Matters," *Proceedings of the National Academy of Sciences of the United States of America* 114, no. 30 (2017): 7784.
39 T. M. Waring and Z. T. Wood, "Long-Term Gene-Culture Coevolution and the Human Evolutionary Transition," *Proceedings of the Royal Society B: Biological Sciences* 288, no. 1952 (2021). "Human long-term gene-culture coevolution is characterized by an evolutionary transition in inheritance (from genes to culture) [so] research should focus on the possibility of an ongoing transition in the human inheritance system."

8

ATTRACTING AUDIENCES

War and Peace, Omar, Song from the Uproar

In February 1948, Sergey Prokofiev traveled to the Kremlin in the freezing cold of winter to receive a government award. The popular composer, 56 years old and in fragile health, had returned to the Soviet Union to live and work a dozen years earlier; and in recognition of his music for symphony, dance, film, and opera, Prokofiev was named a "People's Artist." The Kremlin ceremony and award would have been a matter of some pride for him.[1]

But on that same day, February 10, another group of Soviet authorities was finishing a document that would compromise Prokofiev's creative work. Published later that month, their "Resolution" denounced Prokofiev, Shostakovich, and others for composing music with "formalist distortions and antidemocratic tendencies … foreign to the Soviet people and its artistic tastes."[2]

Prokofiev had plenty of musical plans, including an unfinished opera, and he attempted not to be foiled by the resolution of the Central Committee Propaganda and Agitation Department. He wrote an explanatory letter to them that was part apology, part explanation, and part a vow to do better. Prokofiev was hardly the first opera composer to run afoul of political regimes and bureaucratic censors—Verdi had struggled frequently with this, for example—but the Soviet authorities often determined what kind of art was appropriate for their audiences. This raises the broader question of what sort of audience opera has in the modern world.

"Life is short, art is long … and judgment difficult," as the proverb says, and though it originally applied to medicine,[3] the saying will be taken as a prescription not to draw firm prognoses about the future of opera in the

DOI: 10.4324/9781003254478-12

124 Cultural Considerations Regarding Opera

early twenty-first century. But it is fair to ask questions affecting the persistence of this art. Is there a continuing audience for it? How can it continue to attract?

From the 1890s into the 1940s, opera went through a period of flux and experimentation, with composers going off in several directions and few gaining a broad, international audience. In Europe Richard Strauss sustained the German tradition and Giacomo Puccini the Italian, both conservatively; Alban Berg innovated; each of these men composed operas that have stayed in the repertory of opera houses. But after the World Wars two main factors combined to limit the appeal of contemporary opera.

First, for better and worse, the postwar era of the past three-quarters of a century ushered in increasing competition to opera in the theatrical arts and even more so in the entertainment "market." A new opera is hardly the significant cultural news in the 2020s that it was in the 1620s, 1720s, 1820s, or even might have been in the 1920s. Cinema was a main competitor, having appropriated opera's array of arts and was even evolving in significant ways from operatic models (see chapter 9). And cinema had a great advantage in its sheer productivity, offering a variety and quantity of stories that could appeal to a diverse public.

A second factor for opera's loss of prominence is composers' apparent challenge in finding a contemporary musical style that listeners find as compelling as those of earlier periods. That is likely related, in part, to a move away from tonality and tonality's dependence upon intervals that reflect human speech. Highly dissonant or atonal music can be novel and intriguing, but it appears not to be naturally appealing (as discussed in chapter 3).[4] The musical tradition that Western composers inherited at the end of the nineteenth century was tonal, but Wagner had pushed tonality far with the chromaticism of his *Tristan und Isolde*. Composers of the next decades had continued to challenge tonal structure; Berg's *Wozzeck* shows where some composers arrived by a century ago.

Writing in 1941, the American composer Roger Sessions, then 45 years old, observed a particular challenge for the twentieth-century composer, writing that certain "fortunate" historical periods have "clearly defined standards" that the artist can accept and works within. "Our own is not one of these; today the individual is obliged to discover his own language before he has completed the mastery of it."[5]

"Classical" composers, one can assume, are not without ego nor oblivious to popular taste. They want to be liked or at least appreciated. But there's a catch: how best to proceed? Virtually all serious and ambitious creators of art recognize that they are coming late to a history, or an evolution, of their form and in the wake of their predecessors. Powerful creators, Beethoven and Verdi, for example, can well intimidate, or generate anxiety, in those who come later, confronting them with a challenge of how to go forward past them.[6] Arguably, the somewhat lesser creators might be content with just joining the historical "party" that is well underway. They can join in that party, and if they understand how to get along and contribute to it, they can be well accepted and "successful" (e.g., Salieri, Puccini). This is Plan A: Better in this life to be a secure and prosperous Salieri than a hustling Mozart. (Residuals are not valuable to you once you're dead.) Still, the more ambitious composers want to take the party over to their place, opening a new imaginative space in the culture, creating a new cultural "niche." That's Plan B (e.g., Wagner, Berg); and it's inherently riskier. Sergey Prokofiev tried to work a combination Plan, A+B. But he faced a major problem in his environment.

Born in 1891, Prokofiev was a celebrity pianist and admired composer by the 1920s, presenting a new musical style that pushed the boundaries of tonal convention without entirely breaking them. Featuring rhythmic propulsion that seemed to echo both the Industrial Age and primitive energies and melodies that sounded simultaneously familiar and not quite, Prokofiev's music reflected a European world that was coming apart at the seams. After being abroad for many years he went home to Russia in 1936. In the Soviet Union then, the repressive, murderous regime of Josef Stalin was underway, but apparently Prokofiev believed that he would not be harmed by the regime and that he could continue his composing under his own terms. That was not quite the way it worked out. For all his piano virtuosity and facility with symphonic forms, Prokofiev considered himself mainly an opera composer.[7] As Nazi Germany invaded the Soviet Union in 1941, Prokofiev conceived an opera based on Tolstoy's great novel, *War and Peace*, that concerned itself with Russian life and society at the time of a previous invasion, that of the French under Napoleon.

Prokofiev quickly sketched a plot of 12 scenes, compressing the 1,200-page novel into a manageable drama in two parts. Under more conventional, non-wartime conditions in a more open society, Prokofiev might have been able to follow his own dramatic instincts. But under Stalin's regime in the midst of a brutal and bloody war a protected and comparatively pampered artist was going to be required to hew the party line. While Prokofiev did share patriotic sentiments that Tolstoy's novel could readily be crafted to display, the composer's overseers actually demanded much more. As Simon Morrison details in *The People's Artist: Prokofiev's Soviet Years*, the overseers saw the opera as a tool to affect the Soviet audience as they wished, not just to stir patriotic sentiment but "to represent the larger historical truths of the Russian historical progress toward Communism."[8]

This demand would prove difficult not only as an end but also as a means while the opera was under development. For example, in their 1942 critique of an early version of the opera, the Committee on Arts Affairs focused on beefing up the "War" part and emphasizing an alignment between the

126 Cultural Considerations Regarding Opera

earlier invasion of Russia by the French and the present one by the Nazis: "The victorious people and their exultation need to be shown. ... The listener should discern in your Denisov [character] the many heroes of the Patriotic War against Hitlerism."[9]

For a decade, until his death in 1953, Prokofiev wrote and revised the opera under the advice of artistic advisors but ultimately under the requirements of a succession of arts apparatchiks who determined whether *War and Peace* was to be approved for performance. Audience messaging by political committee apparently could have no end, and, ultimately, Prokofiev admitted to himself in his diary that the endless demands for modifications were "disgusting."[10] The opera was never presented whole in his lifetime, and today the impression of the whole is that the "War" part often veers into patriotic bombast, as in the final chorus:

> The People came forward to fight to the death for our country. We've defended Russia with our blood. Victory is ours. Russia's glory will not fade through all the ages.[11]

Prokofiev's *War and Peace* reflects one moment in cultural history when a pervasive ideology intended to dictate thought. Marxism as practiced by the totalitarian Stalinists might be seen narrowly as a political ideology only. But Marxism-Leninism[12] aspired to be more a comprehensive and dominant belief system,[13] operating throughout the Soviet culture like a religion, and with aspirations of historical inevitability. Thus, for instance, Soviet authorities determined to turn independent farms into farming collectives as part of "the larger historical truths of the Russian historical progress toward Communism" could ignore or minimize the deaths of about four million Ukrainian farmers and peasants in 1932–1933 due to famine caused by the collectivization process and its Soviet direction.[14] Thus also the Soviet authorities would dictate a predetermined message to the audience of *War and Peace*.

Perhaps if the opera had been actually composed by committee, the authorities might have been satisfied with that result. Perhaps wartime Russians, too. A strategy of imposing messages on the creative process and product may have effect in authoritarian societies. But in more open, democratic, contemporary societies, audiences can go where they want, or can afford to go (at least to what's available).

Recently, in most of the countries where Western opera has become established, leaders of opera companies have been worrying.[15] Live, staged opera performances are expensive to produce, in general, and opera companies can reasonably be alarmed by the challenge of drawing audiences. Ticket prices are often high compared to other "entertainment" options; subscribers who buy season tickets have been declining;[16] the average age of opera audiences is increasing; and government subsidies in Europe have lessened.[17]

Still, recent data indicated that an audience in the millions who *attend* opera performances in a year persists.[18] According to a national survey, in the United States 4.7 million American adults had attended an opera performance in a previous 12-month period,[19] and a larger group had used various electronic devices to listen to or watch opera. A conservative estimate would put the latter number at about 10 million adults,[20] some of those the same as went to live shows. So, quite a few Americans—millions—were interested in opera; and the American percentage[21] might be about the same in countries whose music includes classics of the European tradition. More importantly, that US National Endowment for the Arts report showed that about twice as many Americans used various electronic "devices"—described as including both hardware, such as computers and cell phones, and software or online "apps," such as YouTube—to listen to or watch opera. The total number of "views and likes" by American and other viewers of opera videos on YouTube is unknown, but many of these videos garner thousands, even tens of thousands of views. During the coronavirus pandemic in April 2020, the Metropolitan Opera broadcast online a live and free gala with its singers, orchestra, and chorus.[22] That one event attracted approximately 750,000 Internet "views" from one or more viewers in 162 countries.[23]

"I am fairly certain that opera will have to reinvent itself if the species is to survive in the digital age," wrote Nicholas Payne in 2021.[24] Payne, then the head of Opera Europa, a professional association of opera companies, recommended "a sort of Charles Darwin mindset," in his opinion piece, titled "Survival of the Fittest." Payne recommended that opera companies should reform themselves to become more economically sustainable and more equable in all its personnel as well as to exploit the "digital transformation" underway. Yet he recognized that "no amount of repositioning or rebranding will be worth it, if the appetite [of potential audiences] is lacking." But despite his references to species, survival, and Darwin, Payne's framework for solving the "audience-appetite" challenge involved mainly new marketing ideas and strategies to "diffuse the work to a wider and more plural constituency."

Peter Gelb, the general manager of the Metropolitan Opera, was singing the same tune as Payne in late 2022 as the Met, the largest classical music organization in the United States, fell on some economic hard times. "The challenges are greater than ever," Gelb told the *New York Times* newspaper. "The only path forward is reinvention." Accordingly, Gelb planned to stage more contemporary works at the Met and open annually with a new opera. The Met's music director reportedly agreed. "It's our responsibility to generate new works so that people can recognize themselves and their realities on our stage," said Yannick Nézet-Séguin.[25]

128 Cultural Considerations Regarding Opera

Presumably none of these opera professionals believes that *no* "people recognize themselves and their realities" in older, well-established works typically written by White men, presenting heterosexual relations and other common aspects of Western culture. Since the 1970s such works have been decried often as part of a "Western canon" that has dominated literary culture and is seemingly indifferent or even hostile to a "more plural constituency." That canon, or line of masterworks, in English literary studies would include Homer, Virgil, Dante, Shakespeare, Tolstoy, and others.[26] The argument against such artists and works is that "the Western canon is (consciously or otherwise) a product of Eurocentrism and patriarchy, and deserves no particular respect for its antiquity," as historical critic David Richter observed.[27]

A counterargument, the traditional one, would be that these works—*The Aeneid, Hamlet, War and Peace,* for example—are classics not because they are a product and a support of "Eurocentrism and patriarchy." Rather it is because they seem in themselves peerless in expression and because they offer something truly rarer, what canon-advocate Harold Bloom calls a confrontation with "greatness."[28] Their probing offers uncommon insights into common human concerns, often those derived from human biology and evolution. *All* human concerns? No.

Such works, like every other human activity, are both products of their time, with its limitations, and, if they are to stand its test, must also speak, and have spoken, to later generations. As the French essayist Saint-Beuve observed, in 1850:

> A true classic ... is an author who has enriched the human mind, increased its treasure, and caused it to advance a step; who has discovered some moral and not equivocal truth, or revealed some eternal passion in that heart where all seemed known and discovered ... who has spoken to all in his own peculiar style, a style ... new and old, easily contemporary with all time.[29]

Admittedly, many people then, now, and before have felt that such classics still do not speak to them, much less speak for them, and indeed may speak against them. Over the past half-century, a "multicultural" perspective has become ascendant, supported by the various postmodern social "theories" (and often led by them, such that "theory" may seem to take the place of literature). But multiculturalism has brought attention to overlooked works of relevance to groups that have been in the minorities, those of different ethnic backgrounds, sexual orientations, and political views.

For opera, arguably there has also been a canon of composers, including Mozart, Verdi, and Wagner, although what or who exactly is in the operatic canon, and how that canon should be understood, is subject to the same controversy attending literary classics.[30] For all that, some operas addressed to conventionally overlooked "constituencies" may indeed draw fresh audiences.

One example, premiered in 2022, was *Omar*, an opera about an African Muslim scholar's life as an American slave in the nineteenth century. Created by the multiracial musician and librettist Rhiannon Giddens and composer Michael Abels, the opera was presented in major cities, including Los Angeles and Boston. The promotion of *Omar* by LA Opera[31] emphasized the opera's departure from stereotypical fare. "There is a lot of people we don't need more stories about; we could do with a few more 'Omar' stories," said Giddens.[32]

"It broadened the idea of what an American story is," she elaborated. Omar Ibin Said was captured in Senegal, transported across the Atlantic, and sold first in South Carolina, later North Carolina, "and this Middle Passage and Auction Block and all of these things, this is the *reality* for thousands upon thousands of people—that they had to live their lives under the most unbelievable duress."

While saying that Omar's story is ultimately a "triumph" as he stayed true to his beliefs (as recorded in his autobiography), even so, "particularly for people of the African diaspora, African-Americans, I want them to feel, to walk out going, we are all of us feeling pain, feeling trauma, and I understand the trauma that I'm carrying a little bit better because I've seen how this character overcame his."

Members of the racially diverse audience reflected their appreciation and approval of *Omar* in another video produced by LA Opera: "The best depiction of this topic that I've seen in an art-form in a long time," said one attendee.[33]

Although *Omar*'s account of the trauma of slavery is of value to anyone's understanding of the profound effects of this despicable racist behavior, audience members whose own lives were descended from the African diaspora surely might find particular value.[34] The opera's value has been noted beyond the theater. In awarding *Omar* the Pulitzer Prize in Music in 2023, judges cited it for "expanding the language of the operatic form while conveying the humanity of those condemned to bondage."[35]

The topic of identity is foregrounded again in *Song from the Uproar*, a chamber opera composed in 2012 by another American, Missy Mazzoli. *Uproar* concerns the young adulthood of the Swiss explorer and writer Isabelle Eberhardt. Although to what extent this opera about a young woman by a young woman composer can be considered "feminist," it does invite recollection of observations made two decades before in articles developing a feminist criticism of music and opera. "Opera concerns women. No, there is no feminist version; no, there is no liberation. Quite the contrary: they suffer, they cry, they die," Susan McClary lamented.[36] But a "feminist criticism" (and presumably feminist opera) would significantly "focus on those dimensions of music that involve desire and that engage the body."[37]

130 Cultural Considerations Regarding Opera

McClary then asserted a strict postmodern view that only culture affects culture, writing that she did not mean "the body" as "some kind of transhistorical entity" (in which "transhistorical" might be understood as "evolutionary"). Instead:

> Our experiences of our bodies and sexualities are as socially constructed as any other dimension of culture. It is in part because music plays such a prominent role in that fundamental shaping that it needs to be taken so seriously.[38]

Although female sexuality is a key interest of *Song from the Uproar*, for her own part composer Mazzoli has said that she takes a somewhat broader view of her operas, of which *Uproar* was the first. "The thing that I can say consistently inspires me," she told an interviewer, "is …human beings trying to live their lives under insane, impossible circumstances."[39]

Those circumstances, in the case of the Isabelle Eberhardt of the opera, appear largely the consequence of her own choices in her emerging maturity as a woman in her twenties. The opera offers scenes from Eberhardt's life starting with her late adolescence, by which time all of her close family had died, prompting Isabelle to sadly leave her home in Switzerland and journey to Algeria at age 20, where she is shown continuing to grieve her losses, taking on a provisional identity as a man, experimenting with Islamic religion, falling in love with an Algerian soldier, being rejected by him, and dying in a flash flood at age 27.

Isabelle is the one main character in the chamber opera and about the only solo voice (in addition to a small chorus that frequently comments). *Uproar* got its name "because it's her song; this song emerging from the chaos of her life," said the composer.[40] "I was struck by the universal themes of her story," Mazzoli said, "how much her struggles, her questions, her passions, mirrored those of women throughout the 20th and 21st century. Isabelle made a great effort to define herself as an independent woman under extreme circumstances."[41]

Song from the Uproar is one woman's shortened biography, told in an individual way. Although the one-hour opera's 17 scenes have chronological order to them, the listener is more aware of the somewhat disjointed monologue that Isabelle presents through them. Mazzoli said the opera was not like a narrative but rather "more like a fever dream," one that is bewildering and confusing, a nightmare while physically ill. In the original production in New York,[42] that disjointed monologue was accentuated by dream/nightmare-like images (photos, video) and occasional, discursive sound effects projected along with the music. The singer who portrayed Isabelle, for whom the role was written,[43] acted at times congruent to the external circumstances of a scene but often used pantomime to reflect some aspect of her subjective experience.

Attracting Audiences **131**

For example, the New York premiere opened with a video projection of a body attempting to swim, as Isabelle picked up and dropped pieces of paper—these two elements obscure in the moment but presumably alluding to Isabelle's later drowning and the discovery of fragments of her journal. The libretto notes that "a journey of remembering begins."[44] Then, from about three to six minutes into the opera, the audience saw a video projection of a girl child, then barefoot men carrying a casket, and heard a female voice intoning "ah" frequently. But this was a recording, not "live," as the sound broke up. Mourners with wreathes appeared; then a first aria began: "Death moves his hands through me again," as Isabelle made illustrative gestures with her hands.

Musically, Mazzoli's vocal writing would be characterized as minimalist, and Isabelle's solo vocal line throughout is often restricted and limited, which calls attention to the words, the quality of the voice, and the spare orchestration that supports the solo voice. *Song from the Uproar* is unconventional and challenging: minimalism accentuates what is presented but also is vulnerable to its own limitations.

How much or how successfully this chamber opera expresses what Mazzoli called "universal" female themes could be question. Isabelle does sing about her sexuality, her drug and alcohol use, and her encounters with death. Ultimately, the libretto declares that "Isabelle summons the flood that will take her life," and she sings, "Death is familiar / death is my companion / Wash me away."[45] One might ask at the end how much Isabelle differs from conventional operatic women to whom things happen and whom McClary decried: "they suffer, they cry, they die."

Even so, if *Uproar* is identified as an opera about female identity, opera companies may well find an audience, even a new one, for whom this concern is salient. In encountering dramas that appear oriented to heterosexual, middle-class, white males, as Jill Dolan commented, a "feminist spectator might find that her gender—and/or her race, class, or sexual preference—as well as her ideology and politics make [so-called "mainstream" works] alien and even offensive."[46]

Gender, sexual orientation, and race are real identity concerns to be addressed, but may they also put audiences in a box? Hypothetically, if an opera fan is a divorced father of two children, gay, of African ancestry, and a business executive, is there a risk in marketing narrowly as if one of these identities precluded other sympathies and motivations? One would think that producers and marketers would recognize this potential trap. Are people not greater than their identities?

For the society, a broader concern with "identity politics," which came to prominence in America in the 1970s on the political left,[47] is that it likely

132 Cultural Considerations Regarding Opera

stimulated identity politics on the political right, in the extreme leading to a resurgence there of white nationalism. If liberal democracies are to hold together, the political scientist Francis Fukuyama has suggested, the challenge is "not to abandon the idea of identity, which is central to the way that modern people think about themselves and their surrounding societies":

> [I]t is to define larger and more integrative national identities that take into account the de facto diversity of liberal democratic societies.[48]

For opera, specifically, the continuing problem in maintaining and growing the audience for live performances is that a better theory about why people go to the opera at all seems lacking. Empirical research on theater audiences has been very limited,[49] and on opera audiences even more limited and often superficial. It doesn't take a microscope to see that well-to-do, well-educated people have tended to be core opera-goers. What gets measured to define opera audiences has often been demographic elements that are comparatively easy to measure, such as age, income levels, educational attainment, and social status.[50] Producing operas that attract the new "constituencies" of contemporary societies may help, but this is a pragmatic tactic, not an overall strategy grounded in a comprehensive theory.

Why people preferentially attend to certain content in their environment has deep and complex roots. One root taps information. As noted, cultural evolutionists have claimed that humans evolved by learning from others.[51] But *who* information is obtained *from* became a critical consideration for individual success. Dominance ("You will do it my way because I say so") is a default for primates—and Prokofiev's Soviet authorities. But humans typically look for a variety of "prestige" cues to determine from whom to obtain information, cues which include skill, reliability, and success, which may be integrated with cues reflective of the self, including sex and ethnicity.[52]

Perhaps without being recognized as such, this evolutionary perspective sometimes is used in attempting to attract audiences to opera. The LA Opera promotion of *Omar*, for example, could trade on cues of Rhiannon Giddens's success and popularity as a performer (Grammy awards) and as creative artist (MacArthur "Genius" grant award) as well as her multiracial identity.

However, as deep as such information cues may be—on the order of a hundred thousand years for Sapiens as a cultural species—another evolutionary theory finds another root of our choices even deeper and thus likely even stronger. They go back to the origin of life itself.

In choosing any leisure activity, including opera, individuals generally consider three factors—their needs, prior experience, and the "costs and benefits" of the opportunity (here, not exclusively the *financial* costs or benefits but rather the overall weighing of the opportunity). Which begs the larger question of how people weigh and then choose what to do. The cultural-evolutionist understanding is strongly linked to ultimate human goals

Attracting Audiences **133**

of survival and reproduction on scales of years, decades, and longer. But this other evolutionary theory addresses the reality of choice on the timescale of daily living. Evolutionary scientist and learning specialist John H. Falk has developed the research and publications that advance his understanding that all people are trying to extract the greatest sense of well-being from our lives at every moment. We are "born to choose" for our well-being, Falk claims.[53]

"Well-being" arises from meeting one's ever-changing physical, social, intellectual, and personal needs, according to Falk.[54] All of these needs have deep evolutionary roots, ultimately grounded in homeostasis, that internal self-regulating process that biological systems use to maintain stability by continually adjusting to conditions in their environment. Not only organisms but also tissues and cells strive for the best chemical balance between outside and inside themselves, leading some scientists to see homeostasis as the original step in evolution.[55]

Thus, an individual won't go to an opera performance if they're critically ill, for example. But otherwise, they may pay attention to opera because it satisfies their sense of well-being that comes from experiencing creativity and beauty, or from being prompted to reflect on their own life. Or, in the opera house, it might come from enjoying a high-quality social experience with friends; or from enhancing a primary adult relationship with a special person, a spouse, or a "date" (example: in the movie *Moonstruck* the lovers go to see *La Bohème*). The point Falk makes is that the choices we make defy simplifying assumptions—that opera, for example, will attract people with certain demographic characteristics or contemporary "identity" interests. Recognizing the multiple, diverse systems of well-being, from physical survival to social relationships to spirituality,[56] may help marketing be more successful.

Falk's own published research supports his theory,[57] as also, independently, does some research on opera attendance. One study conducted with American "millennials"—those 18–34 years old in 2015—offered insights about what attending opera performances affords them.[58] Three motivations stood out. These were to "feel transcendental, part of something bigger"; to "feel present, de-stress, forget yourself" by attending to the goings-on; and to "dress up for a night out." These would map well to Falk's categories of creativity and spirituality and sociality. More broadly, that 2015 survey found that millennials were seeking two other qualities that opera as well as other performing arts can deliver: "to feel emotional connection and authenticity" and "to enhance sense of identity" by seeing how others, dramatized in a story, handled their difficulties and conflicts. These suggest Falk's well-being systems of reflectivity and individuality.[59]

A second study of frequent opera-goers, conducted in England in 2016, reinforces a number of themes apparent with the American millennials.[60] This study, a set of open-ended interviews with a small group of mostly

134 Cultural Considerations Regarding Opera

retired Britons, explored their reflections on their experience as "highly engaged" opera attendees.[61] Some of the researchers' key conclusions may not require further comment:

> Our respondents describe their experiences in highly emotional terms. They are deeply engaged by the characters and stories of opera ... They have a strong desire to believe in the narratives portrayed, and they make qualitative judgments of productions and performances according to whether or not those aspects interrupt or enhance the believability of narratives. ... Respondents use opera narratives to explore and reflect on human relationships and dilemmas, and they better able to do that when they are captivated by the music.[62]

True, "human relationships and dilemmas" presented through other musical forms, including popular songs in a great variety of styles, command the attention of huge audiences, as any of the online music services[63] or the attendance at live events will attest.[64] But individual songs of a few minutes duration are clearly a different kind from extended narratives of music and drama. Musical theater,[65] epitomized by Broadway shows, draws larger audiences than opera.[66] But opera's music-drama is different because of the expressive potential of its associated arts, which are not merely added together as they are in musical theater with its separation of talking and singing.

Instead, opera integrates its arts on an ongoing, holistic basis. Enduring operas have continuous music and drama that inform each other, compounding and improving the effect of each other, as occurs with the operas discussed in this book. But finally, performance is where opera lives, each performance, with all its "moving parts" ideally of a piece, holding the potential for audience transportation and even transformation.

A theater scholar, Theodore Shank, expressed that transformation decades ago in observing that a dramatic work "articulates for the audience something vital about their own emotive lives that previously they had not been able to grasp."[67]

Today's audiences, just like those of Monteverdi, Mozart, Verdi, and Berg, will respond to a new voice who can offer a musical expression to match the meaning of the drama. Innovation is a value, certainly.

Notes

1 A key source: Simon Morrison, *The People's Artist: Prokofiev's Soviet Years* (Oxford: Oxford University Press, 2008), 296.
2 Morrison, *People's Artist*, 303.
3 The original quote from the Greek physician Hippocrates has been applied to other arts since at least the fourteenth century.

Attracting Audiences   **135**

4 D. Purves, *Music as Biology* (Cambridge, MA: Harvard University Press, 2017), 52.
5 Roger Sessions, "The Composer and His Message," in *The Creative Process*, ed. Brewster Ghiselin (Berkeley: University of California Press, 1952), 48.
6 This psychological dimension is provocatively treated in Harold Bloom, *The Anxiety of Influence: A Theory of Poetry*, 2nd ed. (New York: Oxford University Press, 1997).
7 Morrison, *People's Artist*, 283.
8 Ibid., 282.
9 Ibid., 210.
10 Ibid., 335.
11 Sergei Prokofiev, *War and Peace*, Opéra National de Paris, conducted by Gary Bertini. English translator not noted. TDK DVD, 2000.
12 Overview: Wikipedia contributors, "Marxism–Leninism," *Wikipedia, The Free Encyclopedia*, http://en.wikipedia.org/w/index.php?title=Marxism%E2%80%93Leninism&oldid=1127864841 (accessed December 22, 2022).
13 Kenneth Jowitt, "An Organizational Approach to the Study of Political Culture in Marxist-Leninist Systems," *American Political Science Review* 68, no. 3 (1974): 1171–1191.
14 See Chapter 1, "The Soviet Famines," in T. Snyder, *Bloodlands: Europe between Hitler and Stalin* (New York: Basic Books, 2012). Also: Internet Encyclopedia of Ukraine, "Famine-Genocide of 1932–3," Canadian Institute of Ukrainian Studies, http://www.encyclopediaofukraine.com/display.asp?linkpath=pages%5CF%5CA%5CFamine6Genocideof1932hD73.htm
15 Also performers worry. See Tom Huizenga, "Is Opera Ailing? Assessing the State of the Art," http://www.npr.org/sections/deceptivecadence/2012/08/16/158889694/checking-opera-s-pulse-a-conversation-about-the-state-of-the-art.
16 One public account of the trend: Michael Cooper, "Opera Has a Problem: Fans Aren't Subscribing," *New York Times*, December 21, 2018.
17 Nicholas Payne, "Survival of the Fittest," http://www.operaamerica.org/industry-resources/2021/202102/survival-of-the-fittest/
18 National Endowment for the Arts, "U.S. Patterns of Arts Participation: A Full Report from the 2017 Survey of Public Participation in the Arts" (Washington, DC, 2019). Figure 10.
19 Ibid. In Figure 10, 4.7 million is the listed 2% of a 236 million adult population (18 or older). This document reports "the nation's largest, most representative survey of adult patterns of arts participation in the United States."
20 National Endowment, *Arts Participation*, 57. My conservative estimate is as follows: Figure 29 indicates that 21% of American adults used electronic devices to access "classical music or opera" without specifying separate percentages. My approximation of 10 million is derived from figure 10, which indicated that opera attendance was 22% as large as classical music attendance (2:9). That percentage of 21% is 4.6% × 236 million adults = 10.8 million.
21 About 4% to 5% of the US adult population.
22 While "free," the Met did actively solicit donations: http://www.metopera.org/season/at-home-gala/
23 Lee Abrahamian, Metropolitan Opera, email to author, May 4, 2020.
24 Payne, "Survival."
25 All quotes here in J. C. Hernandez, "Pandemic Woes Lead Met Opera to Tap Endowment and Embrace New Work," *New York Times*, December 26, 2022.
26 Harold Bloom, *The Western Canon*, Riverhead ed. (New York: Berkley Publishing Group, 1995).

136 Cultural Considerations Regarding Opera

27 David H. Richter, *The Critical Tradition: Classic Texts and Contemporary Trends*, ed. David H. Richter, 2nd ed. (Boston: Bedford Books, 1998). Richter may be glossing another critic, but he is not quoting her here.
28 Bloom, *Western Canon*, 489.
29 Charles Augustin Sainte-Beuve, "What Is a Classic?" *Harvard Classics*, Vol. 32 (Bartleby.com), http://www.bartleby.com/32/202.html.
30 See C. Newark and W. Weber, *The Oxford Handbook of the Operatic Canon* (Oxford: Oxford University Press, 2020).
31 "LA Opera" is their styling.
32 "Omar: Behind the Story," LA Opera, YouTube video. October 2022. http://youtu.be/xgYuwXR9TMk
33 "See What Audiences Are Saying about *Omar*," LA Opera, YouTube video. November 2022. http://youtu.be/F3arodJKw-Q
34 Stuart Hall, "Cultural Identity and Diaspora," in *Colonial Discourse and Post-Colonial Theory* (New York: Routledge, 2015), 237.
35 See: http://www.pulitzer.org/winners/rhiannon-giddens-and-michael-abels
36 Susan McClary, "The Undoing of Opera: Toward a Feminist Criticism of Music," in *Opera, or, the Undoing of Women* (Minneapolis: University of Minnesota Press, 1988), 11.
37 Susan McClary, "Towards a Feminist Criticism of Music," *Canadian University Music Review / Revue de musique des universités canadiennes* 10, no. 2 (1990): 9–18. http://doi.org/10.7202/1014882ar
38 Ibid.
39 Frank J. Oteri, "Missy Mazzoli: Communication, Intimacy, and Vulnerability," newmusicusa.org, http://newmusicusa.org/nmbx/missy-mazzoli-communication-intimacy-and-vulnerability/.
40 Ibid.
41 Missy Mazzoli, "Composer Note," *Song from the Uproar*, http://missymazzoli.com/works/.
42 The 2012 video is not commercially available, although excerpts may be online. An audio version with the original cast is available: http://missymazzoli.com/recordings/song-from-the-uproar/
43 Abigail Fischer, mezzo-soprano.
44 Missy Mazzoli, *Song from the Uproar: The Lives and Deaths of Isabelle Eberhardt*, Libretto by Royce Vavrek and Mazzoli. Premiere February 2012, New York City. Private video provided by composer.
45 Mazzoli, *Song*, libretto Vavrek and Mazzoli, scene 16.
46 Dolan, Jill (1988) *The Feminist Spectator as Critic* (Ann Arbor: UMI Press). Research Press: 3–4.
47 Cressida Heyes, "Identity Politics," *The Stanford Encyclopedia of Philosophy* (Fall 2020 Edition), Edward N. Zalta (ed.), <http://plato.stanford.edu/archives/fall2020/entries/identity-politics/>.
48 Francis Fukuyama, "Against Identity Politics: The New Tribalism and the Crisis of Democracy," *Foreign Affairs* 97 (2018): 9.
49 Kirsty Sedgman, "On Rigour in Theatre Audience Research," *Contemporary Theatre Review* 29, no. 4 (2019): 462.
50 National Endowment for the Arts, "A Decade of Arts Engagement," (Washington, DC, 2015), 10.
51 R. Boyd, P. J. Richerson, and J. Henrich, "The Cultural Niche: Why Social Learning Is Essential for Human Adaptation," *Proceedings of the National Academy of Sciences of the United States of America* 108, Suppl 2 (2011): 10918–10925.
52 Joseph Henrich, *The Secret of Our Success* (Princeton, NJ: Princeton University Press, 2016), 37–47.

Attracting Audiences **137**

53 John H. Falk, *Born to Choose: Evolution, Self, and Well-Being* (New York: Routledge, 2018). Falk describes seven human "well-being systems," which arose over 3.7 billion years of evolution.

54 John H. Falk, *The Value of Museums: Enhancing Societal Well-Being* (Lanham, MD: Rowman & Littlefield, 2022). These four categories embrace the seven in the previous book and formulation.

55 J. S. Torday, "Homeostasis as the Mechanism of Evolution," *Biology (Basel)* 4, no. 3 (2015).

56 Falk, *Born to Choose*, part 2.

57 The research was conducted primarily in museums and science centers but appears broadly applicable to other cultural institutions.

58 Marketing Research Professionals Inc., "Building Millennial Audiences: Barriers and Opportunities," (The Wallace Foundation, 2017). The number of participants was not clear from this report.

59 See Falk, *Born*, 51–52, for a description of his seven well-being systems and their evolutionary significance.

60 Sinéad O'Neill, Joshua Edelman, and John Sloboda. "Opera and Emotion: The Cultural Value of Attendance for the Highly Engaged." *Participations* 13, no. 1 (May 2016).

61 Ibid., 29. The researchers noted that the interviewees self-selected to participate, and that they made "no claims that this study is representative of a wider, opera-going public."

62 Ibid., 45.

63 Gabriel Zamora and Jeffrey L. Wilson, "The Best Online Music Streaming Services for 2023," PCMag, December 19, 2022. http://www.pcmag.com/picks/the-best-online-music-streaming-services?test_uuid=05n7gTzbSo0Sh5pVEDljnCi&test_variant=b

64 Herb Scribner, "Live Events Take Off like a Rocket," Axios, September 2, 2022. http://www.axios.com/2022/09/02/live-event-ticket-sales-concerts

65 In 2018–2019, nearly 15 million people attended "Broadway shows": http://www.broadwayleague.com/research/research-reports/. New York's Metropolitan Opera is the largest repertory opera house with 3,800 seats. The Met's annual report for the same period did not disclose in-house attendance, but for the 214 performances, at a listed 75% "paid attendance" the total would appear about 600,000. The Met cited 2.2 million as the worldwide audience for its live telecasts for FY19.Metropolitan Opera, "Annual Report 2018–19" (New York: Metropolitan Opera, 2019).

66 At least in the United States, but that larger attendance is likely similar in other countries with a Western musical tradition.

67 Theodore Shank, *The Art of Dramatic Art* (Belmont, CA: Dickenson, 1969), 172.

9

ORIGINS AND INNOVATIONS

Before and After *La Bohème* (the movie)

When it started and why did it change are intriguing questions for cultural history.

How far back in time does one go to try to understand the origins of a species like music-drama? "Species" is a fair term, since essential similarities and yet "evolved" differences between the operas of Monteverdi and, say, Missy Mazzoli, are apparent. In addition to song, already touched upon, another of the evident changes from *Orfeo* to Mazzoli's *Uproar* is that the latter exploits in a novel way certain contemporary innovations in performance, such as video projections and recorded audio. A prevailing view of innovations is that they are the result of very smart, ingenious individuals who invent something, such as Gutenberg and the printing press, Edison and the lightbulb, Adolphe Sax and the saxophone. But from a cultural-evolution perspective ingenious individuals depend upon all the prior relevant knowledge accumulated and available in a society.

As manifestations of human culture, music-drama would seem to always embody a social communication between those acting as "senders" of the communication and those responding to it. But how far back in time to go to understand how this communication began? In his influential *Opera as Drama*, music historian Joseph Kerman started the clock with the Italian academies of Monteverdi's time—"since the days of the half-literary, half-musical academy that willed opera into being."[1] Dedicating their substantial *History of Opera* to Kerman a half-century later, Carolyn Abbate and Roger Parker began the same: "A history of opera is not lightly undertaken ... when it attempts to survey the entire 400-year period."[2]

Narrowly, if the interest is only the history of what the West conventionally refers to as "opera," then four centuries is the right frame. However,

DOI: 10.4324/9781003254478-13

Origins and Innovations **139**

that opera was "willed into being" by Monteverdi and his contemporaries seems exaggerated. Monteverdi was advancing both a Western musical tradition hundreds of years old and a notion of music-drama that, as noted, he and his contemporaries understood had similarities with that of Athens two thousand years earlier. But music-drama did not spring full-grown out of the head of Aeschylus either, as the Greeks' "ritual-dramas"[3] with music and choreographed movement appear to have emerged from other communal practices, the Dionysian processions, songs, and hymns, which arose earlier.

What difference would it make to our understanding of opera if it was known what gave rise far earlier to expressive voices and movements performed together? If we could say how these fledgling elements of "music" and "drama" could have arisen not four hundred or two thousand years ago, or not even about two hundred thousand years ago when *Homo sapiens* emerged, but double that timeframe, might an inclination to music-drama be more than an art form of a few centuries but built into human evolution?

Evolutionary researchers are trying to piece a history together. It's a complex investigation as evidence-based hypotheses are developed and subjected to scrutiny. As introduced in Chapter 2, the origin of music is being sought in the incremental development of the mental and physical capacities that characterize musicality, including sensitivity to pitch and timbre and the ability to produce and sustain rhythms. Such musicality appears to have slowly arisen over hundreds of thousands of years in the ancestral forebears of our own species.

Over two million years the cranial capacity of hominins increased to the large brains we Sapiens enjoy,[4] such that during evolution of hominins,[5] the neurons in the cerebral cortex, the major part of the brain, increased about ten times. Neurons are information messengers and make everything we think, feel, and do possible, as would have been their vital function along our evolutionary path.

What some distant relatives did with larger brains has been interpreted from, among other places, a coastal location in southern England near the present village of Boxgrove. There, a series of archaeological excavations starting in the 1980s exposed extraordinary evidence of hominin hunting or scavenging activity about 480,000–500,00 years ago. A group of perhaps 30 or more individuals may have killed and definitely butchered large mammals on the site, including a rhinoceros and a horse, the latter in probably only one day.[6]

Fossil bones recovered indicate the hominins were a large and massively built species said to be *Homo heidelbergensis*.[7] At the Boxgrove sites these hominins, with brains about four-fifths of our own size,[8] apparently coordinated on a number of interconnected, time-bound tasks. These included killing or scavenging (recently dead) mammals; the transport of stones to manufacture cutting-tools; the on-site fabrication of those stone hand-axes;

140 Cultural Considerations Regarding Opera

the butchering itself, using them; and protecting themselves and the meat of the butchered animal from roving scavengers such as hyenas.

Lacking anything like language as we know it, the Boxgrove individuals probably communicated by physical gesturing and vocal gesturing.[9] In the multiple tasks of butchering the horse a division of labor between those collecting the stones for the axes, those making the hand-axes, and those using them some distance away likely required urgent gestures. Motions of the arms moving the hands sharply in toward the chest and vocal calls of increasing loudness or repetition would seem to have been called for, and such would have been learned behaviors.

But how would one Boxgrove individual, a half-million years ago, actually understand the vocal or physical gestures that another individual, some distance away, was trying to communicate? The receiver of the communication does not possess language and can't say to himself, "I wonder what that weird arm-flapping is about?" And he can't call out, "Hey there, what are you trying to say?" Evolutionary musicologist Gary Tomlinson has advanced the semiotic interpretation that hominin brains had evolved to recognize and make *signs*—and this crucial capability eventually led to ritual and to what Tomlinson calls "musicking."[10]

His is a complex argument developed over books and articles, and no short simplification can capture its careful sophistication. But "signs" addresses the central question of how cognition—the condition of knowing—can proceed *without* words. "Knowing" has several parts, commonly defined as perceiving, recognizing, conceiving, and reasoning. Tomlinson has argued that hominins exploited the well-developed animal capacity to understand and act in the world by *perceiving* stimuli important to them and *recognizing* them as signs.[11] A robin, for example, recognizes that a berry that is good to eat is bright red. The berry is more than red; it has shape and size, for example. But for the robin, "red" stands in for the whole object, and when the bird sees that "sign" it goes to eat the berry.

Ancestral hominins would have learned to follow signs in the critically important task of fashioning stone hand-axes to cut through animal flesh and bone, to feed themselves. In crafting the edge of a round hand-ax from a flint stone, each flake knapped off the flint might pose, it could be imagined, a question of what precisely to do next. But the Boxgrove makers had learned that the visible *sign* of that edge exposed by the knapping was as an *indicator* pointing to something not yet fully visible, the finished cutting tool. And so they proceeded, one knock on the rock affecting the next in pursuit of a learned outcome. Hand-axes demonstrate the presence then of two crucial hominin attainments: the ability to remember and also to deploy what had been learned by previous generations. This is the essence of culture.[12]

As discussed in chapter 1, archaeological evidence finds that stone tools were in use as long as 3.3 million years ago,[13] and toolmaking behaviors,

Origins and Innovations **141**

involving repeated purposeful gestures that would have proved vital to survival, would have been passed down over a great many generations. This cultural activity over time would have had a significant effect on the environment, as the making of edged tools would have changed what could be hunted and gathered on the landscape. In turn, the control of fire to cook foods has been argued to have dramatically changed hominin diets and ultimately their genetic makeup.[14]

Such appears to be a standard feedback in the coevolutionary cycle of genes and culture. In that cycle an environment affects an organism, putting selective pressure on its genes, and, in turn, the organism affects the environment, creating "niches,"[15] and they coevolve. But in Tomlinson's view the repetition of such purposeful cognitive behaviors by successive hominin generations would have caused the behaviors to take on, in effect, a life of their own, becoming a "feedforward" mechanism (also called an "epicycle").

Feedforward is a crucial hypothesis of how human culture—and music—could have evolved. For example, over time hand-axes did become more sophisticated in their design as the sign-following movements used in making them refined, presumably partly in response to needs and opportunities in the environment.[16] Similarly, as the physical and vocal gesturing demonstrated their usefulness in daily life, the patterns of their signing arguably would have become elaborated and nuanced to express the shades of affect and intention that would be valuable to the increasingly complex social lives of hominins.[17] The various gestures would have cycled "forward" out of their own utility.

Following this logic, the system of signs embedded in physical movements and vocal gesturing would have, Tomlinson wrote, grown to be "more distinct and autonomous from everyday activities. ... They came to be distinct *choreographies* of bodies ... as well as *choruses* of raised voices."[18] The emergent "choreography" and "chorusing," became connected to ritual activities, he suggested.[19] Over time, such ritual practice shaped the emergence of the activities that we consider the arts,[20] including coordinated movement or dance and expressive language repeated to a set pattern, chanted, or sung. Yet for eons these activities would not have been thought of as "arts" but rather as instrumental to ritual.[21]

Evolutionary and learning scientist John Falk has also noted that the evident strong links between music, movement, and religious or spiritual activities in most societies suggest an original interconnection among these behaviors.[22] Philosopher and musician Anton Killin underlines the role of emotion in what he terms "social proto-music";[23] such communal events would have been a means to enhance the expression of emotion and feelings by and between individuals.

A precursor music-drama many tens of thousands of years in the past can be imagined, in which the meaningful gestures and patterned movements

142 Cultural Considerations Regarding Opera

performed arose out of the evolution of communication in the social life of ancestral humans and their need or desire for expression. The musical characteristics of purposeful sounds and pitches, distinctive timbres, and coordinated rhythms in moving bodies could all have served to express feelings and share some imagined realities. Although of course no physical artifact of such a performance remains from so long ago, there are good reasons to believe all these individual behaviors existed and the collective activity likely, as Ellen Dissanayake, the musical anthropologist, early observed.[24]Along with other cultural evolutionists, Joseph Henrich has argued that such a collective, in-person, experience of sharing information was not just an adornment of daily life but essential to who Sapiens are and our success as a species.[25] From the beginning "proto"-music-drama would have brought people together to engage with, learn from, and, presumably, appreciate each other.

Again, the vocal performance of a story always implied both a performer, to present the story, and an observer to watch and hear it and otherwise interact. In nearly all instances, the performance would have needed to be visible. Still today, tribal people gather around a fire, in the evening, to hear a story,[26] although such behavior is hardly limited to tribal communities. Performances do not have to occur this way, but the warmth of a fire can gather people, and its brightness can offer some gradations of lighting, as a performer appears in and disappears from the light. Even daylight with its shadows and changing colors, dawn to dusk, can help tell a story. Even the moon can. The only light that cannot help is no light. This natural condition suggests that light has always helped performance.

Light not only enables but also directs the attention of the listener and viewer. During documented cultural history, it is known that the stages in the ancient Greek theaters were oriented to exploit the changing angle of the sun.[27] Much later, the use of artificial light—oil and candles—and their positioning were developed in Italy in the sixteenth and seventeenth centuries, and refinements slowly occurred to better illuminate the stage and the performers in the following two centuries. Gas lighting, replacing candles and oil, offered a major improvement, with the Royal Opera House at Covent Garden being fitted for its use in 1817. Gas light increased the amount of light available, and its distribution, control, and directionality on stage, all of which affected performances and performers.[28] The pace of lighting technology then accelerated, with limelight, which permitted spotlighting, in use by mid-century, electric light by the 1880s,[29] and continuing advancements since then.

During the performance of operas since the seventeenth century each of these sophistications of lighting technology were innovations, and although talented individuals might be credited with them, each innovation built on earlier ones, all of them in service to a practical result. Innovation, then, is

Origins and Innovations **143**

better understood as not about solitary geniuses; fundamentally it is, again, about our species unique abilities as cultural learners to learn from each other an accumulated body of prior knowledge.[30] All of these innovations in lighting technology have been embraced by both opera composers and directors over the centuries, and they have been the topic of scholarly attention much beyond the overview attempted here.[31] But one example may be suggestive of the embrace.

Verdi had strong and clear views about how his operas should be staged,[32] and when he was not personally able to oversee a production, he often wrote to those involved detailing what he wanted, sometimes concerning the lighting. With a production of his *Macbeth* in 1848, he was explicit about how he wanted the Naples audience to see the moment when the witches expose Macbeth to the lineage of kings who will arise from the murdered Banquo:

> The apparition of the kings must take place behind a special opening at the back [of the stage], with a thin, ash-colored veil in front of it. The kings must not be puppets but eight men of flesh and blood. The spot they pass over must be a kind of mound, and you should be able to see them ascend and descend. The stage must be completely dark ... with light only where the kings are moving.[33]

In the 150 years since electric lighting allowed significant changes to the presentation of opera's stories, the most consequential technology to direct attention has arisen in cinema.

At the beginning of Act 3 of Puccini's *La Bohème*, Mimì has come in the wintry morning to where her friend Marcello is staying, hoping that he might help her by speaking with her lover, Rodolfo, with whom she has had a falling out. Mimì has a terrible cough and looks sickly; Marcello says he will try to help and suggests she go away. But she retreats just out of sight where she can watch and hear what the two men will say. Rodolfo comes out from the house and tells Rodolfo he wants to leave Mimì because of her flirtations with other men. Marcello doesn't believe him: "I have to say, you don't seem sincere."[34]

The music shudders to a pause.

The snow is landing on his hair and the shoulders of his thin coat as Rodolfo, his face in full view and now completely changed, admits, "All right then, no! I know that," he sings. Jealousy isn't the real issue.

The music launches into a minor key as he struggles with his feelings. "In vain, in vain, I'm trying to hide my real agony."

Rodolfo's voice soars to an extended high note with, "I love Mimì more than anything else in the world," the words momentarily breaking through the minor key.

144 Cultural Considerations Regarding Opera

Mimì's tired face suddenly fills the viewer's entire field of view. Mimì's skin is waxy-white, sickly, but her eyebrows rise, her face relaxes, and she smiles. Rodolfo's repeats adamantly, "I love her!" The view quickly returns to his face and his tortured expression, as Rodolfo continues, "but I am afraid ... I am afraid."

The wind whistles, the snowfall seems colder on pale Mimì as the viewer's attention is pulled back entirely to her expression, now wary, no longer smiling, as Rodolfo sings, "Mimì is terribly sick"; and she collapses into the nook in the wall from where she is listening to the men. Another angle of view immediately: Rodolfo slumps down next to his friend Marcello in the snow, "Every day she gets worse. The poor thing is doomed."

Mimì's eyes are wide as she presses herself out from the wall. We hear her think, "What does he mean?"

Unseen by the two men, she begins to walk toward them, unsteadily as if in a trance, teetering and looking toward the next wall for support. Not seeing her yet, Rodolfo continues to confide what Marcello already knows, that "a terrible cough wracks her body."

Turning, leaning against the wall for support, Mimì says softly, puzzled, "Oh my god ... I am going to die."

This summary attempts to convey the cinematic treatment of a scene from a 2008 film of the opera.[35] That perennial story and perennially popular lyric opera of "Bohemian" young love and heartbreak in 1830s Paris is consistently among the operas that receive the most performances annually, although the opera has both modern[36] and postmodern cultural critics.[37] This version of the opera, shot as a feature film (rather than as a film of a stage performance), starred young and telegenic Anna Netrebko and Rolando Villazón, both of them well-cast actor-singers. The production makes apparent several features of cinema that strongly affect how opera is received and appreciated. But modern audiences may be so accustomed to film that the origin of the medium and its use in this instance might not be recognized.

"Motion pictures," a sequence of photographic images, descended from photographic technology, which might appear to be the innovation of Louis Daguerre, who previously was a painter and stage designer for the Paris Opera. But the success of Daguerre's imaging process in 1839 was itself descended from observations and experiments made with silver nitrate in the eighteenth and seventeenth centuries,[38] and before then the understanding by chemists of silver and its reactions stretched back centuries.

When cinema was in its infancy, in 1896, two of its French innovators, the Lumière brothers, showed an audience a simple 50-second silent film in which a train pulled by a steam locomotive rumbled into a Paris train station.[39] The train kept coming forward in the direction of the film's spectators. Some viewers, reportedly, became terrified, apparently unable in the

Origins and Innovations **145**

moment to make the distinction that the film was in another reality, and some are said to have screamed and moved for the exit doors.[40]

Film seems capable of imitating life in a vivid manner that may look, at least initially, "real." The projected image appears to overcome the familiar framing of a physical theater. On the "big screen" the viewer does not see the stage, the wings, the proscenium arch. Space seems to open up, unobstructed (even though the image is framed, as if we are looking through a window).

Puccini offers what could be called a cinematic style of composition in this scene,[41] in which scenes are framed for typical purposes.[42] In cinema, wide and medium shots show the breadth of the scene and relationships of characters. Long and mid-shots show all or part of a single character. A medium close-up focuses on the head and shoulders, and a tight close-up only the face. A successful film director chooses each shot to provide important information. Puccini himself begins with, in effect, a wide shot of the arrival of Mimì, then a medium framing for the conversations between her and Marcello and then the latter and Rodolfo, and intensifies the drama with what would be close-ups of Rodolfo's declaration of love and her response to it. "This opera is very cinematic ... very easy to film," Netrebko noted.[43]

For the viewer, watching a movie involves a different relation to the drama than in an opera house, where each member of the audience has a different view of and connection to the drama on stage, depending on one's seat. The seat determines the angle of view and what one can see; the distance from the stage determines the field and scale of view and what one hears. The seat in the opera house is a constraint. The farther one is from the stage the more the difficulty seeing facial expressions, even though one might hear the singers well enough, though distantly, and understand the meaning of their broad gestures—broad because needing to be understood from a distance. By contrast, watching a movie either on a giant commercial screen or on a home monitor provides nearly everyone the same view, the same sound. Equal proximity brings advantages.

But in an opera house, movie theater, or home, a seat still expresses the same relationship to the drama, one of passive observer to the action happening on "stage." That "fourth wall" dividing spectators from performers stymies a communal experience to expressions of approval—applause, "bravo," standing ovations at the conclusion. What, if anything, to do about "breaking the fourth wall" has received a good deal of attention by theater directors and, in turn, by cultural historians during the past century.[44]

With a movie the spectator is at least gaining the advantage of reduced restriction on what is presented, even though the film's director (and editor) are continually directing where the audience looks and what it sees. Rather than questioning such directed vision or rebelling against it, viewers tend to follow along. One likely reason for this is that in the evolution of forms of communication, pointing gestures arose early, a half-million years ago

146 Cultural Considerations Regarding Opera

or earlier. Our nearest primate relatives, the chimps and other great apes, point, and such behavior also comes naturally to humans, who point and follow the gaze direction of others.

The director of the *Bohème* film, Robert Dornhelm, exploited human pre-verbal and nonverbal understanding[45] by directing the camera, and the audience's attention, selectively to specific framings of each moment in the opera. Consider, for example, the use of the close-up. Unless viewers in the opera house are using "opera glasses" or binoculars to improve their view, the camera can come in close not only more effectively but also with more purpose.

Dornhelm shows Anna Netrebko's face at two critical moments in response to what Mimì is hearing from Rodolfo. First, the few seconds in which Rodolfo declares he loves her "more than anything" is accomplished with a quick "dissolve" to her listening and relieved expression, and then returns to him, in a second, slower dissolve, which for an instant shows both of them. The alteration and composite view of their faces advances the story in a way possible only in film. But this first close-up of her is also a setup to provide a later contrast. As Rodolfo continues to sing he confesses his fear that she will die. Again, Netrebko's face appears, large and shocked.

A viewer understands the dire situation Mimì is in from what Rodolfo and Marcello have been saying and how they are behaving, and what the music sounds like. But seeing the face definitely matters. Mimì's dumbstruck response to Rodolfo's cry that she is "doomed" by her tuberculosis shows a subtle play of expression in her features that would simply not be seen beyond the first rows in the opera house. Such access is valuable because humans preferentially read faces for cues about what's happening in another's mind, doing that extremely quickly, within milliseconds and with very little deliberate effort.[46] Doing so, we generate our interpretation of another's mind (the "theory of mind"), which appears so vital to our competence as social animals.

This close-up of Mimì also exploits another capability that cinema affords that any traditional staged production could not have done. "What does he mean?" Mimì sings, very briefly.[47] But in the Dornhelm production we hear her voice but do not see her singing. She is talking to herself, a "voice-over." This hearing of the mind, though brief, shows how film can intensify the function of soliloquy: the audience obtains that rarity in human life, a "transparent" glimpse of another person's inner life. This bit of crucial interior thought adds to other visible effects of the close-up.

Most observers of these moments, except perhaps for those who have decided that Mimì's predicament manifests a cultural demeaning of women, may have a sympathetic emotional response to her. A scene that focuses on a crisis of courtship gains attention partly because, as noted previously, this is a critical juncture in most human lives. But *La Bohème* intensifies this interest and sympathy in this scene because the romantic crisis is linked to Mimì's terminal illness. By Act 3, she is evidently very sick, which the close shots in the Dornhelm film compel the viewer to see. Their instant effect has to do with the non-thinking functions of our brains. A viewer may also feel her shock and alarm. To a lesser degree, but *actually*.

This happens so commonly in response to performances of dramas that people may not recognize how unusual the phenomenon is. Why should we tear up when we see a character cry, or have a pleasant feeling when we someone else smile? The phenomenon has been recognized for a very long time. Aristotle, writing in 350 BCE, noted that "He who is affected either with joy or grief by the imitation of any objects is in very nearly the same situation as if he was affected by the objects themselves."[48] This was a striking observation, but "imitation" does not quite explain what causes these physical responses. Aristotle could not have known. The discovery of "mirror neurons" in 1992 held the promise of putting on a fundamental biological basis such astonishing social behavior that humans likely always experienced but could not adequately explain.

Neurons, the wiring of the brain, connect incoming stimulus to outgoing response, sensory input to behavioral output. Two qualities of mirror neurons, found in several sections of the brain, make them important. Crucially, they are motor neurons, and they are activated whether one is doing or perceiving someone else doing a particular behavior, such as smiling. Hence, the "mirror" phenomenon, tantalizingly described in 2008 by one of the original researchers, Marco Iacoboni: "When I see you smiling, my mirror neurons for smiling fire up, too, initiating a cascade of neural activity that evokes the feeling we typically associate with a smile."[49]

Rapidly expanding human research followed the discovery of mirror neurons,[50] and scientists and scholars in many fields beyond neuroscience became intrigued and involved in studying this capability of the brain, which seemed so primary in the behavior of social animals. Mirror neurons might help explain the emotional power of dramatic performances—that human feelings *could*, in effect, be engaged automatically. As with every active field of scientific research, details and qualifications continuously emerge about mirror neurons from those studying them.[51] Brain research has found that a mirror neuron "system" is involved in emotion recognition and theory of mind.[52] That system helps us recognize and interpret another's feelings from that person's face.[53] When I see Mimì looking alarmed, instantly I may feel alarmed.

At opera's peak of popularity in the nineteenth century, that popularity depended on generating a rich experience for its viewers, often discussed as a kind of artistic smorgasbord, something for everybody. But opera was the highest art, declared Richard Wagner, in his "The Art-Work of the Future," because all its component associated arts were brought to perfection in their

148 Cultural Considerations Regarding Opera

unity in music-drama.[54] To Wagner's claim, contemporary research can add that opera's power derives from the combination of many arresting modes of communication. As noted, these include the directed gesture of acting, the patterned movement of dancing, the emotive language of song, its complement in instrumental music, and the engagement of a story imitating life, all of which have emerged with humans.

From the perspective of cultural evolution, cinema can be recognized as a "descent with modification" from music-drama. Opera created and occupied a certain cultural niche in its unification and presentation of coordinated arts. Cinema exploited that unification and presentation, unrolling a form that, while different, had the capacity to replace it in that cultural niche. Starting around 1907, as the technical means to produce longer films became available and a broad public audience was emerging, filmmakers turned to opera as a theatrical storytelling mode with which the public was familiar, and which they recognized their own medium had similarities to.

In France, for example, adaptations of operas were extremely popular beginning about 1908–1910, with an estimate of some 70 films produced;[55] and more than 150 opera-related films were produced before 1926.[56] In Italy, the legacy of opera was evident in additional ways. Early "silent" movies were, in practice, not actually silent, as they were screened to the accompaniment of live or recorded music, which in Italy often came from the operatic repertoire.[57] The exaggerated gestures and emotions the early film actors portrayed reflected a cliché of opera; and movies otherwise imitated opera for the dramatic style and the content of early feature films.[58]

Even while the early cinema appropriated from opera significant elements of style and content and theatrical media, not until recorded sound—speech and music, primarily—became an integrated part of cinema starting in the late 1920s could this new "artwork of the future" reach its potential. As it became the more popular theatrical art, at least part of cinema's popularity had to do with its wide range of stories, some of which were sure to relate to the lives of its broad and diverse audience. Economies of scale also favored cinema. Motion picture studios could crank out many more films during the period of time it would take a single qualified composer to compose an opera and have it produced. Moreover, all those films, theoretically addressing a wide range of audiences and interests, could be distributed to many theaters in many countries, dramatically enlarging the cultural niche for this dramatic art. Meanwhile the premiere of that composer's opera might be seen in just one or a very few venues.

Some cinema directors recognized the potential of their medium to offer fresh experiences to opera audiences. Operas conceived as cinema (like the 2008 *La Bohème*) have been produced since the 1930s.[59] Major film directors such as Ingmar Bergman and Franco Zeffirelli have made such opera films.

Audiences may expect new performance styles or even forms of opera, using "moving pictures," such as opera created to be heard primarily or only as a video recording, or made solely for Internet viewing, such as *desert in*, "an operatic, episodic story of love, loss, and redemption" whose eight episodes log almost three hours in duration.[60] In the third decade of this century, the opportunities for entering imaginative virtual worlds are many.

The worldwide users of smartphones numbered more than 3 billion in 2020 and was growing by about 8% per year.[61] Many people are involved playing story-based games, often with others, on those devices or other personal computers. "Virtual Reality" devices, such as enclosing headsets worn by users, appear poised to become another significant entertainment technology. The worldwide market for "VR" is forecast to grow rapidly[62] as people find interest in simulated sensory experiences that are sometimes similar to but sometimes completely different from those of the real world. Perhaps on-site "augmented reality" will strongly engage opera audiences in this century. Both "VR" and "AR" approaches to operas have begun to be tried.[63] In 2023, for example, Wagner's lengthy *Parsifal* was given a full AR treatment at the composer's home theater at Bayreuth (but to mixed reviews).[64] Also in 2023 Google was hosting "Blob Opera," which promised anyone the chance to "create your own opera inspired song!"[65]

Various "species" arise and disappear during the evolution of culture, and presumably always will. Innovations arise from incremental improvements, recombination of existing features, and, occasionally, serendipity.[66] No outcome is certain, but to the degree that music-drama brings performers and spectators closer together it seems more likely to survive, and maybe even flourish.

Notes

1 Joseph Kerman, *Opera as Drama*, New and rev. ed. (Berkeley: University of California Press, 1988), 1.
2 C. Abbate and R. Parker, *A History of Opera* (New York: W.W. Norton, 2015), xv.
3 Eric Csapo and Margaret Christina Miller, "General Introduction," in *The Origins of Theater in Ancient Greece and Beyond: From Ritual to Drama*, ed. E. Csapo and M. C. Miller (Cambridge, UK: Cambridge University Press, 2007).
4 The increase was from about 611 to 1,457 cubic centimeters, i.e., about 2.4 times. Table 2 in van Holstein, "Hominin Evolution," 8.
5 Numerical data, Elisabeth A. Murray et al., "The Story of Your Life: Memories All Your Own," in *The Evolutionary Road to Human Memory* (Oxford: Oxford University Press, 2019), 165.
6 Matthew Pope, Simon Parfitt, and Mark Roberts, *The Horse Butchery Site: A High-Resolution Record of Lower Palaeolithic Hominin Behaviour at Boxgrove* (Portslade, UK: Spoilheap Publications, 2020).
7 However, that species identification has been broadly challenged: Mirjana Roksandic et al., "Resolving the "Muddle in the Middle": The Case for Homo

150 Cultural Considerations Regarding Opera

Bodoensis Sp. Nov," *Evolutionary Anthropology: Issues, News, and Reviews* n/a, no. Online prior (2021).

8 80% calculated from table 2 in van Holstein, "Hominin Evolution," 8.

9 See broad discussion in Iain Morley, "Vocal Control and Corporeal Control—Vocalization, Gesture, Rhythm, Movement, and Emotion," in *The Prehistory of Music* (Oxford: Oxford University Press, 2013).

10 The term favoured by Gary Tomlinson, who provides a succinct account starting at 16:55 in: Yale University, "In the Company of Scholars: 'One Million Years of Music: The Emergence of Human Modernity,'" YouTube video, 1:15:31, April 16, 2014, http://youtu.be/_B5DtgzM-m4.

11 Yale University, "The Third Algorithm: The evolution of human culture," YouTube video, 1:11:48, May 1, 2019, http://youtu.be/HFwUDBYLo9g

12 Tomlinson, *Culture and the Course of Human Evolution*, "Introduction," 1.

13 Jessica C. Thompson et al., "Taphonomy of Fossils from the Hominin-Bearing Deposits at Dikika, Ethiopia," *Journal of Human Evolution* 86 (2015): 112–135.

14 Richard Wrangham, *Catching Fire: How Cooking Made Us Human* (Basic Books: 2009).

15 Felix Riede, "Niche Construction Theory and Human Biocultural Evolution," in *Handbook of Evolutionary Research in Archaeology*, ed. Anna Marie Prentiss (Cham, Switzerland: Springer International Publishing, 2019).

16 Yale University, "The Third Algorithm," lecture by G. Tomlinson discusses evolution from Achulean axes to Levallois "cores."

17 See "the principle of elaboration" in Tomlinson, *Culture*, 149.

18 Ibid., 158.

19 Ibid., 158–159. Emphases in original.

20 Most anthropological/ethnographic research shows that most artistic behaviour in contemporary hunter-gatherer societies is embedded in ritual, and so the assumption is made that this was the case for the ancient hunter-gatherer societies when the arts first emerged. Derek Hodgson and Jan Verpooten, "The Evolutionary Significance of the Arts: Exploring the By-Product Hypothesis in the Context of Ritual, Precursors, and Cultural Evolution," *Biological Theory* 10, no. 1 (2014): 75.

21 See Ellen Dissanayake, "Ritual and Ritualization: Musical Means of Conveying and Shaping Emotion in Humans and Other Animals," in *Music and Manipulation: On the Social Uses and Social Control of Music*, ed. Steven Brown and Ulrich Voglsten (Oxford and New York: Berghahn Books, 2006).

22 John H. Falk, *Born to Choose: Evolution, Self, and Well-Being* (New York: Routledge, 2018), 185–186. For many citations exploring the relationship between rhythmic behaviour and social cohesion, see D. van der Schyff and A. Schiavio, "Evolutionary Musicology Meets Embodied Cognition: Biocultural Coevolution and the Enactive Origins of Human Musicality," *Frontiers in Neuroscience* 11 (2017): 6.

23 Anton Killin, "The Origins of Music," *Music & Science* 1 (2018): 4.

24 Ellen Dissanayake, "The Earliest Narratives Were Musical," *Research Studies in Music Education* 34, no. 1 (2012): 7

25 Joseph Henrich, *The Secret of Our Success* (Princeton, NJ: Princeton University Press, 2016), 5.

26 Killin, "Origins," 4.

27 Linda Essig, "A Primer for the History of Stage Lighting," *Performing Arts Resources* 25 (2007): 1. This useful article goes far beyond my use of it.

28 Ibid., 5.

29 Ibid.

30 Michael Muthukrishna and Joseph Henrich, "Innovation in the Collective Brain," *Philosophical Transactions of the Royal Society B: Biological Sciences* 371, no. 1690 (2016).

31 For example, Tom Sutcliffe, *Believing in Opera* (Princeton, NJ: Princeton University Press, 1996). and P. Fryer, *Opera in the Media Age: Essays on Art, Technology and Popular Culture* (Jefferson, NC: McFarland, 2014).

32 See Frank Walker, "Verdi's Ideas on the Production of His Shakespeare Operas," *Proceedings of the Royal Musical Association* 76 (1949).

33 Charles Osborne, *Letters of Giuseppe Verdi* (New York: Holt, Rinehart and Winston, 1972), 60. Letter 53 to Cammarano.

34 The excerpted translation of Act 3, scene 1 is mine. G. Puccini, *La Bohème*, libretto by G. Giacosa and L. Illica, 1896. Italian libretto: http://www.opera-arias.com/puccini/la-boh%C3%A8me/libretto/

35 G. Puccini, *La Bohème*, libretto by G. Giacosa and L. Illica, 1896. Film directed by Robert Dornhelm, Kultur DVD D4601, 2009.

36 Example: D. H. Lawrence, *D. H. Lawrence and Italy: Twilight in Italy: Sea and Sardinia. Etruscan Places* (Viking Press, 1972), 63. "In every age, in every clime, she is dear, at least to the masculine soul, this soft, tear-blenched, blonde, ill-used thing."

37 Example: Sandra Corse, ""Mi Chiamano Mimì": The Role of Women in Puccini's Operas," *The Opera Quarterly* 1, no. 1 (1983).

38 See "The Evolution of Film" in Time-Life Books, *Light and Film*, Life Library of Photography (New York: Time-Life Books, 1970).

39 *The Arrival of a Train at La Ciotat.*

40 Anecdote in Nimish Biloria and Bernhard Hommel Xin Xia, "From Film Studies to Interaction Design—an Emergent Aesthetic View," in *Embodied Aesthetics: Proceedings of the 1st International Conference on Aesthetics and the Embodied Mind, August 26–28, 2013* (Leiden, The Netherlands: Brill, 2013), 121.

41 Deborah Burton, "Ariadne's Threads: Puccini and Cinema," *Studi Musicali-Nuova Serie*, no. 1 (2012): 2.

42 Evidence is lacking that *Bohème* was affected by cinema in 1896.

43 Jitin Hingorani, "Interview with Anna Netrebko," December 16, 2009. Great Performances, http://www.pbs.org/wnet/gperf/la-boheme-interview-with-anna-netrebko/896/.

44 Susan Bennett, *Theatre Audiences*, 2nd ed. (London: Routledge, 1997). devotes about 80 pages to "the audience and the theatre."

45 A deeper examination of cognition and film: Tony E. Jackson, "Visual Cognition in the Prelude to *Citizen Kane*." *Style* 49, no. 4 (2015): 494–511.

46 Philippe G. Schyns, Lucy S. Petro, and Marie L. Smith, "Transmission of Facial Expressions of Emotion Co-evolved with Their Efficient Decoding in the Brain: Behavioral and Brain Evidence," *PLOS One* 4, no. 5 (2009): e5625.

47 Italian: "*Che vuol dire?*"

48 *Politics*, Book VIII in Aristotle, *The Politics and Economics of Aristotle*, trans. Edward Walford (London: H. G. Bohn, 1853), 280

49 Jonah Lehrer, "The Mirror Neuron Revolution: Explaining What Makes Humans Social," *Scientific American*, July 1, 2008, 2.

50 Hundreds of experiments carried out with a variety of techniques (positron emission tomography, functional magnetic resonance imaging, etc. Pier Francesco Ferrari and Giacomo Rizzolatti, "Mirror Neuron Research: The Past and the Future," *Philosophical Transactions of the Royal Society B: Biological Sciences* 369, no. 1644 (2014): 1.

51 Claims that have appeared too broad have been contested. A scientific review, for example, found that mirror neurons are "involved" in *recognizing* and

152 Cultural Considerations Regarding Opera

discriminating observed actions as part of a complex mental process: E. L. Thompson, G. Bird, and C. Catmur, "Conceptualizing and Testing Action Understanding," *Neuroscience & Biobehavioral Reviews* 105 (2019): 106–114.

52 Stephanie N. L. Schmidt et al., "Fmri Adaptation Reveals: The Human Mirror Neuron System Discriminates Emotional Valence," *Cortex* 128 (2020): 275.

53 Ibid.

54 Richard Wagner, *The Art-Work of the Future*, trans. William Ashton Ellis, The Wagner Library ed., vol. 1, Richard Wagner's Prose Works (1895), 81.

55 Rose Theresa, "From Mephistopheles to Melies: Spectacle and Narrative in Opera and Early Film," ed. Jeongwon Joe and Rose Theresa, eds., *Between Opera and Cinema* (New York: Routledge, 2002). 7.

56 Theresa, *Spectacle*, 7.

57 A. Mallach, *The Autumn of Italian Opera: From Verismo to Modernism, 1890–1915* (Boston: Northeastern University Press, 2007), 361.

58 Grandiose historic melodramas, like the most famous Italian feature film of the 1910s, *Cabiria*, superficially imitated the sets, costumes, and histrionics of grand opera, earning such melodramas the name "silent opera."

59 Charpentier's opera *Louise* was filmed in 1938, for example.

60 As of early 2023 available on Boston Lyric Opera's operabox.tv (http://www.operabox.tv/desert-in).

61 Estimate by Kepios Pte. Ltd., "Digital Around the World," October 2020, accessed November 14, 2020. http://datareportal.com/global-digital-overview.

62 "Virtual reality set to grow significantly," Thomas Alsop, Aug. 2, 2021, http://www.statista.com/topics/2532/virtual-reality-vr/

63 "Welcome to a Virtual World of Opera," Welsh National Opera, archived 2017/2018, http://wno.org.uk/archive/2017-2018/magic-butterfly; and "Follow the Fox with our new AR experience, A Vixen's Tale," Welsh National Opera, October 4, 2019, http://wno.org.uk/news/a-vixens-tale. Both URLs also contain videos to show the VR and AR products.

64 "Snapdragon" (anon. author), "Space and Time experienced anew: *Parsifal* in Augmented Reality at the Bayreuth Festival," Aug. 1, 2023, http://bachtrack.com/opera-event/parsifal-bayreuther-festspielhaus-25-july-2023/379767. See performance review referenced at URL.

65 http://artsandculture.google.com/experiment/blob-opera/AAHWrq360NcGbw?hl=en

66 Muthukrishna, "Innovation," 4–5.

10
AFFORDING EXTRAORDINARY EXPERIENCES

Les Troyens, Akhnaten

After all, if one may be so blunt and risky, what is art?

Often it is recognized as a form (drama, poetry, opera, etc.). Often it is defined by certain qualities (beauty, skill, etc.). But at root art is a human behavior that, broadly, calls and sustains attention, and makes something special.[1] Art is said to open the doors of perception[2] and reveal something not so recognized before, typically novel, often surprising. One means by which this occurs with narrative arts like opera is to transport the observer into its imagined world and afford extraordinary experiences there. Operas of Hector Berlioz and Phillip Glass provide examples.

Berlioz was a leading example of a nineteenth-century "Romantic" artist,[3] one who emphasized emotion, aesthetics, and individual imagination in comparison to the emphases on dispassionate reason, science, and philosophy of the previous era, the Enlightenment.[4] Too much can be made of a sharp break between the two eras.[5] Nonetheless, clear differences in subject matter and style are evident between Mozart and Berlioz, for example; and the writers Voltaire and Victor Hugo; and the painters Jacques-Louis David and Caspar David Friedrich.

Starting with his semi-autobiographical *Symphonie Fantastique* in 1830, Berlioz's unconventional behavior and music kept him from being embraced by the French musical establishment. Nevertheless, he persisted on his own path as a music critic and essayist, conductor, and, chiefly, composer. His operas are distinctive and culminate with his masterwork, *Les Troyens* (*The Trojans*), completed in 1858. The two-part, five-act opera is a retelling of the violent end of the legendary Trojan War and the flight of the surviving Trojans to Carthage, where they briefly help the Carthaginians, themselves a recently displaced people, defeat an enemy. But the Trojans depart to a

DOI: 10.4324/9781003254478-14

154 Cultural Considerations Regarding Opera

new homeland for themselves, Italy, which ultimately will destroy Carthage. So, this ambitious opera concerns itself with nothing less than a key recurring pattern in human history, the fall and rise and fall of peoples and civilizations.[6]

One reason that rise and fall has enduring resonance as a story is that it is the experience of humans in social groups for at least 15,000 years[7] and probably longer. Evolution collected this mid-sized mammal with the large brain into extended family groups to defend themselves, survive, and successfully reproduce, but that process put groups in contact with each other. Cooperation or competition inevitably followed, with danger to the group and to the individual always a possibility, never more real than in an attack on one's home.

That attack is the comprehensive subject of the first part of *The Trojans*, subtitled "The Fall of Troy." Berlioz drew his story from the Roman epic poem, *The Aeneid*, completed by Virgil about 19 BCE. *The Aeneid* built on that earlier seminal epic of Western culture, *The Iliad*. All that story, which is considered to be, in part, about a historic event in the twelfth century BCE, was first the subject of an oral storytelling tradition and later written down and attributed to Homer in about the eighth century BCE. The composer had known the story of the Trojan War since his childhood—in fact, he was named for the hero Hector—and he could have reasonably assumed that many literate Europeans of his own time would be at least somewhat familiar with the *Aeneid*, as for centuries it was a core text in education, especially of the elites.[8]

Berlioz wrote both the opera's libretto and music. In his telling, the great movements of history and whole civilizations are ultimately moved by individuals who have complicated allegiances not only to their social roles but also—very clearly—to their own physical selves. This is exactly what one might expect in the course of war and from an evolutionary understanding of well-being with our constantly negotiating physical survival, individual needs, and social responsibilities. But Berlioz emphasizes the living body, its triumph and sensuousness, along with its pain and loss.

An early illustration of this emphasis occurs in the fifth and sixth scenes of Act 1. In the former, the Trojan people celebrate what they believe is the departure of the Greeks after ten years of war, as the Greek ships have left the beach where they were long docked—and they have left behind a giant wooden horse, which appears to be a peace offering. So, in believing themselves victorious, the Trojans praise their gods through a hymn and then through a high-spirited dance of their warriors, moving to music with Berlioz's characteristic, idiosyncratic rhythmic energy. Often staged as quite a rough-and-tumble affair of proud men with strong and lithe bodies watched by happy onlookers, the knowing theater audience nevertheless will witness the "Wrestlers' Dance" with some misgiving. The celebration

Affording Extraordinary Experiences **155**

quickly changes as the wife and young son of Hector arrive, in mourning. Hector, prince of Troy and its main defender, has recently been killed by the Greek champion, Achilles.

This next, sixth scene is likely emotionally affecting, for several reasons. First is the dramatic action itself, which is in stark contrast to the preceding dance but again gives priority to the movement of bodies. Andromache, Hector's wife, is still grieving him, but silently, and she seeks and takes comfort by reaching out and embracing other Trojans gathered there. "This immense sorrow," the chorus of men and women observes softly; "Oh, destiny!"

Andromache next approaches the king and queen to accept the silent condolences expressed in their faces; and her young son, Astyanax, is presented to and blessed by the king and queen. In Berlioz's own stage directions, Andromache then is overcome by tears, and the Trojans sympathetically draw apart to let weeping mother and son pass slowly away from them. In some productions, such as one introduced at the Metropolitan Opera in 2003, the body of Hector is also present in the scene. Carried in by his comrades, the soldiers then lay hands on the body in a sign of respect for the best of them, and some women begin to weep. Andromache kneels down to put her face next to her dead husband, and she cries out when, after some moments, the men begin to raise the body for its final transport. Many of the warriors, linked arm to shoulder, follow Hector's bier away.

How often such a scene of mourning over a fallen leader must have occurred in human history. An audience may be moved, as Berlioz's Trojans are, in recognizing this repeated "imitation" of life and its significance. Over eons of history such a loss has often meant greater danger to those who remain.

Contemporary research also finds that, in general, people tend to attribute greater meaning to emotionally extreme life experiences,[9] which this scene imitates, offering an explanation for the scene's impact.[10] Why story meaning and emotional extremity would be linked in evolution was proposed in Gottschall's notion that a purpose of stories is to allow understanding troubles before they occur.[11]

The second extraordinary and potentially moving feature of this scene is that, except for occasional hushed comments by the choral onlookers, there is no other singing and only a spare orchestral accompaniment for nearly all the stage action. Given the acoustic tumult of other scenes, the very subdued music of this "pantomime"[12] marks a brilliant contrast that likely surprises and draws the viewer in. A solo clarinet sets the overall tone of lament, leading the pacing of the onstage movements through a few changes in sonority. But it is the pantomime itself that arguably goes deepest to move the audience. Berlioz's detailed stage directions guide not only the actions but also the feelings of those actions. For example, Andromache is described as

156 Cultural Considerations Regarding Opera

holding her son to her with "convulsive tenderness" (l'embrasse avec une tendresse convulsive).

Any description of the scene of mourning must be a pale substitute for the actions an audience observes, especially when those actions mimic significant human experiences. But the specific movements, the actors' gestures, again matter greatly. As discussed in the previous chapter, gesture may speak louder than words because our species likely communicated by gesture long before language as we know it had evolved.[13] Still today, without any words, we follow in the direction of a pointing finger or appraise a relationship in an embrace. With pantomime Berlioz appears to be communicating by very ancient, instinctive means, a third likely cause for the scene's emotional resonance.

These scenes offer a type of rare experience. The first, with the lively dancing, sets up a pointed contrast to the second, with its stunned, deliberate processional, illuminating great love, disastrous loss, and human respect.

In the first century CE, an essayist known as Longinus[14] wrote that "The Sublime, wherever it occurs" in literature, "consists of a certain loftiness and excellence of language."[15] But "a lofty passage does not convince the reason of the reader, but takes him out of himself, [as] the Sublime, acting with an imperious and irresistible force, sways every reader whether he will or no." Then "having acquired a certain ... loftiness, [the reader or observer] is filled with joy as if [he or she] had created what was heard."[16]

Berlioz's sixth scene with Andromache, her son, her dead husband, the defender of his community, and the community itself, possesses all the dramatic ingredients lending to a sublime experience for the audience. But "joy," while it may be too quickly criticized here, is amended by a definition of the sublime offered by the essayist Edmund Burke seventeen centuries after Longinus: "Whatever is fitted in any sort to excite the ideas of pain and danger ... is a source of the sublime; that is, it is productive of the strongest emotion which the mind is capable of feeling."

"The most powerful of all the passions," Burke wrote, are those that are caused by pain and danger, because they threaten "the preservation of the individual."[17] In such a moment of life as scene 6 presents, the real participants—any embattled human community since our species' history began— would likely feel the "strongest emotions." Sublime experiences, despite the apparently rarified cultural name, are at root physical phenomena.

In research during recent decades, scientists from various psychological disciplines, evolutionary biology, and neuroscience describe what appears to add up to identical or very similar findings with slightly different terms about this phenomenon. That is in the nature of scientific disciplines, their specialty training, their focus, methods, and jargons. But whether they are studying "sublime" experiences or experiences of "awe," "peak" experiences or "strong experiences with music," certain findings are repeated and a common picture begins to emerge.

Recent research summarizes the features of a sublime or awe experience as follows.[18] It usually arises unexpectedly or suddenly, as a kind of surprise that directs attention[19] to some situation or circumstance that the observer perceives to be of great size, magnitude,[20] or significance.[21] Furthermore, it precipitates a stunned response[22] of astonishment, often with a sense that time is suspended or slowed. This response is accompanied by distinctive physiological reactions, such as "goose bumps," teary eyes, or hair standing up on neck.[23] A feeling of *being moved* arises,[24] which usually crests to an emotional peak[25] of joy or, sometimes, fear. The emotional response usually transitions to a comprehension[26] and interpretation[27] of the moment that may have initially overwhelmed the observer, including some better understanding of human life.

Acute listeners to music know this experience. A moment (or scene) of "lofty" expression exerts an "imperious force" that "sways" or moves the observer into something inexpressible, "ineffable," at least temporarily. So thought Charles Darwin: "These powerful and mingled feelings [accompanying music] may well give rise to the sense of sublimity ... We can concentrate ... greater intensity of feeling in a single musical note than in pages of writing."[28] The twentieth-century philosopher Vladimir Jankélévitch added, "The ineffable, thanks to its properties of fecundity and inspiration, acts like a form of enchantment. ... Ineffability provokes bewilderment [and] unleashes a state of verve."[29]

"Many people experience intensely positive affective states in response to music," the psychologists Alf Gabrielsson and John Sloboda summarized in 2016 about "peak experiences with music":

> The intensity of these experiences often brings about a sense of transcendence and transformation, and their relative rarity makes them greatly prized in the minds and lives of the individuals experiencing them. People tend to retain vivid memories of such experiences many years after they have occurred, and they are often cited as a major reason for continued involvement with music.[30]

Another such moment occurs later in *Les Troyens*. Aeneas is the major character of Virgil's *Aeneid* and of Berlioz's opera (though a minor character in the *Iliad*, very second in prestige to Hector.) When the Greeks emerge from the "Trojan Horse" and sack Troy, it is Aeneas who rallies the surviving Trojans and helps them escape across the Mediterranean to Carthage, a new city founded by Queen Dido after she and her compatriots from Tyre fled from another war. But almost immediately after the Trojans land there, the Carthaginians are attacked by a neighboring African people. Aeneas and the Trojans help defeat the attackers.

158 Cultural Considerations Regarding Opera

Victorious in battle, Aeneas returns to Dido, and the two become lovers. During a unique and daring wordless scene composed for orchestra, dancers, chorus, and pantomime, Berlioz has Dido and Aeneas appear on stage during a royal hunt and take refuge together in a cave during a storm. In case there is any doubt about what happens inside the cave, two of Dido's courtiers discuss the romance of the leaders in the scene immediately following.

One minister frets that Dido has given up building her nation in pursuit of pleasure with Aeneas, even though the Trojan will be drawn "inexorably by fate to Italy" to found Rome. And so for the remainder of the opera the conflict between private love and public duty comes center stage, here between leaders of their people, who have their own ambitions and desires—and those motives having consequences of harmony or danger for them all.

Dido had put all her energy into creating a new life for her people in Carthage following the death of her husband. But when Aeneas tells Dido that Andromache herself has, since Troy's demise, become the wife of her Greek captor, the shocked Dido says in an aside, this "absolves her heart" from her previous sense of obligation to her husband, also killed in war. She repeats and absorbs this change of perspective while those around her, Aeneas and others, observe and comment; and the absolution of Dido's heart is dramatically and musically achieved. At this moment, along with a change in the musical key to a very different tonality,[31] Aeneas invites Dido to "banish sad memories" and go outside with him into a "night of splendor and enchantment." She does, and the others attending these two, backed by an offstage chorus, join them in a remarkable septet, singing:

> All is peace and enchantment around us;
> Night spreads its veil and the sleeping sea
> Murmurs the softest harmonies.

The French of Berlioz is inspired, with soft and murmuring vowel-sounds and their echoes underlining the meaning:

> *Tout n'est que paix et charme autour de nous!*
> *La nuit étend son voile et la mer endormie*
> *Murmure en sommeillant les accords les plus doux.*[32]

An equally rhapsodic presence is the orchestra, which establishes a harmonic thrumming in imitation of the murmuring sea. In its wave-like, repetitive, yet peaceful rocking between tones, the orchestra creates a kind of hypnotic ground of enchantment, while the singers' voices wrap caressingly around each other in long, repeated phrases. The length of the musical phrases and their general downward motion also imitate the characteristic voice-pattern of people wanting to be calm.[33] A love duet for Dido and Aeneas follows the septet, their voices weaving together celebrating a "night of rapture and boundless ecstasy" (Nuit d'ivresse et d'exstase infinie!). If paced rather slowly, on stage the duet may suggest what Berlioz wrote at the end of his *Memoirs,* that while "love cannot give an idea of music," music "can give an idea of love."[34] This scene of temporary timelessness, rapture, and joy again meets characteristics of a sublime experience, sweetly though strongly presented.

Psychologist Alf Gabrielsson has studied "strong experiences in music," whose key features he describes as "their positivity, powerfulness, rarity, nonvoluntary nature," and "strong, intense emotions and some emotional, physical, perceptual, and cognitive correlates." Finally, "the peak has even been called indescribable."[35]

An audience member simply may *feel* "moved" by the love duet; and feeling moved by art deserves attention, as it appears a common desire of audiences. A team of researchers led by Winfried Menninghaus reported their findings on the psychology of being moved in 2015, noting that the great majority of the scenarios that moved participants in their studies are associated with "significant relationship and critical life events (especially death, birth, marriage, separation, and reunion)" and:

> Sadness and joy turned out to be the two preeminent emotions involved in episodes of being moved. ... Moreover, being moved ... was experienced as an emotional state of high intensity; this applied to responses to fictional artworks no less than to own-life and other real, but media-represented, events.[36]

Why people would *want* to be "moved" by art, by opera, may be suggested by the English word itself and by this research. People want to be moved up and out of a lower-intensity emotional state by observing "critical life events" just as those might happen to them. However, the preceding discussion, largely from a scientific and cultural-evolution perspective, would be challenged by a cultural-history perspective expressed by musicologist Susan McClary, generally discussing "romantic" operas:

> There is nothing sillier than seeing a love story sung on stage. Opera is grotesque when one takes the slightest distance on it and sublime when one goes along with identification. The plot works quietly, plainly visible to all. ... It is totally dull, always setting in play vague philosophical premises, ordinary banalities, life-love-death; it is all familiar and forgettable. But, beyond the romantic ideology lines are being woven, tying up the characters and leading them to death for transgression—for transgressions of familial rules, political rules, the things at stake in sexual and authoritarian power. That is what it is all about.[37]

160 Cultural Considerations Regarding Opera

True, Dido is soon abandoned by Aeneas. He is driven by a nightmare in which his kin call for him to lead the Trojans to Italy where they can establish their own progeny as Romans.[38] As the last surviving hereditary leader of his Trojan tribe, Aeneas finds it impossible to walk away from this responsibility; the consequence might be the end of the Trojans as a distinct group. This matters, as Berlioz in the nineteenth century, Virgil 20 centuries before, and Homer 7 centuries before him would have recognized. Sapiens learned long ago about the risks of losing group prerogatives, most decisively through warfare. No group, tribe, or nation wants to be erased by war, as the Trojans in Carthage risk.

Asking Dido's forgiveness, Aeneas departs, and, at the end, Dido commits suicide. Whether that death is "all about" McClary's "transgressions of familial rules, political rules, the things at stake in sexual and authoritarian power" sounds plausible. But in this opera itself, Dido's suicide seems more willful, an extreme act by a proud individual, a queen who feels humiliated.

So-called new historicist criticism has been labeled one of those postmodern theories[39] that view human events and, in this case, fictional human events, as "texts" subject to interpretations that may be at odds with what the original creator apparently intended. "New Historicism has a motto," wrote Michael Warner: 'The text is historical, and history is textual': the first part means that meaning does not transcend context but is produced within it."[40]

From that postmodern perspective *Les Troyens* can be considered a text about, and in agreement with, Western imperialist dominance.[41] This mid-nineteenth-century music-drama about the fall and rise of civilizations lands on Roman, and, by extension, European dominance, while the Trojans at Troy, the Tyreans, the Carthaginians, their African opponents—all from the Near East or Africa—are swept into the dustbin of history. During the 1850s France was indeed colonizing parts of Africa, and Berlioz seems to end on the side of public duty, colonizing glory, and the inevitability of a particular Eurocentric history, despite the human costs.

However, that triumphalist Eurocentric conclusion is too pat, too much a reduction and simplification of *Les Troyens*. The opera is deeply sympathetic to the victims—all the Trojans, the Carthaginians, Dido, Aeneas himself—who do as well as they can, struggling in the grip of an "*inexorable loi*"—the apparently inexorable law, the power of forces seemingly beyond control, which the prophet Cassandra laments at the start of the opera.[42] Berlioz and the French of his time would have received sufficient exposure to the consequences to them of forces beyond their control, including the French Revolution and "Reign of Terror," Napoleon Bonaparte, and King Louis-Philippe and the Revolution of 1848.

What forces push history? A "new historicist," a Marxist, an anti-imperialist, a feminist would have their own perspectives. An evolutionist would include the evolved human drive to survive and to perpetuate kin, first of all, and our dispositions to fight, to cooperate, to believe in illusions and imagined realities, and to value now more than the future.[43]

Perhaps a contemporary example is not out of place. In the 2020s, human civilization is facing the extreme, unprecedented risks associated with global warming. Some people can imagine the future and its dangers, like Cassandra in our earliest Western story. But most people do not attend to future risks and stay in the grip of now, as did the imagined Trojans. Blame today could be centered on the lack of global political leadership or an ideological fealty to economic growth at any cost, or the absence of a persuasive Cassandra[44] who offers a motivating story of collective action and advantage.[45] Overall, we humans apparently have not *seen* how extraordinary is the challenge of this time nor how to respond in time.

"My task which I am trying to achieve is, by the power of the written word, to make you hear, to make you feel — it is, before all, to make you *see*," wrote the novelist Joseph Conrad.[46] In presenting the extraordinary, art has the potential to change our ordinary and accustomed minds, or, perhaps. to reveal what we've always possessed.

With opera, the extraordinary has to do with voice, and not solely or even primarily the voice of performers. In *The Composer's Voice*, musicologist Edward T. Cone called that voice "an intelligence in the act of thinking through the musical work."[47] Music and opera historian Carolyn Abbate praised Cone for "insisting upon a conception of music as 'sung' through time, as originating in an oscillating, sonorous body—both literally in performance, and figuratively, as music issuing from what might be called the composer's throat."[48] The insight of scholars Cone and Abbate about voice may have been held before by many practicing composers. For himself, Aaron Copland declared that "the largest part of our emotive life [is] the part that *sings*. Purposeful singing," Copland continued, "is what concerns most composers most of their lives."[49]

A claim can be made that persuasive music-dramas sound as if they came whole and continuously from a particular voice. That voice, like a speaker telling a story to others, might display various tones, rhythms, and inflections but would clearly be "issuing from" the same throat, that same person in telling the story. In doing so, such a manner might echo the experience, long before opera, of listeners attending preferentially to persons who were persuasive, first because they were consistent, coherent, and distinctive in utterance, but more importantly because they spoke, from knowledge and experience, of matters of value and importance to the group. Cultural evolution would have favored such prestigious individuals as leaders who would be willingly attended to[50] (as was noted with Verdi's Simon Boccanegra in his plea for community peace).

162 Cultural Considerations Regarding Opera

One modern opera presenting a consistent, distinctive voice is Philip Glass's *Akhnaten*. Composed in the early 1980s and premiered in 1984,[51] the opera concentrates on that pharaoh of ancient Egypt who attempted to change his society by introducing a new religion, a revolutionary one—monotheism. Revolutionary thinkers appealed to Glass; *Akhnaten* is the culmination of a set of three operas about visionary men. The other two concern Mahatma Gandhi (*Satyagraha*) and Albert Einstein (*Einstein on the Beach*).

Glass was one of the originators and composers of "minimalist" music in the 1960s, which was recognized as a kind of experimental music and first called the "New York Hypnotic School." Minimalism earned that label by its limited means, which focus attention on its subtly changing internal processes within an overall framework of repetitiveness. The music seems' often to be going nowhere fast.[52] So it seems like a strange choice for conventional narration, for most music-drama. But minimalism is a persuasive fit to *Akhnaten*. Glass's music in the opera is often described as "hypnotic"; and like the proverbial pocket watch swung on a string to hypnotize a patient is the music's insistent prolonged repetitive movement.

While *Akhnaten* audience members are presumably not actually hypnotized, the music does have the strong effect of increasing awareness of the present moment. In this strangeness, the opera is not just presenting a composer's voice and vision but engaging the audience in a potentially new experience. If one were listening to an audio recording only and not actually seeing a staged performance, this musical approach might not work well, particularly since *Akhnaten* offers very little sung language that most listeners would recognize, as Greek, Egyptian, and Hebrew are the main languages.

"I wanted the overall experience of the opera to come through movement, music, and image," Glass wrote.[53] A sequence of tableaux, linked together by a narrator and by scene-names that the audience sees projected, organizes the story. Glass's Egypt of Akhnaten is not *of* conventional time, secular time, when the clock is always running. It is primarily myth time, in which time seems to almost stand still. In certain tableaux, such as the opening ones of the entombment of the previous pharaoh (Amenhotep) and his movement to the spirit world, Glass goes all the way back beyond the origins of opera to ritual.

In a production seen at the Metropolitan Opera in 2019,[54] as the orchestral repetition very slowly changed, a visual scrim that suggested a highly figured funeral garment for a mummy became slowly transparent, revealing on stage a shadowy group of figures wearing headdresses of Egyptian gods and moving in hieratic patterns. Simultaneously these god-figures juggled balls in the same patterns at the same time, suggesting, perhaps, some suspension or circularity of time. The body of the dead pharaoh was seen being wrapped in white linen. Out came a Speaker, who intoned:

Open are the double doors of the horizon
Unlocked are its bolts
...
Clouds darken the sky
The stars rain down
The constellations stagger
The bones of the hell hounds tremble
The porters are silent
When they see this king
Dawning as a soul[55]

In this Prelude actions and music are performed precisely, with great ceremony and coordination, as is common in all ritual, which intends to make the uncertain, the troubling, or even the inexplicable, less so, thereby giving the participants some sense of control over messy experience.[56] In doing so, the death of the god-king Amenhotep perhaps is transformed into something momentarily beyond the grasp of time. Is this not a common aspiration of funeral rites?

Amenhotep's son and successor, Akhnaten, Glass strives to make a rather mysterious and even tragic figure, compelling for his novel vision. That vision is presented mainly in one long aria and scene, Akhnaten's "hymn to the Sun," his one god. That aria, the only one sung in the language of the theater audience (German in Germany; English in the United States and the United Kingdom), is also distinctive for two musical reasons. First, it is agreeable and somewhat familiar in its musical style, in fact beginning with what sounds like the introduction to an aria in a sacred work by Bach. Second, the singer commands attention by his unique sound. Akhnaten is a countertenor, a high male voice with the approximate range of a woman mezzo soprano. As Glass wrote, when the audience hears Akhnaten he wanted them to think, "Oh my god, who can this be?"[57]

The hymn to the Sun (Aten) begins with veneration ...

Thou dost appear beautiful/ On the horizon of heaven / Oh, living Aten / He who was the first to live ...

And after praising all the life which the Sun created, "according to thy will," the aria ends in an ecstasy of identification of self with god:

There is no other that knows thee / Save thy son, Akhnaten / For thou hast made him skilled/ In thy plans and thy might / Thou dost raise him up for thy son/ Who comes forth from thyself.[58]

The religious ecstasy of the hymn alludes to, and perhaps achieves for some viewers, the extraordinary experience of awe associated with peak religious

164 Cultural Considerations Regarding Opera

experience and the mingling of self and god. That mingling may be more familiar from the communion in the Roman Catholic Mass with its magical transformations not only of matter but also in the consciousness of the communicants, who will be "blessed":

> The Priest takes the host [bread-wafer] breaks it, and places a small
> piece in the chalice, saying quietly:
> May this mingling of the Body and Blood
> of our Lord Jesus Christ
> bring eternal life to us who receive it. [59]

A group of psychologists in 2017 led by David Yaden conducted sophisticated survey research with 1,137 adult participants, which led to confirmation of factors associated with awe experiences.[60] Their six factors are a close match to the stages and conditions summarized previously about sublime experiences: a perception of "vastness" and of "altered time"; "physical sensations," such as freezing in place and goose bumps; reduced self-importance ("self-diminishment") and "connectedness" to something greater than the self; and a need to change thinking to process and integrate the experience ("accommodation"). The "triggers of awe" that the participants selected from a list included "Encounter with God." An "encounter," though, may be considered a rare and specific event, much less common than more-general religious feelings and behavior, which other research has found awe associated with.[61]

So: what do people want most from opera? As the previous chapters suggested, they want an experience that is special, including by showing them something meaningful they had not seen or recognized before.

"Poetry," the American poet Wallace Stevens wrote, "is a revelation in words by means of the words. A poet's words are of things that do not exist without the words."[62] The poet's imagination can become a "light in the minds of others." Similarly, the opera composer's imagination can become the listener's, as the sounds the composer provides at particular dramatic moments create an imaginative insight that would not exist without the sounds combined with the words and actions.

The imagination of the director who visualizes and presents the opera can matter in the same way, can light the mind. Just as the deus ex machina descending onto stage claimed audience attention in the seventeenth century, and operas presented as cinema gave audiences new perspectives in the twentieth, perhaps virtual or augmented reality, or some presentation not yet imagined will engage opera audiences in this century.

More broadly, will audiences in coming decades still be attending performances mainly written by "dead white men," from Monteverdi on? Will operas by women, by persons of color and every diversity, obtain and retain

Affording Extraordinary Experiences **165**

audiences with new works of novelty and quality? Beyond these, will operas address the personal and social concerns that may be prompted by large-scale political or environmental challenges, such as unprecedented planetary disruptions brought by a changing climate?[63]

"Life is short, art is long, and judgment difficult" for the momentary observer. But here are some beliefs. If opera continues to be drama married to continuous music that illuminates critical moments and junctures in human life-history, it will attract an audience. If opera has the power to move audience members and provide extraordinary experiences, it will be valued. If attending to opera, as a whole, meets the needs of the audience to enhance their individual and social well-being, opera can thrive.

Notes

1 These distinctive qualities are advanced in Ellen Dissanayake, "The Artification Hypothesis and Its Relevance to Cognitive Science, Evolutionary Aesthetics, and Neuroaesthetics," *Cognitive Aesthetics*, no.5, Special Issue on Aesthetic Cognition (2009): 136–158.
2 Not necessarily as meant in Aldous Huxley, *The Doors of Perception* (New York: Harper & Brothers, 1954).
3 See Jacques Barzun, *Berlioz and the Romantic Century*, 1st. ed. (Boston: Little, Brown, 1950).
4 William Bristow, "Enlightenment," *The Stanford Encyclopedia of Philosophy* (Fall 2017 Edition), Edward N. Zalta, ed., http://plato.stanford.edu/archives/fall2017/entries/enlightenment.
5 Keren Gorodeisky, "19th Century Romantic Aesthetics," *The Stanford Encyclopedia of Philosophy* (Fall 2016 Edition), Edward N. Zalta, ed., http://plato.stanford.edu/archives/fall2016/entries/aesthetics-19th-romantic.
6 Illuminating development of this idea in P. A. Robinson, *Opera & Ideas: From Mozart to Strauss* (Ithaca, NY: Cornell University Press, 1986).
7 A succinct review and additional sources: "War and the State" in S. Condemi and F. Savatier, *A Pocket History of Human Evolution: How We Became Sapiens*, trans. Emma Ramadan (New York: The Experiment, LLC, 2019).
8 P. Hardie, *The Last Trojan Hero: A Cultural History of Virgil's Aeneid* (London: I. B. Tauris, 2014), 2.
9 Sean C. Murphy and Brock Bastian, "Emotionally Extreme Life Experiences Are More Meaningful," *Journal of Positive Psychology* 15, no. 4 (2020): 531–542. doi.org/10.1080/17439760.2019.1639795
10 Brock Bastian, Brodie Dakin, and Sean Murphy, "The Evolutionary Function of What People Find Meaningful," *Evolutionary Studies in Imaginative Culture* 4, no. 1 (2020).
11 Jonathan Gottschall, *The Storytelling Animal: How Stories Make Us Human* (Boston: Houghton Mifflin Harcourt, 2012), 58.
12 Berlioz's direction.
13 For a measured, recent evaluation of the evidence, pro and con, see A. Kendon, "Reflections on the "Gesture-First" Hypothesis of Language Origins," *Psychonomic Bulletin & Review* 24, no. 1 (2017): 163–170.
14 Today no one really knows who Longinus was, or even if that was his name. What is definite is that this author wrote in Greek and shows familiarity with the Hebrew Bible, and so it is likely he was from the Mediterranean region; and

166 Cultural Considerations Regarding Opera

from internal references his long essay was written in about the first century of the Christian era.

15 Longinus, as he wrote in Greek, did not actually use the word "sublime," which was introduced in the title of Longinus's rediscovered text published in 1554 by an Italian Renaissance humanist, Francesco Robortello in *Dionysii Longini rhetoris praestantissimi liber de grandi sive de sublimi orationis genere.* Demetrio St. Marin, "Bibliography of the Essay on the Sublime [Peri Ypsoys]" (The Netherlands 1967), http://books.google.com/books?id=6yUVAAAAIAAJ. 7.

16 In an English translation Longinus, *Longinus on the Sublime,* trans. H. L. Havell (New York: Macmillan, 1890).

17 Edmund Burke, *A Philosophical Inquiry into the Origin of Our Ideas of the Sublime and Beautiful* (New York: P. F. Collier & Son, 1909–1914; Original 1759), online at http://www.bartleby.com/24/2/.

18 Each of the items that follows is also treated in a detailed review by Gabrielsson, "Peak Experiences," 748–749. For a recent summary of awe, see David B. Yaden et al., "The Development of the Awe Experience Scale (Awe-S): A Multifactorial Measure for a Complex Emotion," *Journal of Positive Psychology* 14, no. 4 (2018): 474–488.

19 "Both surprise and novelty increase an animal's level of arousal, direct its attention, enhance learning, and elicit other appropriate behavior." A. Barto, M. Mirolli, and G. Baldassarre, "Novelty or Surprise?," *Frontiers in Psychology* 4 (2013): 9.

20 Humanists such as Longinus, Edmund Burke, and Immanuel Kant have long argued for magnitude, as have recent psychologists. For examples, see Dacher Keltner and Jonathan Haidt, "Approaching Awe, a Moral, Spiritual, and Aesthetic Emotion," *Cognition and Emotion* 17, no. 2 (2003): 297–314. and Vladimir J. Konečni, "Aesthetic Trinity Theory and the Sublime," *Proceedings of the European Society for Aesthetics* 2 (2010).

21 The estimation of "significance" by the observer derives from the initiating surprise, which may stimulate an instinctive, though quickly moderated "threat response." Joseph E. LeDoux, "Feelings: What Are They & How Does the Brain Make Them?," *Daedalus* 144, no. 1 (2015): 102. Also: John Onians, "Neuroscience and the Sublime in Art and Science," ed. R. Hoffmann and Iain Boyd Whyte, *Beyond the Finite* (Oxford: Oxford University Press, 2011). 95.

22 Sublime experience seems a relic of an adaptive response to threat as historically claimed by humanists such as Burke writing about "terror," in Edmund Burke, "A Philosophical Inquiry into the Origin of Our Ideas of the Sublime and Beautiful" (New York: P. F. Collier & Son, 1909–1914; Original 1759), Online at http://www.bartleby.com/24/2/. Neuroscience confirms stunning—"freezing"— as part of an initial animal response to threat Joseph LeDoux, *Anxious* (New York: Viking, 2015), 54–55.

23 Oliver Grewe, Reinhard Kopiez, and Eckart Altenmüller, "The Chill Parameter: Goose Bumps and Shivers as Promising Measures in Emotion Research," *Music Perception* 27, no. 1 (2009). Also: Gabrielsson, "Peak Experiences," 748–749.

24 See Vladimir J. Konečni, "Being Moved as One of the Major Aesthetic Emotional States: A Commentary on 'Being Moved: Linguistic Representation and Conceptual Structure,'" *Frontiers in Psychology* 6 (2015). Also: W. Menninghaus et al., "Towards a Psychological Construct of Being Moved," *PLoS One* 10, no. 6 (2015): e0128451.

25 A. H. Maslow, "Peak Experiences in Education and Art," *Theory into Practice* 10, no. 3 (1971): 149–153. Also: Gabrielsson, "Peak Experiences," 748–749.

26 Neuroscience observes that after being overwhelmed in the perception of a threat, once that threat is mitigated learning can occur. See LeDoux, *Anxious*, 69.

27 Humans have a species-typical need for "finding and making 'meaning.'" Joseph Carroll, "An Evolutionary Paradigm for Literary Study," *Style* 42, nos. 2–3 (2008): 125. Again, see Gabrielsson, op cit. "Many, for example, describe their experience as having resulted in a better understanding of the human condition, or offered a glimpse at God."

28 Charles Darwin, *The Descent of Man, and Selection in Relation to Sex* (Princeton, NJ: Princeton University Press, 1981; repr., Reprint of 1871 first edition), 335.

29 Vladimir Jankélévitch, *Music and the Ineffable*, trans. Carolyn Abbate (Princeton, NJ: Princeton University Press, 2003), 72.

30 Alf Gabrielsson, John Whaley, and John Sloboda, "Peak Experiences with Music," in *The Oxford Handbook of Music Psychology*, ed. Susan Hallam Ian Cross and Michael Thaut (2016), 745.

31 The key change is from D-flat major to C major, i.e., from a tonality of five flatted tones to C, which has none.

32 (Act 4) no. 36.

33 C. T. Snowdon, E. Zimmermann, and E. Altenmuller, "Music Evolution and Neuroscience," *Progress in Brain Research* 217 (2015): 24.

34 Quoted in Peter Bloom, *The Life of Berlioz* (New York: Cambridge University Press, 1998), 98.

35 Gabrielsson, "Peak Experiences," 738.

36 Menninghaus, "Being Moved," 1.

37 Susan McClary, "The Undoing of Opera: Toward a Feminist Criticism of Music," in *Opera, or, the Undoing of Women* (Minnespolis: University of Minnesota Press, 1988), 9–10.

38 These are the urgings of the dead Priam, Corebus, Cassandra, and Hector (No. 42).

39 Paul H. Fry, *Theory of Literature* (New Haven, CT: Yale University Press, 2012), 246ff.

40 Cited in Richter, *Critical Tradition*, 1205.

41 Edward Said, "Les Troyens," in Edward Said, *Music at the Limits* (New York: Columbia University Press, 2008), 183.

42 Cassandra foresees the Greeks have tricked the Trojans by leaving behind a giant wooden horse on the beach. "The die is cast," she asserts; "it is necessary to submit to fate!" (Il faut subir l'enoxorable loi!).

43 For an evolutionary discussion of "future discounting" see Martin Daly and Margo Wilson, "Carpe Diem: Adaptation and Devaluing the Future," *The quarterly review of Biology* 80, no. 1 (2005).

44 The fictional Cassandra was not persuasive. In recent years, the young Swede, Greta Thunberg, has tried to be.

45 Despite the efforts of many individuals and organizations to offer a persuasive story., e.g., the Post Carbon Institute (http://www.postcarbon.org/).

46 Joseph Conrad, "Preface" to *The Nigger of the 'Narcissus'* (1897): http://www.gutenberg.org/files/17731/17731-h/17731-h.htm

47 Edward T. Cone, *The Composer's Voice* (Berkeley: University of California Press, 1974), 58. This Cone is no relation to the present author.

48 Carolyn Abbate, *Unsung Voices: Opera and Musical Narrative in the Nineteenth Century* (Princeton, NJ: Princeton University Press, 1991), 12.

49 Aaron Copland, *Music and Imagination*, 1980 paperback ed. (Cambridge, MA: Harvard University Press, 1952), 2.

50 See discussion of prestige and persuasion in Joseph Henrich, *The Secret of Our Success* (Princeton, NJ: Princeton University Press, 2016), 122ff.

168 Cultural Considerations Regarding Opera

51 The production of *Akhnaten* in London and New York in 2019 emphasized its remote period and unusual protagonist.
52 See Timothy A. Johnson, "Minimalism: Aesthetic, Style, or Technique?" *Musical Quarterly* 78, no. 4 (Winter 1994), 742–773.
53 Philip Glass, *Words without Music: A Memoir* (New York: Liveright, 2015), 317.
54 Production by Phelim McDermott; pattern-juggling routines by Gandini Juggling.
55 Glass, *Akhnaten*, Act 1, Prelude. http://www.opera-arias.com/glass/akhnaten/libretto/
56 Nancy Easterlin, "The Functions of Literature and the Evolution of Extended Mind," *New Literary History*, no. 44 (2013): 671.
57 Glass, *Words*, 318.
58 Glass, *Akhnaten*, Act 2, scene4. http://www.opera-arias.com/glass/akhnaten/libretto/.
59 The Roman Catholic Church permits slightly different forms of communion text, but what's extracted here is standard. "The Order of Mass," Catholic Bishops, accessed December 21, 2018, http://www.catholicbishops.ie/wp-content/uploads/2011/02/Order-of-Mass.pdf
60 Yaden, "Awe Experience Scale," 1.
61 P. O. Kearns and J. M. Tyler, "Examining the Relationship between Awe, Spirituality, and Religiosity," *Psychology of Religion and Spirituality* 14, no. 4 (2022): 436–444. Advance online publication. http://doi.org/10.1037/rel0000365
62 "The Noble Rider and the Sound of Words," in W. Stevens, *The Necessary Angel: Essays on Reality and the Imagination* (New York: Vintage Books, 1965), 31.
63 See Aaron Matz, "Flaubert's Planet," *The New York Review of Books*, July 21, 2022.

INDEX

Abbate, Carolyn 138, 160
Abels, Michael 129
adaptations 14–15
Adès, Thomas 99
The Aeneid (Virgil) 154
affective states 28
African-Americans 129
aging: *The Tempest* 100; *Lear* 103; *Falstaff* 107
agreeableness 71–72
Akhnaten (Glass) 162–164
Alceste (Gluck) 36
allostasis 28
antisemitism 89–90
arias 32–33; *Akhnaten* 163; *Lear* 104; *Le Nozze di Figaro* 61–62; *Rodelinda* 35–36; *Simon Boccanegra* 92; *Turandot* 20
aristocrats, *Le Nozze di Figaro* 56
Aristotle 16, 46, 57, 147
art 15, 153
attracting audiences 126–127
attraction 43–44
audience research 33
audience response 14; to *L'Orfeo* 14; to *Le Nozze di Figaro* 64; to *Don Giovanni* 81; to *Wozzeck* 81
audiences 132; attracting 126–127; "being moved" 157; communication 7, 14, 43, 50, 76, 138, 142, 145; directed attention 74, 93, 102, 143, 157, 162–164; mourning 155; peak experiences with music 159; joint attention 13–14
augmented reality (AR) 149
awe 157, 164

Barrett, Lisa Feldman 31
basic emotion theory 31–32
beauty 48
behaviors 3–4; adaptation 14–15; awe 157, 164; big five personality traits 71–72; imitation 13–14, 16–17; life cycle 4; mate selection 20, 44–45, 56; monogamous mating 57; morality 74; peak 157, 159; social bonding 35; sublime 156–157, 164; toolmaking 13; wisdom 100, 104, 108; *see also* courtship; emotions; parenting
"being moved" 157
benefits of attending opera 133
Berg, Alban, *Wozzeck* 78–80, 124
Berlioz, Hector 19, 153; *Les Troyens* 153–160; *Symphonie Fantastique* 153
"big five" personality traits (openness, conscientiousness, extraversion, agreeableness, neuroticism) 71–72
biocultural perspectives 5
biological evolution 3–4, 118–120
biology, culture and 5
Bloom, Harold 105, 128
Boito, Arrigo 105–108

170 Index

Boxgrove sites 139–140
Boyd, Brian 15
Boyd, Robert 115
Brahms, Johannes 65
Büchner, Georg 78
Burke, Edmund 156
Burney, Charles 29
Buss, David 44

care of parents 104–105
Carroll, Joseph 77, 102
Caruso, Enrico 119
castrati 27
catch-phrases (memes) 118
catharsis, *L'Orfeo: Favola in Musica*
  (*Orpheus: A Tale of Music*) 16–17
characteristics (physical) 3–4
"chemistry" between performers 44
childbirth/childbearing 47, 85
childrearing 47
children 84–85; fall from parental
  grace 87–89; relationships with
  father 90–91, 102–104; *see also*
  parenting
chills (goosebumps) 21
chorus: *Falstaff* 109; *L'Elisir d'Amore*
  44, 46; Greek chorus 46; *Le Nozze
  di Figaro* 64;
cinema 124, 147–149; close-ups
  146–147; fourth wall 145–146; *La
  Bohème* (Puccini) 143–146
classics 128
close-ups in cinema 146–147
coevolutionary process 5
cognition, signs 140
collective learning 5
comedy 41, 46; *Le Nozze di Figaro*
  55–66; *L'Elisir d'Amore* 40–51;
  Merry Wives of Windsor 105–106;
  see also romantic comedy
commercial distribution of music 119
commitment (marital) 56; *L'Elisir
  d'Amore* 47
common wisdom model 104
communication 7, 14, 43, 50, 76, 138,
  142, 145
Communism 126
composers: Adès, Thomas 99; Berg,
  Alban 78–80, 124; Berlioz, Hector
  153-160; Donizetti, Gaetano 40–41;
  Giddens, Rhiannon 129, 132; Glass,
  Philip 162–164; Handel, George
  Frideric 26, 29–34; Mazzoli, Missy

129–131; Monteverdi, Claudio
  11–12, 16–17, 22, 138–139; Mozart,
  Wolfgang Amadeus 54–55, 69–78,
  81; Prokofiev, Sergey 123, 125–126;
  Puccini, Giacomo 124, 143–144;
  Reimann, Aribert 102–103; Verdi,
  Giuseppe 95, 123; Wagner, Richard
  84–94, 147–148
Cone, Edward T. 160
conscientiousness 71–72
construction theories (emotions) 31
Cooke, Brett 65
Copland, Aaron 160
courtship 19; *L'Elisir d'Amore* 42–49;
  L'Orfeo: Favola in Musica 15;
  singing 20–21
cultural evolution 58, 116–120; kin
  selection 93
Cultural Evolution Society 118, 120
cultural learning 5, 13, 100
cultural species (humans) 5, 65,
  115, 132
culture 4–5; biology and 5; defined 115;
  hominins 139–141; "two cultures"
  among scholars 7, 116
Curtis, Liane 71

da capo 33
Da Ponte, Lorenzo 55–58, 70, 72,
  74–75
dancing 62–63
Darwin, Charles 19–20, 157
Dawkins, Richard 118
De'Calzabigi, Ranieri 36
deformity 48
desert in 149
Didion, Joan 14
Die Walküre (*The Valkyrie*) (Wagner)
  84–94
directed attention 74, 93, 102, 143,
  157, 162–164
discourse 117
Dissanayake, Ellen 30, 35, 142
distribution of music 119
Dolan, Jill 131
Don Giovanni (Mozart) 69–71,
  81; moral judgments 73–75;
  psychological processes to assess
  character of others 73; rape 69–71;
  reproduction 70; theory of mind
  72–73
Donizetti, Gaetano, *L'Elisir d'Amore*
  40–41

Index **171**

dopamine 21
Dornhelm, Robert, *Bohème* film director 146
drama 14; Greek tragedy 18; punctuations 16; singing 18–20
"dramma giocoso" (comic operas with serious elements) 75
duets 43, 91, 92, 101, 104
Duprez, Gilbert-Louis 19

Eberhardt, Isabelle 129–131
Einsten, Albert 55
emotional intimacy 43–44
emotional power of dramatic performances 147
emotions 27–30; as affective state 28; evoked or expressed by music 29–32; basic emotions, questioned 31–32; for fictional characters 57; happiness 31–32; in *Rodelinda* (Handel) 29–31; sadness 32
emotion theories 28
environmental influences 7, 119
epicycle 141
Euridice (Peri) 18
evolution 3–4, 20; adaptations 14–15; coevolution 5–6, 13, 141; cultural evolution 58; culture 5; feedforward mechanism (epicycle) 141; fitness 102; gene-culture coevolution 5–6, 13, 122n39; gesturing 140–141, 145–146; hominins 41, 139–140; *Homo sapiens* 13; of lighting 142–143; of music distribution 119; memes 118, 120; musicality 34; natural selection 5, 19; psychology 5–6; reproduction 42, 47–48, 56; sexual selection 19–22, 48; survival 34–35; theory of mind 72–73; well-being 133; *see also* biological evolution; cultural evolution
evolutionary psychology 6, 8, 65
extraversion 71–72

Falk, John H. 133, 141
Falstaff (Verdi) 106–109
father, relationships with children 88–91
feedforward mechanism (epicycle) 141
feelings 147; *see also* emotions
female sexuality, *Song from the Uproar* 130
feminism 129–131

fiction 65, 77–78
fictional characters (paradox), *Le Nozze di Figaro* 57–58
fidelity, *Le Nozze di Figaro* 59–60, 63–64
fitness (in evolution) 102
"flow" 33–34
forgiveness, *Le Nozze di Figaro* 63–64
"fourth wall" 145–146
Fry, Paul H. 117
Fukuyama, Francis 132

Gabrielsson, Alf 157, 159
Gelb, Peter 127
gene-culture coevolution theory 5, 13
genetic influences 6
gesturing 140–141; pointing gestures 145–146
Giddens, Rhiannon 129, 132
Glass, Philip, *Akhnaten* 162–164
Gluck, Christoph Willibald 36
gods, *Die Walküre* 86–87, 89
Gonzaga, Vincenzo 11, 18
Gottschall, Jonathan 65
Greek chorus 46
Greek tragedy 18

Haidt, Jonathan 73
Handel, George Frideric 26; *Rodelinda* 29–30, 32–34
happiness 31–32
"Happy Birthday" song 30
Harari, Yuval Noah 77, 116
harmonic series 49
healing social divisions, *Simon Boccanegra* 92–93
Henrich, Joseph 58, 77
Henry IV (Shakespeare) 107
heritable traits 119–120
heterosexual characters, *Don Giovanni* 70
homeostasis 28
hominins 41, 139–140
Homo sapiens 3, 13, 77, 84, 139
honor, *Falstaff* 106–107
human life, stages of human life 4
human life-history 4
human nature 6–7
human psychology 5–6
human relations 89
humanities 116–117
Hume, David 73
humiliation 81

172 Index

humor 100
hymns, *Akhnaten* 163

Iacoboni, Marco 147
identity 131
identity politics 131–132
imitation 13–14; *L'Orfeo: Favola in Musica* 16–17
ineffability 157
infants, communication with mothers 30
innovation 142–143
Internet culture 118
Italian rhyming, *Le Nozze di Figaro* 60

Jankélévitch, Vladimir 157
joint attention 14

Kahneman, Daniel 73
Kerman, Joseph 138
Kierkegaard, Søren 76
Killin, Anton 141
kin selection 93
King Lear (Shakespeare) 102
King Louis XVI 56
Kivy, Peter 76, 95
knowledge of life 100

La Bohème (Puccini) 143–146
laughter 41
Le Nozze di Figaro (*The Marriage of Figaro*) (Mozart) 54–55, 62–64; chorus 64; fictional characters 57–58; fidelity 59–60, 63–64; forgiveness 63–64; marriage 58–59; music 61–62
leadership, *Simon Boccanegra* 93
Lear (Reimann) 102–105
L'Elisir d'Amore (*The Elixir of Love*) (Donizetti) 40–41; commitment 47; courtship 42–49; rivalry 45
Les Troyens (*The Trojans*) (Berlioz) 153–160
life cycle 4
life-history theory 4, 64, 89
lighting 142–143
long-term relationships 47
Longinus 156
L'Orfeo: Favola in Musica (*Orpheus: A Tale of Music*) (Monteverdi) 11, 22; catharsis 16–17; courtship and marriage 15; imitation 16–17; reversal of fortune 16–17

love: father and child 90–91; in *L'Elisir d'Amore* 41–42; in *Les Troyens* 158–159; in *The Tempest* 101; *see also* courtship; marriage

Macbeth (Verdi) 143
male dominance, *Simon Boccanegra* 93
Marie-Antoinette 56
marriage 55; in *Le Nozze di Figaro* 58–59; in *L'Orfeo: Favola in Musica* 15
Marxism 126
Marxism-Leninism 126
mate selection 20, 44–45, 56; monogamous mating 57
Mazzoli, Missy 129–131
McClary, Susan 129–131, 159–160
memes 118, 120
Merry Wives of Windsor (Shakespeare) 105–106
Metropolitan Opera 127
millennials, benefits of attending opera 133
Miller, Geoffrey 21
minimalism 162
mirror neurons 147
Mithen, Steven 34
moment of discovery 58
monogamous mating 57
Monteverdi, Claudio 22, 138–139; *L'Orfeo: Favola in Musica* 11–12, 16–17
mood 29
Moonstruck (1987) 42, 133
moral judgments, *Don Giovanni* 73–76
morality 74
mothers, communication with infants 30
motion pictures 144–145 *see also* cinema
mourning, *Les Troyens* 155–156
Mozart, Wolfgang Amadeus 54–55; *Don Giovanni* 69–78, 81; *Le Nozze di Figaro* 55–65
multiculturalism 128
music 49–50; atonal 124; in *Die Walküre* 88–89; distribution of 119; in *Don Giovanni* 76; in *Falstaff* 107–108; harmonic series 49; as language 60–61; in *Le Nozze di Figaro* 61–62; in *Lear* 103–104; overtones 49–50; peak experiences with 157, 159; speech 16, 18, 32, 50, 60–61, 107, 124; tonality 50, 79, 124–125, 158

Index **173**

musical language 79
musical repeats 35–36
musicality 34, 139
music-drama origins 138–139
music-emotion link 34
"musicking" 140

natural selection 5, 19
neurons 147
neuroscience 28, 31, 57, 147, 166n26
neuroticism 71–72
New Criticism 116
New Historicism 160

Oakes, Meredith 99
Omar 129
openness 71–72
opera (origins) 18, 138–139
opera houses 26, 145
opera seria (serious opera) 29
overtones 49–50

pantomime 130, 155–156, 158
paradox of fiction 57–58
parenting 84–85; care 104–105;
   children who fall from parental
   grace 87–89; in *Falstaff* 106–107; in
   Lear 102–103; in *Simon Boccanegra*
   88–94
Parker, Roger 138
Parsifal (Wagner) 149
passions 29; *see also* emotions
Payne, Nicholas 127
peak experiences with music 157, 159
performances 142; emotional power
   of 147
Peri, Jacopo, *Euridice* 18
phallic song 46
Plato 57
plot 15
Poetics (Aristotle) 18
pointing gestures 145–146
polygamy 57
postmodern perspectives 116
prediction 31
pregnancy 47
program music 32
Prokofiev, Sergey 123, 125–126
proto-music-drama 142
Prum, Richard 20
psychological processes to assess
   character of others, *Don
   Giovanni* 73

psychology 5–6
Puccini, Giacomo 124; *La Bohème*
   143–144
punctuations in dramas 16

rape, *Don Giovanni* 69–78
reasons for attending opera 133–134
recitativo 18
regular rhythm, *Le Nozze di Figaro* 62
Reimann, Aribert, *Lear* 102–103
relationships: father and child 88–94; in
   Lear 102–104; long-term 47
reproduction 42, 47–48, 56; in
   Don Giovanni 70; mate selection
   44–45
reversal of fortune *L'Orfeo: Favola in
   Musica* 16–17; *Rodelinda* 35
Richerson, Peter J. 115
Richter, David 128
Ring of the Nibelung (Wagner) 85–87
rituals 43–44, 141
rivalry in *L'Elisir d'Amore* 45
Rodelinda (Handel) 22; emotions
   29–34; survival 34–35
Romani, Felice 42
romantic comedies, *L'Elisir d'Amore*
   40–51
romantic operas 159

sadness 32
Saint-Beuve 128
Sapiens 116, 142
Savage, Patrick 117
self-engagement 57
sense of humor 100
Sessions, Roger 124
sex 19; dopamine 21; *L'Orfeo: Favola
   in Musica* 15
sexual desire 70, 76–77
sexual reproduction 47–48; *see also*
   reproduction
sexual selection 19–22, 48
Shakespeare, William 99, 102, 105;
   Henry IV 107
Shaw, George Bernard 86–87
signs 140–141
Simon Boccanegra (Verdi), 90–94
singing: castrati 27; drama 18–20;
   sexual selection 19–22
Skank, Theodore 134
slavery, *Omar* 129
Sloboda, John 157
Snow, C. P. 7

174 Index

social bonding 35, 62, 64
social cognitive processing 104
social intuitionist model 73
social media 118
social norms 77; *Simon Boccanegra* 93
social ordering 77
social performance 71–72, 74
social proto-music 141
soliloquies, *Le Nozze di Figaro* 61–62
Song from the Uproar (Mazzoli) 129–131
Soviet Union 123, 125–126
spectacle 18, 22
speech 16, 18, 32, 50, 60–61, 107, 124
stages of human life 4
stone tools 5, 13, 139–141
stories 14–15; catharsis 16–17, 105; comedy 41, 46, 55–56, 65, 75, 105, 107–108; pantomime 130, 155–156, 158; paradox of fiction 57; purpose of 155; reversal of fortune 16–17; rituals 43–44, 141; romantic comedy 46; soliloquies 61–62; spectacle 18, 22; tragedy 15–16, 18, 44, 46, 80, 103, 105; transportation 33–34, 48, 105
storytelling 89
Strauss, Richard 124
Striggio, Alessandro 11
sublime 156–157, 164
suffering in *Lear* 105
suicide in *Les Troyens* 160
survival in *Rodelinda* 34–35
suspension of disbelief 57
Symphonie Fantastique (Berlioz) 153
System 1 thinking (Kahneman) 73, 75
System 2 thinking 74

The Tempest (Adès) 99–100
Theory (in humanities; sciences) 117

theory of mind, *Don Giovanni* (Mozart) 72–73
Tomlinson, Gary 140–141
tonality 124, 158; apparent preference for 50
toolmaking 13, 139–141
tragedy 15–16, 18, 44, 46, 80, 103, 105
transparency 61
"transportation" (by media) 33–34, 48–49, 105
Tristan und Isolde (Wagner) 124
Trump, Donald 118
"two cultures" among scholars 7, 116

Updike, John 46

Verdi, Giuseppe 95, 123; *Macbeth* 143; *Falstaff* 105–106; *Simon Boccanegra* 90–94
Virtual Reality (VR) 149
vocal performances 142
vocalizations 50, 140
vocal register 43
voice (composer's voice) 161
voices 49–50; *see also* singing

Wagner, Richard 147–148; antisemitism 89–90; *Die Walküre* 84–94; *Parsifal* 149; *Tristan und Isolde* 124
Walküre (Wagner), gods 86–87
War and Peace (Prokofiev) 125–126
Warner, Michael 160
well-being 133
Western canon 128
William Tell (Rossini) 21
wisdom 104; *Falstaff* (Verdi) 108; *The Tempest* (Shakespeare) 100
Wozzeck (Berg) 78–80, 124

YouTube 127

Printed in the United States
by Baker & Taylor Publisher Services